AWAKE AS IN ANCIENT DAYS

Sat Nam Har Dyal,
May your journey be filled
with joy and many alive
moments.
           My best,
               Nam Joti Kaur

AWAKE
AS IN ANCIENT DAYS

The Christ-Centered Kundalini Yoga Experience

by Nam Joti Kaur | FELICE AUSTIN

No tips, instructions, exercises, or commentary included in this book should be considered medical advice. The intent of the author is to offer information to assist individuals on their own personal quests for emotional, physical, and spiritual enlightenment. Individuals who choose to implement anything from this book take full responsibility for their own health and well-being. All testimonials shared in this book are personal experiences. Results and experiences vary. In no way is the information included in this book intended to diagnose, cure, treat, or replace any medical advice or treatment from a health care professional. As always, seek the advice of a trained health care professional before implementing any exercise program.

The teachings of Yogi Bhajan that have been quoted or reproduced in this book are used with permission from the Kundalini Research Institute, however all commentary and interpretation are my own and are not approved or disapproved of by KRI.

Published by MADISON & WEST PUBLISHING

Cover Design by Marie Reese
Cover Photography by Felice Austin

For photograph credits, see page 311

www.treeoflifekundaliniyoga.com

Library of Congress Cataloging-in-Publication Data
Austin, Felice
Awake as in ancient days: the Christ-centered kundalini yoga experience/ Felice Austin
1. Kundalini Yoga 2. Meditation 3.Christ consciousness 4. Spirituality 5. Meditation Stories 6. Mantra meditation 7. The Word 8. Prana 9. LDS stories

ISBN 978-0692381823

I humbly dedicate this book to my Savior Jesus Christ
in gratitude for His redeeming love.

And to three men I admire who are still dedicated to liberating the captives:
Joseph Smith, Abraham Lincoln, and Yogi Bhajan.

And to the women who exist within me and I in them:
my Heavenly Mother, Mother Eve, and all my female ancestors who have
supported me and blessed me with strength and spiritual gifts.

Table *of* Contents

Table *of* Contents

INTRODUCTION

My name is Felice Austin. I am happy, healthy, and holy. My name is also Nam Joti Kaur. I am the princess-lioness who walks in the light of God's divine name. I am beautiful, I am bountiful, I am blissful.

I am a faithful and active member of The Church of Jesus Christ of Latter-day Saints. I am also a Kundalini yogini and spiritual teacher. Through my life's journey, which I will share more about in this book, I have learned that all truth can be circumscribed into one great whole.

One of my spiritual gifts is the gift of translating truth. When I hear truth, whatever the source, my heart recognizes it. My mind, which has always loved words, can then translate the truth into the language that others need in order to understand, whether that person be Jewish, Sikh, Muslim, Hari Krishna, or atheist. My ability to speak truth to people in their own language is one of the reasons I was so successful in my hypnotherapy practice, and this gift contributes to my success now as a spiritual teacher. Because of this gift, I have attracted many dear friends of faith, and I am so grateful for the light they reflect from God.

There is a poem by Joy Harjo titled "The Path to the Milky Way Leads through Los Angeles," and I think I love the title even more than the poem because, ironic though it may seem, the city of Los Angeles has been a big part of my spiritual journey. This city is the fixed point I have traveled from and returned to many times on my journey. Los Angeles has been the backdrop to many lows and highs that have shaped my path. This city is also where I started my Kundalini Yoga journey at the feet of Yogi Bhajan. It is where I went to the Latter-day Saint temple weekly, where I chanted Kirtan with Sikhs, and where my daughter went to an Orthodox Jewish preschool. Los Angeles is where my daughter and I ate with Hari Krishnas every Sunday. It is where I taught mommy-and-me yoga and pregnancy yoga at the YMCA. Los Angeles is also where I studied hypnotherapy and then owned a private hypnotherapy practice for three years, during which I saw clients from every walk of life. I saw every kind of case imaginable—and some that are not imaginable. I also belonged to an organization of business professionals and regularly spoke at their gatherings.

I am grateful for the skills and certifications that Los Angeles gave me access to. And I am most grateful to the saints and yogis everywhere who have elevated me on my path.

When Yogi Bhajan first came to America in the late 1960s, he started teaching Kundalini Yoga in Los Angeles, mostly to hippies because they were the people who had flexible belief systems and were listening. If they stuck around, the yoga, meditation, and Yogi Bhajan's firm but loving guidance changed them. They stopped doing drugs.

They learned the value of personal purity. They came to see their divine lineage and to understand their bodies were temples. They became spiritual teachers.

Indeed, the fruits of a regular Kundalini Yoga and Meditation practice are beautiful. If members of any organized church have any concerns about Kundalini Yoga As Taught by Yogi Bhajan®, I hope these concerns will be alleviated by reading the information in this book, which includes personal stories from faithful members of The Church of Jesus Christ of Latter-day Saints..

The man affectionately known as Yogi Bhajan was the highest master of Kundalini Yoga in the world, and he was also a religious person. He became the head of the Sikh religious dharma in the United States, and many Sikhs love and revere him. Yogi Bhajan repeatedly taught that Kundalini Yoga is not a religion, and he tried to some extent to keep the yogic teachings separate. But because of his religious affiliation, many people who loved his yogic teachings also became Sikh, and many Sikhs in America practice Kundalini Yoga. The technology of Kundalini Yoga, however, is for everyone, including members of organized religions of all kinds. Some of the most beautiful results I have witnessed have come when people who already live a life of devotion begin regularly practicing Kundalini Yoga As Taught by Yogi Bhajan®.

Though I emphasize in this book the message of Jesus Christ as recorded in the scriptures, sacred Latter-day Saint temple ordinances, and the science of Kundalini Yoga, I honor all the diverse ways that God leads His children to grow in light and truth.

I anticipate that a good portion of my audience for this book will be Latter-day Saints who are looking for ways to enhance their spiritual journey and to remain Christ centered. I also hope that members of other Christian denominations and practitioners of Kundalini Yoga from any background will find it interesting and encouraging to see how this technology truly is for everyone. Yogi Bhajan taught that it was for everyone, and we have finally lived to see it come to pass. I hope it will be useful for teachers with students who are members of The Church of Jesus Christ of Latter-day Saints.

Though I have made every attempt to be consistent with the doctrine and teachings of The Church of Jesus Christ of Latter-day Saints, this book is an expression of my own thoughts and pondering the truths of the gospel that I treasure. This is not an official declaration of the doctrine in regard to the The Church of Jesus Christ of Latter-day Saints to which I belong and cherish my membership. Please make sure you pray about and ponder everything you read.

All the kriyas and meditations in this book are exactly as Yogi Bhajan taught them, and they have been approved through the Kundalini Research Institute's review process.

MY STORY

I was born to a family who had been members of The Church of Jesus Christ of Latter-day Saints (Mormon) for generations. Both sides were pioneers from England and Europe and crossed the plains and helped to build temples and found cities, like Salt Lake City and Cedar City, Utah. I was baptized into The Church of Jesus Christ of Latter-day Saints when I was eight years old, as is custom. I wore a white dress and wore my hair in a French braid so that it wouldn't float to the top when I got dunked. (We do baptism by total immersion.)

I was raised praying daily and going to church every Sunday. My parents taught me the scriptures, and I knew all the answers in Sunday School, but I was hardly the teacher's favorite. In fact, at my own baptism I talked back to the person giving the talk about baptism. I also mortified my parents by publicly picking my toes as my Sunday School teacher spoke about the Holy Ghost. I was smarter than most adults I knew, or so I thought, and I was sassy.

I was also shy when I was uncomfortable. I liked to live in my imagination, whether this was in outdoor play with my siblings or in books. My imaginary worlds were intricate. They were peopled by fairies, witches, werewolves, talking birds, portals to other worlds, and occasionally a romantic interlude on a baseball mound. As Annie Dillard might say, my reading had gone to my head. Perhaps this helped me to cope with the truth that my mother was dying.

I see now that I was angry. And afraid. The few years after my mother died were dedicated to these emotions, covered only by a lot of sass and a little style.

When I was old enough to start high school, I was expected to go to early morning seminary class, a religion class for all the Mormon kids that was held at a church near our school. Seminary started at 6:30 a.m. My father dropped me off every morning and right after the roll was taken, I would excuse myself to go the bathroom, where I would hang out with a few other strays for the rest of the hour doing anything but studying the scriptures. The following year, my dad gave up the fight and didn't make me go.

By then, however, I was already an incurable morning person. I found that I liked the quiet of the early morning ambrosial hours, and no matter how late I stayed up, I couldn't sleep in. I loved rising at 5:30 in the morning and taking a half-hour bubble bath and listening to sappy music in peace before the rest of the family rose. This was my first form of meditation.

A few months into my sophomore year, however, I began to have trouble falling asleep at night, which is bad for a morning person. So I did what someone suggested: read something boring to fall asleep. At this point in my life, the scriptures were the most boring literature I could imagine. I started with the Book of Mormon.

Reading to fall asleep worked well for a time, until it stopped being boring, and began to change me, and change my heart. The Book of Mormon is a special book, and I became awake to its power and started to like it and its epic stories and truths. When I finished it, I then read the Bible (also not boring when you are awakened), but when I got to the New Testament book of Revelation, I didn't understand a word of it.

I wanted to though. I had a feeling that it was of great import to me.

My friend Juli told me that in seminary they were studying the book of Revelation, and their new teacher was good. She invited me to come, but my dad wouldn't drive me. So I walked. It was a good half-hour walk at six a.m. in the chilly morning. By the time I arrived, I was probably the only student present who was wide awake. I rarely missed a day of seminary afterward, and I walked most days. (I still did not understand the book of Revelation until twenty years later when I became a yogi, but I will get to that later.)

My transformation was noticeable. Though I still had some inner anger, and I frequently challenged authority, I had a testimony of the truth of the restoration of the gospel of Jesus Christ, the Book of Mormon, the Bible, and Jesus Christ's Atonement. I became a lovely young woman.

Twenty years later, I am still a young woman, only more radiant. But let me go back a decade. One of my good qualities is that I can be very loyal, but this also became a source of pain, when I made a bad choice in marriage. I spent four years being loyal to a man who physically abused me on occasion and mentally abused and belittled me daily. I was too embarrassed to admit that I had become "that woman," whatever stereotype I may have had for her, and so I lived in total denial.

My only form of meditation at that time was my daily writing practice, which I began early in the morning like *sadhana*, and wrote for hours. This practice may be what kept me alive, even if it was living in an alternate reality.

By the grace of God, my husband left me when I became pregnant. Although my troubles didn't end there, I was no longer living without oxygen. I got a fresh breath of air and awoke from four years of sleep. I realized I had a choice. I could become bitter, or I could become better. As soon as I chose better, the rest started to happen on its own.

Somehow, I found myself at Yoga West in Los Angeles, staring at an image of Yogi Bhajan on the wall of the dimly lit yoga room with wood floors and Christmas lights on the ceiling. I was there for pregnancy yoga. Over the course of many Tuesdays there, I discovered, or rather remembered, that I had all the tools I needed within myself. I decided to birth my baby naturally. I took a hypnosis for childbirth class. I started to meditate. I had always been good at praying (after all, worry is a form of prayer), but when I started to meditate, I started hearing back from God. Personal revelation became more recognizable, and I had the strength to follow it.

Grace for grace, I walked the valiant path where it led me. Creating life was amazing. Birth and motherhood transformed me into my true self. I started singing again (I stopped when I married). I had such a spiritually amazing experience with birth, that I wanted to help other women of my faith have a great birth, too. So I began to gestate a second baby, a spiritual birth book. I published it six years later with four coauthors.

The five of us all say that *The Gift of Giving Life: Rediscovering the Divine Nature of Pregnancy and Birth* was really written by God; we were just the transcribers. In the book, I dedicated a whole chapter to meditation and the importance of meditation while pregnant. When Mormons everywhere read the book and wanted to learn more about meditation, they were suddenly looking to me.

Thankfully, God has a plan, and in that six years between the birth of my daughter and the birth of our book, I had graduated from a college of hypnotherapy and completed several Kundalini Yoga teacher trainings. I didn't always know why I was doing these things at the time, but God knew. While I once thought that working with pregnant women was my destiny, it was actually preparing me for my higher destiny, which is to teach people of my faith about the technology of Kundalini Yoga and Meditation As Taught by Yogi Bhajan®.

Kundalini Yoga and Meditation changed me from a hollow husk of a woman to a radiant spiritual being who is awake and whole. I still have all the duties and challenges of a householder in the modern era. I clean my house, run a business, pay bills, do laundry, and try to cook nutritious meals. My daughter and I have a great relationship, but I still have to teach her manners and remind her to do her chores. I have to watch out for gopher holes when I walk through the orange groves, remember to put gas in my car, dress for the weather, and choose how to respond to grouchy people who work in customer service. I deal with grief, discomforts, loved ones' burdens and traumas, and global tragedy. But I now deal with these things differently.

Kundalini Yoga gave me the tools to access a fulness of what I already had a bit of (the gospel, the Atonement, joy, etc.). It hasn't made my life tragedy proof, but my daily practice has transformed me such that I walk through fire or sunshine or rain with grace. And I feel happy—which is the meaning of my given name. It took many years to live up to that name.

Now I also have a spiritual name, which I grow into each time I use it. Nam Joti Kaur means the princess-lioness who walks in the light of God's divine name. As a teacher, I have been blessed to witness hundreds of students also transformed through communion with God. They are faithful members of the Church of Jesus Christ of Latter-day Saints who found my online class, took a chance on something weird, and are happy they did. You will read many of their stories and more of mine in this book.

Before my baptism, years ago, I memorized the thirteen Articles of Faith, which begin with "We believe..." and summarize the church's theology in very simple terms. The thirteenth and crowning article of faith ends with this statement: "If there is anything virtuous, lovely, or of good report, or praiseworthy, we seek after these things." I have spent most of my life taking this statement to heart, and I am better for it. The Prophet Joseph Smith said, "One of the grand fundamental principles of 'Mormonism' is to receive truth, let it come from whence it may."[1]

I love Kundalini Yoga As Taught by Yogi Bhajan®! I love Jesus Christ's gospel and His restored church. I am a covenant-keeping, temple-going member of The Church of Jesus Christ of Latter-day Saints who wears a turban and practices daily sadhana during the ambrosial hours. I live a consecrated life. I hope that the technology of Kundalini Yoga spreads to all the reachable and teachable everywhere.

Yogi Bhajan taught that everyone should create a teacher ten times greater than themselves in their lifetime and that every student should be a teacher. That is why I have written this book. It is my hope that the sacred science that Yogi Bhajan so generously and freely gave us can be easily and accurately shared. I also hope that for those with little access to a Kundalini class or to others with common interests, the stories I have included will help you to know that you are not alone. The stories included are all from people who have taken my class or found my videos online and accepted my 40-day challenge (which is meant to be only the beginning, of course). They are are active, covenant-keeping members of The Church of Jesus Christ of Latter-day Saints. I hope that they inspire you to what is possible as they continue to inspire me.

---

1 Joseph Fielding Smith, ed., *Teachings of the Prophet Joseph Smith* (Salt Lake City, UT: Deseret Book Company, 1976), 313.

ABOUT KUNDALINI YOGA AND YOGI BHAJAN

In ancient days there was a sacred science of God-realization called Kundalini Yoga. Yogi Bhajan sometimes called Kundalini Yoga the science of humanology, and stated that "only God knows what it will be called in the future."[1]

The sacred kriyas and meditations that make up Kundalini Yoga have been preserved for thousands of years. They were handed down through a royal, priestly lineage from master to student, but only after the student had proven himself trustworthy—sometimes after months or years. This practice kept the technology from being misused or diluted.

Despite the secrecy, or perhaps because of it, people in certain circles knew about Kundalini Yoga and there were plenty of rumors. In the 1920s, Kundalini Yoga attracted the attention of renowned psychotherapist and author Carl Jung, who referred to Kundalini Yoga as inexpensive psychotherapy because of the way the kriyas and meditations cleaned out the subconscious mind. He acknowledged, however, that the West was not ready for this technology.[2] A few decades later, in 1969, when Yogi Bhajan arrived in Los Angeles for a weekend visit, the West was both ready and in desperate need of Kundalini Yoga. Yogi Bhajan saw and courageously filled this need.

Yogi Bhajan was born Harbhajan Singh to a family of healers and community leaders in what is now known as Pakistan. When he was just eight years old, he began his yogic training with an enlightened teacher, Sant Hazara Singh, who proclaimed Yogi Bhajan to be a Master of Kundalini Yoga when he was only sixteen and a half years old, a feat in itself. He was also a master of Hatha Yoga and White Tantric Yoga.

During the turmoil of partition in 1947, when Yogi Bhajan was eighteen, he led the

---

1   Yogi Bhajan, *KRI International Teacher Training Manual, Level 1* (Santa Cruz, NM: Kundalini Research Institute, 2007), 196.
2   Carl Jung, *The Psychology of Kundalini Yoga* (Princeton, NJ: Princeton University Press, 1996), 26.

7,000 people in his village 325 miles on foot to safety in New Delhi, India. He arrived with only the clothes on his back. Later, when he was able to continue his education, he studied comparative religion and Vedic philosophy, and he received a master's degree in economics, with honors, from Punjab University. Many years later, he earned a doctorate in communication from the University of Humanistic Studies in San Francisco.

When he came to North America in 1968, he was one of the highest living masters of Kundalini Yoga, yet he was virtually unknown. In 1969, while in Los Angeles, he met a number of young hippies who were experimenting with drugs and alternative lifestyles. He recognized that the experience of expanded consciousness and community they were seeking could be achieved by practicing Kundalini Yoga. At the same time, these youth would rebuild their nervous systems, which were being fried on drugs.

Breaking the centuries-old tradition of secrecy surrounding the science of Kundalini Yoga, Yogi Bhajan began teaching it publicly. When people discovered that it provided the natural peace and euphoria they were seeking, they flocked to his classes, where they found an alternative to the drug culture. He called it the 3HO (healthy, happy, holy) way of life.[3]

In explaining his reasons for breaking with tradition, Yogi Bhajan stated, "We are in the desert and I have some water."[4] He also was familiar with the scriptures and yogic prophecies, and he knew that the world was about to enter a new age (the Aquarian Age, which began in 2012), where the world would be in great turmoil and people would need Kundalini Yoga to sustain themselves and survive the calamities that would precede the Thousand Years of Peace. He was sharing the technology for the future.

By sharing the teachings, he risked his life. His straightforward manner of speaking also made a few enemies, but I know him as a man with loving intentions, infinite compassion, and a sense of humor. Just like my beloved prophet Joseph Smith and America's beloved president Abraham Lincoln, Yogi Bhajan had the courage to follow a divine mission, which has resulted in a vast legacy.

He said, "I've come to train teachers, not get disciples."[5] He served tirelessly in this capacity and also as a religious leader. As a deeply devoted Sikh and leader of the Sikh Dharma in the Western Hemisphere, he has met with other religious world leaders to discuss interfaith dialog and to foster world peace.[6]

His motto: "If you can't see God in all, you can't see God at all."
His credo: "It's not the life that matters, it's the courage that you bring to it."
His challenge to students: "Don't love me, love my teachings. Become ten times greater than me."[7]

---

3 Kundalini Research Institute, "Yogi Bhajan," accessed March 18, 2014, http://www.yogibhajan.com.
4 Dharma Singh Khalsa and Cameron Stauth, *Meditation as Medicine: Activate the Power of Your Natural Healing Force* (New York: Fireside, 2001), 7.
5 3HO Foundation, "About Yogi Bhajan," accessed March 18, 2014, http://www.3ho.org/womens-camp/experience/about-iwc/yogi-bhajan.
6 Kundalini Research Institute, "Yogi Bhajan."
7 The Kundalini Research Institute, accessed March 18, 2014, http://www.yogibhajan.org

Awake, awake, put on strength,

O arm of the Lord; awake, as in the ancient days,

in the generations of old. . . .

Therefore the redeemed of the Lord shall return,

and come with singing unto Zion;

and everlasting joy shall be upon their head:

they shall obtain gladness and joy;

and sorrow and mourning shall flee away.

— ISAIAH 51:9, 11

It is something of
a misnomer to call the
New Testament the
'Christian' Bible,
for it does not belong
exclusively to any one sect.
Truth is meant for
the blessing and upliftment
of the entire human race.
As the Christ Consciousness
is universal, so does
Jesus Christ belong to all.

— **Paramahansa Yogananda,** The Yoga of Jesus

LOS ANGELES: SELF-REALIZATION FELLOWSHIP, 2007

Christ's Yoga

Christ's Yoga

TRYING TO BE LIKE JESUS

When I was growing up, I went to to Primary (the children's Sunday School class at church). In Primary, we would sing children's hymns, and there are a few that I remember well. One is "I Am a Child of God." We sang that one so often that it could be called my first mantra. Another, "I'm Trying to Be Like Jesus," is still among my favorites.

As a child, I was fascinated by the idea that Jesus was perfect. He had never messed up or taken a backward step. I had heard that little children were also considered perfect (or innocent), but I was a child and I knew I had done plenty wrong—sometimes even on purpose. I wondered about Jesus often. Was He really never mean to His siblings? Did He always obey His mother?

I tried to be perfect sometimes—just for one day—but I never made it more than a few hours, at best. I was in awe at how Jesus did it. I felt a little hopeless that I'd ever be totally perfect like Jesus, but I was continually drawn to the idea.

As I grew up and continued to go to church, it seemed to become okay not to be perfect. Everyone said that we should just do our best—perfection was not possible, and we could become perfect someday after we died. I didn't buy it. I saw lots of people not doing their best and using all kinds of excuses. I knew that most of us could do better. Why else did Jesus command us to be perfect? Why would He promise, as He does in the Gospel of John, that if we are willing, we can do even greater works than He did? His exact words: "Verily, verily, I say unto you, He that believeth on me, the works that I do shall he do also; and greater works than these shall he do; because I go unto my Father" (John 14:12).

Even as a child I longed for this. Perhaps because I knew I had an important mission and that perfection was something I not only could achieve but was expected to achieve in this life.

It wasn't until years later that I understood that one of Christ's definitions of *perfect* is "whole." I realized that because of Jesus Christ, I could be made whole on every level, if I followed His example and applied His gift, the Atonement. But it was more years later before I learned how.

When looking to follow Christ's example, the first place to start is in His youth. Though He was perfect, He was not born with a perfect knowledge of everything. At a young age He showed spiritual maturity beyond His years, but it is also clear that He spent a great deal of time studying and learning. The scriptures say that Jesus did not receive a fulness at first, but rather grew "grace *for* grace" (implying an exchange) and then "grace *to* grace" (implying steps or increasing degrees) (Doctrine and Covenants 93:12–13). Wouldn't you like to know more details about that growth? I sure would. It seems that the learning and training He completed in preparation for such an intense and important mission would be good for us to know about, especially if we are to do "greater works than these." Unfortunately, the details are missing: He disappears from the Christian canon from age thirteen to thirty years old.

When I, as a youth, asked about these "lost years," I was told that Jesus was probably just quietly working with His father as a carpenter. I also heard speculation that maybe He had gone back to Egypt for a while. These answers didn't make sense to me. Why would a youth like Jesus, who drew crowds even at twelve years old, suddenly shut His mouth and leave no record? If you know Jesus, then you know He wouldn't. At age twelve, He gently reprimanded His parents for their lack of understanding, saying, "[Know] ye not that I must be about my Father's business?" (Luke 2:49).

As a Latter-day Saint, I have the blessing of having the Book of Mormon: Another Testament of Jesus Christ as part of my canon, in addition to several other ancient books of scripture that have been restored in modern times. The idea of newly discovered ancient records shouldn't be a new concept to Latter-day Saints. In fact, since 1830, when Joseph Smith restored the gospel of Jesus Christ and His authority on the earth, many ancient things that were "lost" have been restored. Most of the world has heard of the Dead Sea Scrolls, discovered between 1946 and 1956. Latter-day Saints should be familiar with the papyrus scroll that surfaced in the early 1800s and eventually came into Joseph Smith's hands. That scroll was translated and is now included in our canon as the Book of Abraham.

Among these many cool rediscoveries, of particular interest to me are ancient scrolls from Tibet that tell of Jesus's doings in India from ages thirteen to twenty-nine. Though the scrolls surfaced in the late 1800s, they were not well received in the West, and it took many years and more evidence before they became more widely known and accepted.

Of course, the lore about Jesus in India was not a new idea to the folks in India. Along the route He likely traveled and in the places He lived, there is plenty of oral tradition, folklore, and myth surrounding His life. He was known there as Master Issa, and to this day, there is a pool named after him, where supposedly He once stopped and washed His feet.

While I was reading the Tibetan scrolls, three translations of which are now available in book form,[1] I recognized the truth in them and felt the Spirit confirm it. It seemed so obvious to me: *Of course Jesus would go to India.* I thought. *He went there to study and perfect His knowledge of the divine word and of the sacred science of God-realization.*

Jesus Christ has been so Westernized that some people may find it hard to believe that He was ever in India, so it might be good to begin with some basic geography. Born in the heart of Palestine, Jesus was positioned in the exact center of the known world (at that time) and at the crossroads between East (India and the Orient) and West (Europe). Almost all trade routes from Europe to India and back went through Israel. And in truth, Jerusalem was more of an Oriental city than a Western city, but the Christian world has forgotten this.

At the time of Jesus Christ's birth, "wise men from the East" (Matthew 2:1) came to visit Him and worship Him. These distinguished Eastern men are believed to be kings from India (possibly why King Herod granted them an audience) who were known for their scientific, astrological, and esoteric knowledge. Their scriptures had foretold Christ's coming, and they had watched the stars and used scientific knowledge to find him. They traveled far and were inspired to bring Him specific gifts. These gifts were not mere symbolic tokens but may have been very important in helping Jesus fulfill His life's mission. For example, the gold they brought was a huge sum of money. This gift likely funded His family's move to Egypt and their sojourn there during His early years. (The gifts of frankincense and myrrh are discussed on the left.) It makes sense that Jesus would reciprocate the visit from these Eastern wise men.

FRANKINCENSE AND MYRRH

What was the significance of this duo of gifts brought to Jesus by men from the East? One writer suggests both practical and symbolic meanings.

Frankincense

Practical use: Aside from its considerable monetary value, frankincense was used as a sweet-smelling incense and perfume.

Symbolic meaning: Frankincense comes from a sweet tree resin and was used in priesthood ordinances, in burnt offerings (see Leviticus 2:1), and in oil for anointing priests. Thus, frankincense can represent the Lord's priesthood and His role as the Lamb of God to be sacrificed on our behalf (see John 1:29).

Myrrh

Practical use: Myrrh, a bitter oil from a tree resin, was economically valuable but was probably more beneficial to Mary and Joseph for its medicinal uses.

Symbolic meaning: In the New Testament, myrrh is usually associated with embalmment and burial because of its preservative qualities (see John 19:39–40). Myrrh's medicinal uses can symbolize Christ's role as the Master Healer. The oil's use in burials can symbolize "the bitter cup" He would drink when He suffered for our sins (see Doctrine and Covenants 19:18–19).

---

1 Elizabeth Clare Prophet, *The Lost Years of Jesus: Documentary Evidence of Jesus' 17-Year Journey to the East* (Livingston, MT: Summit University Press, 1984), 191–221.

Though Judaism and Christianity have largely given our civilization its present shape, according to scholars, these religious traditions "were influenced by ideas stemming from countries further east, especially India."[2] The scriptures of India are known as the oldest and most all-encompassing of the the human race. India is widely regarded by religious scholars as the mother of religion.[3]

But let's go back to Jesus, age thirteen. In Jewish culture, age thirteen was when a boy reached manhood and could be married. Jesus, already known for His intelligence and excellence, was probably a candidate for marriage. According to the Tibetan scrolls (which for now, let's just assume are factual), His parents were arranging a marriage for Him. But Jesus had His own plans. He arranged to travel with a caravan of merchants to India and He secreted away with them.

JESUS IN INDIA

The records say that Issa was fourteen when He crossed the Sind. His fame spread quickly, as it had in Israel. The Jains asked Him to stay with them, but He went to Juggernaut, where the Brahmin priests taught Him to understand the Vedas and to teach, heal, and perform exorcisms.

He spent six years in Juggernaut and other holy cities. He became involved in a conflict with the Brahmins and the Kshatriyas (the priestly and warrior castes) because He was teaching the holy scriptures to the lower castes. The lower castes were not allowed to hear the scriptures at all or were permitted to hear the scriptures only on special holidays.

If you know Jesus, then you will not be surprised by His response: "God the Father makes no difference between his children; all to him are equally dear."[4]

Jesus ignored the injunction of the upper castes, and they plotted to kill Him. After being warned by the people, He left during the night and went to the foothills of the Himalayas in southern Nepal. After six years of study, Issa "had become a perfect expositor of the sacred writings."[5] He then journeyed west, preaching against idolatry along the way. At age twenty-nine he finally returned to Israel, where He found John the Baptist and received the ordinance of baptism to officially begin His ministry. (The scrolls go on to describe Christ's ministry and crucifixion, though this part is very brief and varies a bit from the New Testament as this information appears to have come back second hand from traveling merchants who witnessed some of the events.)

As one comes to understand the East, Eastern scriptures, and the ancient science of Kundalini Yoga, many of Jesus's familiar teachings become richer. As you experience

---

2 Georg Feurerstein, Subhash Kak, and David Frawley, *In Search of the Cradle of Civilization: New Light on Ancient India* (Wheaton, IL: Quest Books, 1995), 12.
3 Ibid.
4 Nicolas Notovich, *The Unknown Life of Jesus Christ* (Radford, VA: Wilder), 5:11, quoted in Prophet, *The Lost Years of Jesus*, 198.
5 Notovich, *The Unknown Life of Jesus Christ*, 6:4, quoted in Prophet, *The Lost Years of Jesus*, 200.

the awakening power of Kundalini Yoga and Meditation, things that have remained mysterious can suddenly be perceived through intuitive understanding.

EYES TO SEE AND EARS TO HEAR—AWAKENING INTUITION

But blessed are your eyes, for they see: and your ears, for they hear.—Matthew 13:16

Many of Jesus Christ's most sacred teachings are embedded deep in layers of symbolism. However, careful study shows that He did not shroud these deeper truths in mystery when speaking to the individuals close to Him. As recounted in the book of Matthew, the disciples ask Jesus, "Why speakest thou unto them in parables?" Jesus answered, "Because it is given unto you to know the mysteries of the kingdom of heaven, but to them it is not given. Therefore speak I to them in parables: because they seeing see not; and hearing they hear not, neither do they understand" (Matthew 13:10–11, 13).

Jesus is basically saying, "You—who are ordained, who are my real disciples, and who are living spiritually disciplined and consecrated lives according to my teachings— you have meditated and your spiritual eyes and ears have been awakened. You deserve to know the mysteries of God. But ordinary people, unprepared or unwilling, are not able to comprehend or practice these deeper truths. So I give these truths to them in symbolic stories with many layers, and all people can glean what they will. And if they apply it, they will make some progress."

In teaching this way, He was being merciful and also realistic. If we are to be realistic, we must accept, as Christ did, that the reachable and teachable are a small percentage: "For this people's heart is waxed gross, and their ears are dull of hearing, and their eyes they have closed; lest at any time they should see with their eyes, and hear with their ears, and should understand with their heart, and should be converted, and I should heal them" (Matthew 13:15).

To illustrate this point, He gave the parable of the sower. While the sower (teacher) sowed seeds everywhere without prejudice, only a few seeds fell on good ground. If we are to be among the percentage whose soil is deep and rich, we must open our eyes and ears, or in other words, awaken our intuition.

The dictionary definition of *intuition* is "direct perception of truth, fact, etc., independent of any reasoning process; immediate apprehension."[6] Many people of faith have experienced flashes of intuition—the moments when you *just know*. Yet flashes of intuition are just the beginning. By actually awakening intuition, we have the ability to receive divine insight/personal revelation at all times, not just in flashes and spurts.

Regarding intuition, Paramhansa Yogananda said, "All bona fide revealed religions of the world are based on intuitive knowledge. Each has an exoteric or outer particularity

---

6 *Dictionary.com*, s.v. "intuition," accessed January 3, 2014, http://www.dictionary.com.

and an esoteric or inner core."[7] The exoteric aspect is the external public image, which includes the doctrines, ceremonies, dogmas, and culture. The esoteric aspect focuses on the actual communion of the soul with God. For example, in The Church of Jesus Christ of Latter-day Saints, the doctrine of personal revelation is the core of the religion. God revealed himself to a young boy, through whom He restored the gospel of Jesus Christ and His authority on the earth in this dispensation. Regarding this and all other truths, each

> We pay too little attention to the value of meditation, a principle of devotion. In our worship there are two elements: One is spiritual communion arising from our own meditation; the other, instruction from others, particularly from those who have authority to guide and instruct us. Of the two, the more profitable . . . is the meditation. . . . Meditation is one of the most secret, most sacred doors through which we pass into the presence of the Lord.
>
> —David O. McKay, Teachings of the Presidents of the Church: David O. McKay (Salt Lake City, UT: The Church of Jesus Christ of Latter-day Saints, 2003), 31.

member of the church is encouraged to seek confirmation through personal revelation—a witness from God. Because this core of experiential understanding is individually applied, there are varying degrees of dedication and success. The outer is for the many, the inner is for the few.

We know, through scriptural records, that having an inner experience of the divine is possible. The enlightened prophets had a firsthand knowledge of God and of reality. They were able to see through the façade that the ancients called *maya* (a Sanskrit word meaning "illusion").

How these prophets became awakened and God-illuminated was twofold, and Jesus laid out the steps in His simple statement to Nicodemus: "Except a man be born of water and of the spirit, he cannot enter the kingdom of God" (John 3:5).

In the first step, the prophets entered in. They had to be purified. To do so, they had to physically receive the ordinance of baptism. Baptism by immersion is both a symbolic and literal cleansing, as well as a symbolic rebirth. As part of the ordinance, the prophets made a *covenant* to follow God and keep His commandments. Keeping commandments is an important key to purity and advancement: "He that keepeth [God's] commandments receiveth truth and light, until he is glorified in truth and knoweth all things" (Doctrine and Covenants 93:28). One could say that the ordinances and the commandments are part of

---

7 Paramahansa Yogananda, *The Yoga of Jesus* (Los Angeles: Self-Realization Fellowship, 2007), 45.

the exoteric aspect of religion. They are absolutely necessary, but they are the outer gate.

In the second step, the prophets were "born of the spirit." In this case Jesus is referring to a second birth of the soul—which occurs in a personal, esoteric way. It is the awakening of intuition. Some people call this awakening the baptism of fire and the Holy Ghost. Others call it enlightenment. Whatever you call it, awakening is accomplished with the aid of the Holy Spirit: "For by my Spirit will I enlighten them, and by my power will I make known unto them the secrets of my will. Yea, even those things which eye has not seen, nor ear heard, nor yet entered in to the heart of man" (Doctrine and Covenants 76:10).

The Holy Spirit is available to all people everywhere; however, because of the fallen state of humankind's consciousness and because of maya, everyone—regardless of religious affiliation—can lack the companionship of this member of the godhead. The Book of Mormon prophet Alma implied as much when he posed the following questions to a crowd of converted believers: "Have you spiritually been born of God? Have ye received his image in your countenances? Have ye experienced this mighty change in your hearts?" (Alma 5:14).

Let's return to Nicodemus, who was a Pharisee and held the title of a "master of Israel." He came to Jesus by night, probably to avoid social criticism, and declared that he knew Christ was teaching and working miracles by the power of God. It was an act of courage for a man of his position to approach Jesus, a controversial teacher, and declare faith in His divinity. But Nicodemus didn't understand what Christ meant by "born again." And so Nicodemus asks, "How is it done?" Holding a ceremonial office did not guarantee him an understanding of the mysteries of God. He had an intellectual knowledge of the scriptures but not of things that could be perceived only by intuitive understanding.

In reply, Jesus states: "We speak that we do know, and testify that we have seen; and ye receive not our witness. If I have told you earthly things and ye believe not, how shall ye believe if I tell you of heavenly things?" (John 3:9–12). The phrase "we speak that we do know" refers to knowledge deeper than that derived from intellectual reasoning. Jesus, and those closest to Him, *knew* how to achieve this awakening, and Jesus shared this knowledge with Nicodemus in veiled language.[8]

---

8 Christ's answer to Nicodemus is discussed in greater detail in the Kundalini chapter.

CONSCIOUSNESS AND COVENANTS

Jesus teaches that the route to mighty change and second birth/awakening is through regular, disciplined comm*union* with God: "Take my yoke upon you . . . for my yoke is easy and my burden is light" (Matthew 11:29–30).

The word *yoga* means "union" and comes from the same root as the word *yoke*. Anciently, yoga[9] was about the practices, principles, and disciplines that led one to a state of union with God. In our day, many people have come to think of yoga only as a physical discipline. But the *asanas*, or postures, that have gained popularity in recent years are actually the most superficial aspect of this profound science of unfolding the infinite potential of the human mind and soul.

Because of the many layers in Jesus's teachings, it is reasonable to assume that when Jesus taught "take my yoke upon you . . . for my yoke is easy and my burden is light," He could have been saying, "Take my *yoga* upon you." Indeed, the experience of yoga, with its royal lineage, does make one's burdens light and has the power to awaken the devoted disciple.

Yoke also could also imply union with God through covenants. Covenants are two-way promises with God. In the Church of Jesus Christ of Latter-day Saints, we make our first covenant at baptism. We promise to follow Him and keep His commandments, and He promises to forgive us of our sins as we repent, to give us the gift of the Holy Ghost, and to give us eternal life.

After baptism, however, on the journey to greater light and knowledge, God requires additional, deeper covenant making from the heart. When we make these covenants, he promises us blessings even more magnificent than those that come with baptism. These promises include obtaining godhood, becoming joint-heirs with Christ, achieving perfection—being like Jesus! These deeper covenants are made in the Lord's holy temples as part of sacred ceremonies that are called *ordinances*. (The term has a meaning roughly similar to that of the term *sacrament* in other Christian denominations.) The LDS church's Guide to the Scriptures defines *ordinances* as "sacred rites and ceremonies. Ordinances consist of a*cts that have spiritual meaning*s."[10] The Prophet Joseph Smith explained that "by the Spirit of God through ordinances," we are born again.[11] Truman G. Madsen added, "All ordinances, therefore, are channels of his Spirit. But the crowning ordinances are those of the Holy Temple."[12]

According to my understanding and experience, becoming like Jesus requires both consciousness and covenants. Each is powerful but is not enough alone. No matter how

---

9 If the word *yoga* triggers images of gym yoga and body cult, just mentally replace it with the concept of union.

10 Guide to the Scriptures, s.v., "ordinances," accessed March 21, 2014, https://www.lds.org/scriptures/gs/ordinances?lang=eng&letter=o. Ordinances are discussed more in "The Body and the Temple" chapter.

11 Joseph Fielding Smith, ed., *Teachings of the Prophet Joseph Smith* (Salt Lake City, UT: Deseret Book Company, 1976), 162.

12 Truman G. Madsen, "Foundations of Temple Worship" (devotional, Brigham Young University–Idaho, Rexburg, ID, October 26, 2004), accessed March 21, 2014, http://trumanmadsen.com/media/FoundationsofTempleWorship.pdf.

purified and awakened we might be, we cannot make the final ascent to godhood without the ordinances and covenants of the temple. Similarly, making covenants and participating in "acts that have spiritual meanings" in temples or elsewhere is not enough if our hearts are not purified and if we don't filter those meanings through awakened consciousness.

Yes, we need the essential ordinances, but we also need the essential attributes. Yes, we need to keep our covenants, but we also need to develop our character.

Neal A. Maxwell, "Apply the Atoning Blood of Christ," *Ensign*, October 1997, 22

Opening My Eyes to See and Ears to Hear | Nancy Holbrook

I started meditating after I had an excruciating surgery to repair a broken ankle. I broke my ankle the middle of February and tried the casting, but my ankle never healed so I had to do surgery at the beginning of May. This year and last have been tough, tough, tough.

I practiced Qigong before I broke my ankle, but it requires standing and movement, so Qigong was out. I was looking for some other modality to help me heal. Basically, the entire month of May I was off my feet and stuck in bed after the surgery. My soul sister Robyn had told me about the book *The Gift of Giving Life*, and so I signed up on the newsletter. I got the e-mail about the meditation class, and once I read about it I couldn't stop thinking about it. I read Felice's entire blog about meditation and still kept putting off the class. Yoga and meditation are *not my thing*. I've tried to do yoga before, but I have a really difficult time sitting still. I ended up signing up for the class late but getting in. My intention for doing meditation was to help heal my ankle and recognize and receive personal revelation more easily.

I started with just Kirtan Kriya but pretty quickly added the anger and prosperity meditations. When I started meditating with Kirtan Kriya, I would cry almost every time I meditated. When I added the other meditations, I would sometimes cry through all three, or sometimes one or two. Sometimes I would have to stop because I was crying so hard, and I would start over again. When I would meditate, all the unpleasant emotions I was trying to hold in or ignore or press down would come bubbling up to the surface, and I would have to feel them and deal with them.

I was really angry that I broke my ankle and that it didn't heal. I was frustrated and angry that I had made the wrong choice and not gotten surgery right away. I was angry that my best friend, who I love, was moving away. I was angry that even though I was doing everything I could to keep the commandments and my covenants, challenge after challenge after challenge were breaking on my head and my family. I was angry that I had a new, very overwhelming, challenging calling. I was angry that God didn't give me a miracle and heal me. I felt like He was picking on me and my family and had way more confidence than I did in my abilities to manage everything.

After I started meditating, I felt like my ankle finally started to heal. I wasn't in so much pain all the time. But meditating was helping to heal my spirit too. I have been learning a lot about myself, my body, and how much more intertwined and connected our emotional/spiritual self is with our bodies.

I started doing the anger meditation because I have four kids, and sometimes it seemed that out of nowhere I would have this white hot rage after the twentieth tantrum of the day or some other small thing (like the straw that broke the camel's back). The anger was like lightning—quick, loud, and destructive. And I would always feel bad afterward and beat myself up for being a bad mother.

Through many sources, including meditation, I came to understand that anger is a secondary emotion. It was my manifestation of feeling helpless, lonely, constantly worried, overwhelmed, unloved, or all of the above. Many emotions were unpleasant and difficult, and I wouldn't acknowledge or address them, trying to will them away. But when I thought I was safe, they would come popping up like a ball held underwater that finally wiggles its way out unexpectedly. They were expressed many times through anger. Once I had worked through why I was currently angry, memories and emotions from my childhood starting coming up. I would relive how I felt sometimes as a child—helpless, lonely, confused, unloved.

I came to realize why I have difficulty really listening and learning through hearing. As a child, I was rascally and would do anything to get out of chores or work, and I would make messes wherever I went. When I was really young, I didn't understand when I would get yelled at, be called names, or feel a burning resentment/anger from my mother. I know that is why I learned to tune out what I was hearing—it hurt too much to take it in. As I got older, I learned how to get positive attention from my parents by cleaning the house, watching my siblings, and so forth. But until I was about nine years old, when I started helping around the house, I didn't think my mother liked me (not that I blame her). This tuning out was a problem when I first got married—and still is because I can completely tune out and be somewhere else entirely when things are tough in the moment, and I don't consciously do it.

All these memories and clarity of thought have not made me angry or resentful of my parents. They did the best they could with what they had. And I feel more compassion for them because I understand how difficult parenting is. I wish I could go back in time and hug them and give them what they needed.

This growth has helped me tremendously with my own children. I think it has been a gift from God, because now I remember what it feels like to be on the receiving end, and I can change these patterns in my own parenting. I can break these destructive traditions in my life.

In the past I had struggled to parent differently from how I was parented. When I would find myself yelling and screaming and demeaning my children to get their compliance, using anger and fear as the whip, I would then go to the library and check out more parenting books. I would listen to parenting techniques and books in the car as I ran errands until I had the techniques memorized. I would listen to general conference. I would pray. I would try to implement the new techniques and make new goals. But now through the help of the Atonement and meditation, I am changing from the inside out. With Christ, I am rooting out my old heart and replacing it with a new heart. I am changing from the inside out, which is light years more effective. I am finally understanding better how to access the power of the Atonement to heal and change. This process started years ago, but with meditation it is much faster and for some reason easier.

Don't get me wrong. All is not butterflies and rainbows at my house. I am a work in progress. I still have adult temper tantrums and yell and stomp my feet. But I think they are fewer and further between, and the knee-jerk reaction of anger is fading. I can consciously choose my reaction. I can chose to react with love instead of anger.

With meditation, my eyes are finally open. I can see the way things really are in the world. I can see my children. I can see my husband. My understanding of the gospel, the scriptures, prayer, and faith are opening wide up. I'm not asleep. I pray often that I can see my children for who they really are. I feel like I have eyes to see and ears to hear, like the scriptures say. I realize who and what is influencing me and those around me and how to better protect myself and my loved ones.

Meditation, Myrrh, and Rebirth | Name Withheld

I just got back from the most wonderful retreat. My friend Felice came here to teach us Kundalini Yoga and Meditation. It was a spiritual weekend, full of learning, healing, and spiritual guidance. God spoke to my heart many times and taught me what I needed to know.

I have been an avid user of essential oils for over two years. I was excited to share some of my knowledge with the ladies at the retreat. In preparation, I listened to a CD about emotional healing with essential oils. It was a powerful message and so timely. He explains two particular ways to use the oils to facilitate emotional healing. I knew that I was supposed to share these two methods with the women at the retreat. The first activity was to select three oils that you are drawn to, read the descriptions of their emotional properties, and then ponder the messages that your body is giving you—the physical ailments that are manifesting in your body and how they are communicating some emotional pain.

The second activity was to select the oil that repulses you, the smell that you cannot tolerate. After consulting the book, you are to consider the emotions associated with that oil. Which emotions have you avoided, ignored, or repressed? He suggests that you journal, pray, and meditate until you have an understanding of this emotion and what it is that you need to release.

On Saturday the five of us did these two exercises. Each of us had a powerful experience with our "oil of avoidance." I knew that my oil was myrrh. I had always disliked the smell of myrrh. It nauseated me. I knew that I was avoiding something big.

I read from the book about myrrh. This oil is known for healing the relationship between mother and child when it has been severed. Myrrh heals the disturbance and feelings of abandonment. "Myrrh assists individuals in letting go of fear. Through reestablishing a healthy connection to the earth and to one's own mother, myrrh rekindles trust within the soul. As the individual learns to once again live in trust, confidence in the goodness of life returns and the soul feels more safe and at home in the earth."[1]

I have never had a close connection with my mother. She was a good mom, and she always took good care of my family. I love her, but I have always felt some resentment and anger toward her, without understanding why. I blame her for many of my faults, even my body issues and weight gain. I am not proud of these feelings, but I feel them nonetheless. Clearly, I had some things to release.

So there I was, reading about myrrh and contemplating my relationship with my mother. I applied some myrrh to my hands, cupped them around my nose and mouth, and breathed deeply. Yuck! I kept breathing. Felice suggested we tune in and do some simple alternate-nostril breathing as a meditation. I could smell the myrrh on my hands as I did so. I continued for about three minutes. I felt an immediate shift.

I began to write in my journal: "Dear Mom, I forgive you. I accept you exactly where you are. I came to you at the right time. I take the best you gave me and I let the rest go. I can move on in peace. I love you how you are right now. You are enough. I am enough. We have lessons to teach each other."

Although five of us were sitting at the table together, we were each having a powerful experience of our own. We were each letting our special oil teach us about our emotional pain and then journaling about our thoughts. Many quiet tears were shed.

Next, Felice led us in a rebirthing meditation. As part of the meditation, we had to imagine that we were in heaven, preparing to come to earth for our mortal experience. We imagined our joy and excitement. We imagined ourselves coming into our mother's womb and how wonderful it was to have a body. We felt safe and secure in the womb; we felt loved. We also imagined what our mother was experiencing during the pregnancy and how she felt to be carrying us. This was a beautiful and powerful experience for me. I started to feel greater love for my mother and to understand her a little more. I began to accept her and to accept my body.

During this experience I was given some new knowledge. God spoke to my heart and helped me understand an important part of my life story. I was a *castaway*—a spirit that had been sent into a mother's womb but had not been born because of an elective abortion. My spirit returned to heaven and was "reassigned" to another mother. This realization gave me

---

1 Daniel McDonald, *Healing with Essential Oils* (Vauxhall, NJ: Enlighten, 2012).

many feelings of abandonment and fear. Also, I was angry that I got this body instead of the body I was meant to have. I was meant to have a better, more thin and beautiful and healthy body. I was meant to have a better, more thin and beautiful mother. In an instant, I understood why I harbored such anger and resentment toward my mother and my own body. This understanding was both disturbing and enlightening.

God showed me a glimpse of what I felt in my mother's womb—the confusion, the anger, the feelings of abandonment. He also explained to me that I didn't want to come out, that I wasn't ready to be born. The doctor, who thought I was overdue, had induced labor even though I was really six weeks premature. I weighed just over 4 pounds, so I was bottle fed and in an incubator for the first few weeks of my life. I think this only added to my feelings of abandonment and separation. The words I had read in the book about myrrh came flooding into my mind: "Myrrh helps the soul to feel the love and nurturing presence of mother. Similar to the nutrient-rich colostrum found in mother's milk, myrrh oil inoculates individuals from the adverse and harmful effects of the world. Like the warmth of a mother's love for her child, myrrh assists individuals in feeling safe and secure."[2]

In that moment, God inspired me to start rubbing myrrh on my stomach daily, that this would heal and repair my digestion—as if I were getting the colostrum I needed after my birth. He told me that it would help me to release the anger, heal emotionally, and strengthen my relationship with my mother.

Tears ran down the sides of my face. This was a revelation. A message straight from God. I felt so connected to Him and so loved. I was overwhelmed with gratitude and humility.

That night, as I prepared for bed, I applied some myrrh oil to my stomach. Then He instructed me one more time: "Put it on your tongue, and suck your thumb."

Felice had just been talking about how pressing the tongue (or thumb, in this case) to the roof of the mouth stimulates the hypothalamus to get a better signal from the pituitary gland.

I followed the instruction and crawled into bed and sucked my thumb. Myrrh was the "colostrum" that I needed at that moment. Words cannot describe how amazing I felt. I felt soothed and consoled in a way that I never had before. Following this inspiration filled a hole in my soul that had been there for forty years. I wept with joy and felt the love of God surrounding me.

I awoke the next day feeling like a brand-new person. I now feel comfortable in *this* body, the body I had resisted and resented for most of my life. I am now reprogramming my brain and treating my body like the precious gift it is. I praise God for guiding me that day and for the knowledge He gave me. I am so grateful for the gifts of essential oils, prayer, journaling, and meditation, all of which helped me to receive that knowledge.

---

2 McDonald, Healing with Essential Oils.

God hath both
raised up the Lord,
and will also
raise up us by his
own power.

— 1 Corinthians 6:14

The Mysterious Kundalini

The Mysterious Kundalini

From the scriptures we learn that God created man in His image, from the dust of mother earth, and then "put into him his spirit, the spirit of the man" (Moses 3). I imagine that the best way to fill a vessel (in this case, a man) is through the top, starting at the Crown Chakra and allowing the spirit to descend through the trap doors of the chakras, which knot the physical and ethereal bodies together (see the Yogic Anatomy chapter, pp. 38).

Because of the Fall of Adam, not only were humans separated from God, but their consciousness also *fell,* quite literally. The pure, true, spiritual self that was flowing through Adam and Eve's physical bodies fell toward the lower chakras and earthly desires. With this fall, most of the spiritual life force (Kundalini energy) became coiled and knotted at the base of the spine, creating the "natural man" state. However, our Father, being all knowing and loving anticipated the Fall and prepared a way for fallen man to come again into the presence of God—namely a Savior—Jesus Christ. All they had to do was to covenant with God to obey His laws and when they erred, repent.

Repentance means literally to *re-turn* to God, and in fact, all acts of sincere repentance literally return some of the energy in the body to the upper, spiritual centers. The ultimate form of returning occurs when the Kundalini energy awakens from its coiled sleep at the base chakra and rises through the straight path of the central spinal channel (*shushmana*) to the spiritual centers of the body (*chakras*) and ultimately to God. This upward shift in energy is truly enlightening and is what allows each of us to "put off the natural man" (Mosiah 3:19). When our divine Kundalini energy rises through the body to the crown chakra where it can meet and mingle with God's energy and then returns back through the body, it is life changing. If you keep in mind Jesus's teaching that "the Kingdom of God is within you," (Luke 17:21) then this may be a deeper layer of meaning for what is described in Doctrine and Covenants 65:5: "The Son of Man shall come down in heaven, clothed in the brightness of his glory, to meet the kingdom of God which is set up on the earth."

This may also be an explanation for what occurred on the day of Pentecost, as described in described in Acts 2:3–4: "And there appeared unto them cloven tongues of fire, and it sat upon each of them. And they were filled with the Holy Ghost." I have experienced this kundalini rising/baptism of fire many times, and the only way to describe how it feels is like being reborn.

Kundalini energy is real and is flowing through your body right now. This energy feeds your entire nervous system and is very powerful, though most of this power is locked below the fourth vertebra. The majority of people never tap into even the smallest bit of this energy. This lack of use has been likened to having a Ferrari and never taking it out of first gear. The word *Kundalini* means "the curl of the lock of the beloved's hair." It is considered "the nerve of the soul."

Knowledge of Kundalini energy has existed for centuries, but for most of that time, the knowledge was kept secret from the general populace. Because of this secrecy, many inaccurate representations of Kundalini energy have made their way into the world's web of information. Kundalini energy is powerful, but it is not dangerous when a person's body has been prepared to properly use and integrate the energy. In fact, when a person practices Kundalini Yoga As Taught by Yogi Bhajan®, the Kundalini rises quite naturally and easily and is never forced to rise.

When the Kundalini energy rises, amazing things happen. As it flows through the straight path of the spine and reaches the top of the skull, the pineal gland starts to radiate, and major changes in our consciousness take place. The energy then returns down into the body like nectar flowing down through the chakras, and major changes take place in a person's life[1]—changes that might previously have seemed impossible, such as the happenings in Acts 2 and in the stories shared in this book. When the Kundalini is awakened, our true spiritual nature unfolds, accompanied by the Christ-like attributes that we have been striving to attain. Keeping the Kundalini raised and balanced is another matter and requires discipline and daily practice.

With limited spiritual technology, this kind of awakening can take decades—maybe even centuries—of repentance, disciplined spiritual practice, service, more repentance, slow growth and struggle against the natural man, and so on. But through the practice of scientific meditations and specific yoga kriyas that have been preserved by dedicated holy men since ancient days, raising the Kundalini can occur easily and naturally. A person's true divine nature gracefully unfolds.

The Kundalini energy is often referred to as the serpent force. In fact, the Kundalini rises through three central *nadis* (ethereal nerves): the *shushmana*, which runs straight along the spine, and the *ida* and *pingala*, each of which make two-and-a-half turns as they spiral upward from the base of the spine. You may recognize that motif because it is the symbol printed on medical documents and buildings. This symbol, called the *caduceus*, shows two snakes intertwined around a staff. The caduceus

---

1 Shakti Parwha Kaur Khalsa, *Kundalini Yoga: The Flow of Eternal Power* (New York: Berkeley, 1996), 49.

was likely inspired by the the biblical story of Moses and the brass serpent, and is a perfect representation of the flow of Kundalini.

Serpent symbolism is highly prevalent in the Christian canon and is of a dual nature. Many scholars suggest that the symbol was used anciently, and maybe even before the foundation of the world,[2] to represent Jesus Christ; but Satan distorted the symbol and became known as the "old serpent," thereby creating this paradox.[3]

Many scriptures, however, refer to the serpent as the true symbol of deity. My favorite example is when Moses throws down his staff; it turns into a snake (for the second time); and then, in a kind of serpent showdown, it swallows the snakes of Pharaoh's magicians (Exodus 7:10–12). And in John 3:13–14, Jesus clears up any confusion about the serpent symbolism when He tells Nicodemus, in veiled language, the way to be born again: "And no man hath ascended up to heaven, but he that came down from heaven, even the Son of man which is in heaven. And as Moses lifted up the serpent in the wilderness, even so must the Son of man be lifted up."

There is historical evidence (and I personally believe) that Jesus knew and taught yoga technology to his closest disciples. Christ often gave sacred teachings in a veiled fashion. While the scripture in John 3 reminds us to look to Christ and live, there is an even deeper symbolism.

Jesus Christ was the great crossover artist. He was both God and man. Throughout the Gospels, Christ refers to His mortal body as the "Son of Man," as distinguished from His divine identity and consciousness, regarding which He refers to himself as the "Son of God." Therefore, *Son of Man* not only refers to Christ's body, which would be raised on the cross, but also refers to all people, who must raise the divine spark within them, the metaphorical serpent coiled at the base of the spine (the Kundalini energy).

Christ's answer to Nicodemus's question of "How is it done?" has many layers. His answer shows that He is both the *power* through which this second birth occurs (the Atonement) and the model of what must occur within us. Our consciousness must be "lifted up" (reversing its downward flow and sending it back up to divine consciousness) through the straight path of the spine. Perhaps this process is what Christ was referring to when He advised us to take up our own cross and follow Him. As Paul explained, "God hath both raised up the Lord, and will also raise up us by his own power" (1 Corinthians 6:14). Eternal life is predicated on our ability not just to have intellectual knowledge of God, as Nicodemus had, but also to elevate our consciousness to Christ consciousness, to be "raised in immortality" (Alma 5:15).

---

2 In speaking of the dove as an identifying symbol of the Holy Ghost, Joseph Smith said, "The sign of the dove was instituted before the creation of the world, a witness for the Holy Ghost, and the devil cannot come in the sign of the dove." One implication of this statement is that other signs, symbols, and tokens may have been instituted in premortality to represent deity. And though Satan could not usurp the symbol of the dove, he could and does usurp other symbols, especially the snake. See Andrew Skinner, "Serpent Symbols and Salvation in the Ancient Near East and the Book of Mormon," *Journal of Book of Mormon Studies* 10, no. 2 (2001): 54.

3 Skinner, "Serpent Symbols and Salvation," 42–55.

KUNDALINI QUICK REFERENCE GUIDE

- Kundalini: The essential true self, your divine potential, and consciousness. The energy of the soul itself.

- Kundalini energy is flowing through your whole body, but most of it is locked at the base of the spine.

- Kundalini Yoga teaches that the Kundalini is raised from the base of the spine through three main *nadis* (ethereal nerves): the *sushmana*, or central spinal channel, and the *ida* and *pingala*, which coil around the spine in a serpentine fashion, ending at the right and left nostril.[1] The path of the Kundalini resembles the healing serpent symbol, called the caduceus.

- When the Kundalini energy rises to the Crown Chakra, the Kundalini energy blends with cosmic energy (God/Holy Spirit) and then travels back down through the body, creating major changes in consciousness. Many people describe this process as a rebirth into Christ consciousness.

- Some people think Kundalini Yoga and the Kundalini energy are dangerous. According to Yogi Bhajan, the only danger is when you force something external and artificial, like a drug, into you. The Kundalini energy is God's energy and is already within you. Yogi Bhajan explained, "It is a normal capacity that you are not utilizing. If you start utilizing the energy, where is the danger?"[2] He added, "as long as you practice a balanced kriya, there is no problem. The truth is Kundalini Yoga produces whole human beings"[3] who cannot be manipulated.[4]

- When a person practices Kundalini Yoga As Taught by Yogi Bhajan®, the Kundalini rises naturally and easily and is never forced to rise.

- Sometimes people feel physical sensations, such as tingling or heat, or see flashes of color. These experiences may be indicators that something good is happening, but Yogi Bhajan called them "glitter at the bottom of the ladder" and not evidence the Kundalini has risen. When a person maintains a daily practice, the Kundalini unfolds so naturally that it may be imperceptible at first. The true indicator that the Kundalini has risen is in the "consistent character and noble behavior of an individual."[5]

- The Kundalini rises not just because of exercises but because of a total lifestyle of consciousness, including faith, repentance, covenant making and keeping, selfless service, and healthy eating. Everything we do affects our vibration and our Kundalini energy, and our Kundalini energy affects everything in our lives.

---

1 Khalsa, *Kundalini Yoga*, 48.
2 Yogi Bhajan, *The Aquarian Teacher: KRI International Kundalini Yoga Teacher Training Level I* (Santa Cruz, NM: Kundalini Research Institute, 2007), 26.
3 Ibid.
4 Khalsa, *Kundalini Yoga*, 49.
5 Ibid., 50.

Meeting Christ In My Heart | Beth Hughes

My name is Beth, and I'm twenty-eight years old. I am a mother first and foremost. I have two delightful boys, and by delightful I mean that they are energetic, loving, busy, and all boy. I have a daughter who is still "zero," as my boys like to say. They are also happy to say that she is zero and a half. I also tutor math to high school students in the neighborhood. I taught middle school for three years before I had children. And I always say to people that I love middle schoolers and high schoolers because I never really matured past that age. I have a little, but I have a similar attention span as them, I have the same energy level, and I like to read what they read. I teach a youth Sunday School class right now, and I *love* that I am teaching absolute truth to teenagers. It's awesome. We live in West Lafayette, Indiana, while my husband attends Purdue University to get a PhD.

I discovered meditation through *The Gift of Giving Life*. I had always heard the apostles and prophets talk about meditation and pondering, and I had tried to do it on my own, but I couldn't keep it up. I wanted the peace and the knowledge that we have been promised that comes to those who ponder and meditate. When I found Felice's website and saw that she was going to do a webinar teaching you how to meditate, I signed up.

When I started doing Kundalini Yoga, I found it a little different, but I loved it. As I mentioned earlier, I have always had a hard time being still. And it made me feel guilty whenever I read, "Be still and know that I am God" (Psalm 46:12), because I don't sit still. I am always twiddling my fingers, moving my toes or my feet, or bouncing. Doing the mudras and chanting the mantras were enough movement and repetition for me to be still. I have always set my intention on being closer to God. And I envision that, as I am chanting out loud, I am letting God know that I am preparing for Him to enter into my heart. As I whisper, I envision all the things that I love about God as I prepare to lower myself and enter into my heart and meet God there. While I am silent, I envision being in my heart with God, and then I slowly come out of it, singing praises and gratitude for God and his goodness.

Then I start reading my scriptures. And I study them, and I'm slower about it. I like to be quick and I like to gobble things up, but after I've done the meditation I feel like I can savor the words and ponder them better. I also ask more questions about how different people feel in the stories, or why different words were chosen. Or what questions I should ask my Sunday School class. And then I try to find the answers. And I know that God is listening to me ask better questions and helps me answer those questions.

I also say my longest prayer of the day before I tune out. I list many things that I'm grateful for. Little things, like my oldest son whispering to me how much he loves his sister or the younger son's sense of humor developing. And big things like how grateful I am for the gospel and for revelation and for specific revelations. Then I ask for blessings for everyone else. Since I've started meditation, I feel like I don't have to ask for things for myself. Or if it is for myself it's also for my family, like asking to help me become the best mother for my children. Or asking for the Atonement to cover my mistakes so that my children still have a good experience with families and can still love me despite my sins. I started this when I was five months pregnant with my daughter. And I noticed that I was in a lot more control. I have felt that I don't fly out of control, even with the shift in hormones, and believe me—my hormones have shifted *a lot*. I have also noticed that I am kinder to myself and to my children (which, as my husband says, "is saying a lot because you've always been kind, patient and loving"). I feel lots more at peace. I also have slowed down enough to ponder and think about things. I practice conversations if I know that they'll be loaded, because I don't want to offend with my lack of tact (which I still do, but not every day like I did before.)

My personal relationship with God is solid now. It has always been strong. I have been blessed with a gift of faith, but this has just made my faith like Job's. I feel that I'm not afraid to ask for blessings because I know that God wants to give them to me. I'm quicker to thank Him for those blessings, and I'm quicker to work for them. I feel the love of God strongly, and I feel like I've made my home more like a temple because of meditation. I have had a hard time getting to the temple, because it's three hours away and it becomes an eleven-hour day, and it's hard with a newborn, but I still feel like I'm participating in temple worship with meditation. I feel like I've been able to make my home a temple where God and I visit and commune with each other. Don't get me wrong, we are still striving to attend the temple, but I feel more at peace with my limitations.

I have noticed that my family is all happier. My husband has noticed in me that I seem more at peace. He says the changes are subtle because I was already full of light, peace, and happiness. My boys will break out in singing Sa Ta Na Ma or walk around doing the prosperity meditation. I love it. They are happier on the days that I meditate because I set the tone of the day. They like to watch the life of Christ movies while I meditate. And then we play Resurrection or carrying the sick palsy man around, which strengthens their testimonies. I also am more in tune with the Spirit and can find the moments that I can testify about Christ as we are playing and growing.

I am not perfect, but meditating is the springboard to higher learning for me. I am closer to God when I invite Him into my home, and I do that through meditation. I am in better control of my body, and my body works better when I meditate. I feel close to God and I can feel His love for me and for everyone around me.

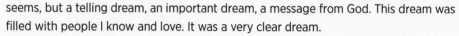

I Had a Dream | Janice Madsen

About six months before Felice started offering online meditation classes, I had a dream. This is what I wrote in my journal:

I had a dream last night. Not a regular kind of dream where nothing makes sense and nothing is quite what it seems, but a telling dream, an important dream, a message from God. This dream was filled with people I know and love. It was a very clear dream.

The most important part of this dream was the feeling I had of peace and tranquility that was repeated throughout my dream. I felt so loved and so happy. These feelings are not often present in my daily life. In my dream, I was filled with the knowledge that I was doing exactly what Heavenly Father wanted me to do to best serve and help those around me—to share with them the love of Heavenly Father.

I woke up knowing what I am to do with my life—or rather, what would make me the most happy and what Heavenly Father would have me do [my life's mission]. This is something I have spent a great amount of time trying to figure out through high school and college.

I am to study natural healing—particularly the mental/subconscious/spiritual side. I know nothing about this and don't even know what to call it for sure. But I know I will be led to the specifics when the time is right. I need to learn all I can in the areas of yoga, meditation, and hypnosis healing. This will be for my benefit and for the benefit of those around me. Now for my dream.

In my dream, I was in a class. I am not exactly sure what all this class entailed, but it was on the subject of yoga and meditation, along with some degree of hypnosis and offering suggestions to the mind on a subconscious level. I was taking this semester-long class and was feeling very frustrated because I had joined late and had missed some important information. I felt I has missed so much of the class and didn't know what was going on.

The teacher didn't mind at all that I had missed part of the class. She was just so happy that I was there. She was someone I knew very well, a dear friend. During our meditation, she spoke directly to my mind and spirit. The words she spoke were very specific and distinct. During my dream, I could remember them word-for-word, although I wasn't sure what the words meant. It was almost as if it was in another language that only my spirit and heart could understand. Now that I am awake, I can no longer remember the words. But what I do remember is the great feeling of peace and happiness and the love that came over me as my teacher impressed these words upon me. These feelings stayed with me throughout the rest of my dream and when I first woke up....

Upon waking from this dream, I felt it was so important and was compelled to get up immediately and write it down. As I have thought through this dream and what it means, the thing that keeps coming to me is that I am to study and learn to meditate. Through this, and more so through the associations and great friends I will meet on my journey, I will be able to best help and serve others. I will gain a great knowledge and testimony of the Savior and the love, peace, and happiness He has to offer. Through my journey I will be able to share His love with others and bless their lives as well.

After I had this dream, I spent some time thinking about what specifically I should do. I looked into different yoga teacher certifications, but nothing felt right. Six months after I had this dream, I came across Felice's online meditation webinar. I immediately knew that this is what I needed to learn and the direction I should take. Up until that point, I had never heard of Kundalini Yoga and had no experience in meditation.

It was a year ago this month that I started my first forty-day meditation. It has been a year of learning and growth, a year of healing and forgiveness, and a year of understanding and drawing nearer to my Savior. Through this journey, I have been reminded time and time again of the love that our Heavenly Father has for me and for each of His children. I have been blessed many times to feel the same feelings of peace, happiness, and love that I felt in my dream as my teacher spoke to my heart. I still have so much to learn, but I am beginning to be truly happy each day and to trust and rely on my Savior. I am so happy to be on this meditation journey. What a wonderful journey it is.

I beheld the
Ancient of Days...
and his wheels were
as burning fire.

— Daniel 7:9

The Chakras
and the Two Trees

The Chakras and the Two Trees

The Sanskrit word *chakra* means "wheel." The chakras are perceived as swirling vortexes of energy. The vortex is one of the most powerful forces in nature, and this vortex motif appears everywhere, from twisting galaxies to tornadoes, the shape of the DNA double helix, and the serpentine path of the rising Kundalini. The chakras are believed to be the doorways to divine consciousness and are centers of transformation. They essentially knot the physical and etheric bodies together, and they exchange energy and communication from physical to nonphysical (ethereal/spiritual) and back.

There are seven major cerebrospinal chakras, beginning at the base of the spine and going all the way to the top of the head. Their common names are: Root Chakra, Sacral Chakra, Solar Plexus Chakra, Heart Chakra, Throat Chakra, Third Eye, and Crown Chakra. Each one correlates with a different color of the rainbow, beginning with red at the Root Chakra and ending with purple at the Crown Chakra. Yogi Bhajan also taught that the Aura is a chakra, the eighth, and the color associated with it is white. Though the chakras are ethereal, they are real, and some people are able to see them with their spiritual eyes. The ancient prophet Ezekiel recorded a vision in which he saw "living creatures," which he later identified as cheribum (Ezekiel 10:20), with different colored "wheels" inside of them that were the colors of the rainbow.

> And when the living creatures went, the wheels went by them: and when the living creatures were lifted up from the earth, the wheels were lifted up . . . for the spirit of the living creature was in the wheels (Ezekiel 1:19–21; see also Ezekiel 10:17).

> And I saw as the colour of amber, as the appearance of fire round about within it, from the appearance of his loins even upward . . . as the appearance of the bow that is in the cloud in the day of rain (Ezekiel 1:27–28).

The chakras are indeed "the spirit of the living creature." When the chakras are open and balanced, the Kundalini is able to rise, which allows a powerful transformation, good health, and happiness. When the chakras are weak or closed, unhappiness, misery, and disease can result.

To understand the chakras fully, we must go back to the Garden of Eden and the two trees planted there.

THE TREE OF KNOWLEDGE

When Adam and Eve partook of the Tree of Knowledge of Good and Evil, our planet became a polarity planet, with "opposition in all things." Some Christians condemn Adam and Eve for the Fall, believing that were it not for this transgression, mankind could have existed forever in Eden. However, Latter-day Saints have an enlightened and different perspective about our first parents and the choice they made in the garden. Latter-day revelation makes clear that the Fall is a blessing, without which humankind could not have come into existence. The Fall was the process by which Adam and Eve became mortal,[1] meaning they were physically changed. Blood began to circulate through their veins, and they became subject to death, but this change also enabled them to give life. "Eve, his wife, heard all these things and was glad, saying: Were it not for our transgression we never should have had seed, and never should have known good and evil, and the joy of our redemption" (Moses 5:11).

Like Eve, I cannot discuss the Fall without rejoicing in the Atonement. Of course, an all-knowing and loving God foresaw Adam and Eve's choice, and He had already prepared a way for Adam and Eve to reenter His presence. As part of God's great plan, we were given the freedom to choose between good and evil, and we were also given a Savior and the ability to repent. It is through Jesus Christ and His infinite Atonement that human kind's fallen consciousness can be returned to God and our bodies will be changed again and become immortal.

Before the Fall, I believe the chakras may have existed in some form, but they did not become the powerful centers of transformation that they are today until after the Fall. As mentioned, the chakras are swirling vortexes of energy. A vortex, the most powerful force in nature, is caused by opposing forces, like the clash of cold and hot air that creates a tornado. Thus, the polarity force—opposition—makes the chakras swirl.[2]

I am awed by the brilliance in God's design. The bitter consequence of the Fall is the very thing that can be harnessed to create the power to overcome it. It is through the pressure of opposition and faithful obedience that potential and growth are created.

---

1 The Church of Jesus Christ f Latter-day Saints, "Fall of Adam and Eve," accessed March 8, 2014, https://www.lds.org/scriptures/gs/fall-of-adam-and-eve.
2 2 Nephi 2:11–16.

Transformation occurs in the same way through the science of Kundalini Yoga. The two opposing forces of the prana (life force) and apana (destroying, eliminating force) are harnessed by pressurizing them below the navel, within the temple of our body. Through this process, we can open and balance the chakras and unlock the Kundalini (the divine True Self) and raise it back up to the higher centers and to God.

President Joseph Fielding Smith said, "Now this is the way I interpret Moses 3:16–17: The Lord said to Adam, here is the tree of the knowledge of good and evil. If you want to stay here, then you cannot eat of that fruit. If you want to stay here, then I forbid you to eat it. But you may act for yourself, and you may eat of it if you want to. And if you eat it, you will die."[1]

President David O. McKay explained that to man "is given a special endowment not bestowed upon any other living thing. . . . God gave him the power of choice. Only to the human being did the Creator say: 'thou mayest choose for thyself, for it is given unto thee' (Moses 3:17). . . . Thus man was endowed with the greatest blessing that can be given to mortal beings—the gift of free agency. Without this divine power to choose, humanity cannot progress."[2]

1 Joseph Fielding Smith, "Fall—Atonement—Resurrection—Sacrament," in Charge to Religious Educators, 2nd ed. (Salt Lake City, UT: The Church of Jesus Christ of Latter-day Saints, 1982), 124.

2 David O. McKay, "The True Purpose of Life," Conference Report, October 1963, 5.

The reason I refer to Kundalini Yoga as a technology is because the word *technology* means the application of scientific knowledge for practical purposes. The purpose of Kundalini Yoga and Meditation, sometimes called "the science of God-realization"[3] is the same as God's purpose for temples and sacred ordinances: to bring humankind back into the presence of God. In The Body And The Temple chapter, you will read more about the similarities between these two technologies.

Because God is an all-knowing God and also the Creator of our bodies and ethereal anatomy, it makes sense that He would have the technology to help Adam and Eve awaken and return the sleeping Kundalini. And it is quite possible that before He sent Adam and

---

3 Paramahansa Yogananda calls it "Kriya Yoga" and "the science of God-realization" throughout his book *The Yoga of Jesus* (Los Angeles: Self-Realization Fellowship, 2007), and I like the second term.

Eve out of the garden, He gave them a little bit of this sacred technology. Later, when they proved trustworthy and faithful, He gave them more light and knowledge.

You may understand this concept if you are an endowed member of The Church of Jesus Christ of Latter-day Saints and go to the temple often with an awakened understanding of what we do there. I will cover this concept more throughout the book, particularly in the chapter titled, The Body and the Temple.

For now, suffice it to say, when we combine a raised consciousness with the power of sacred ordinances that God has revealed in His latter-day temples, we can rise to a level of purity and power that is above and beyond the façade of polarity (maya), we can literally come into the presence of God, and we can become like God.

THE TREE OF LIFE

That brings me to the other tree: The Tree of Life. In its simplest symbolism, this tree represents eternal life and the presence of God. When Adam and Eve partook of the other tree and fell, God barred them from the Tree of Life to prevent them from coming to God on their fallen terms. He did so by putting two barriers between them and eternal life: "I drove out the man, and I placed at the east of the Garden of Eden, cherubim and a flaming sword, which turned every way to keep the way to the tree of life" (Moses 4:31; cf. Genesis 3:24).

Because eternal life is the ultimate goal of God's plan of happiness for His children, there must necessarily be a way past these two barriers. The first barrier mentioned is *cherubim*. Cherubim are sentinel angels; they guard the way to the presence of God. To pass by them, we need the appropriate *technology*. We can receive this technology in the temple when we make covenants. As alluded to above, Adam and Eve received their first bit of this technology when they made their first covenant[4] before they left the garden.

However, even with the technology to pass the sentinel angels, there is still the flaming sword. Nephi and Lehi's vision of the Tree of Life suggests that the flaming sword may represent the justice of God.[5] As we know, the justice of God cannot allow sin. To come into God's presence, one must be pure in both mind and body. If there is any enmity, ill will, or hostility toward someone or something, it will make the nervous system weak and unable to handle the glory of God. One will quite literally fry, and enmity is the fuel for the fire.

---

4 This first covenant was the one in which God promised Adam and Eve a Savior if they promised to obey God's laws and repent when they erred. The technology they received is sacred and only revealed in the House of the Lord.

5 Royal Skousen, as part of his critical text project on the Book of Mormon, has reached the conclusion that 1 Nephi 12:18 in the original Book of Mormon manuscript (which still exists for that passage) says the following: "And a great and terrible gulf divideth them yea even the *sword* of the justice of the eternal God" (italics added). Note that this text differs from our current edition of the Book of Mormon, which reads "word" instead of "sword." This passage describes that which divides the wicked in the "great and spacious building" from the Tree of Life, namely, "the sword of the justice of the eternal God." Combining Nephi's descriptions of his (and Lehi's) vision of the Tree of Life, we have "the justice of God" represented as both a sword and a flaming fire—combined, a flaming sword.

I like the way LDS scholar M. Catherine Thomas explains the weakening effects of enmity in her book *Light in the Wilderness*:

> Enmity makes us impure and corruptible. The reason that beings with enmity will be destroyed seems to be that enmity decreases a person's ability to endure holiness, being in a contracted, self-absorbed, toxic, and blind state. The nervous system of a spiritually underdeveloped person cannot withstand the higher energy field of purified beings and conditions. Enmity then puts us at risk and makes us perishable in the presence of holiness.[6]

So we must purify our bodies of enmity and anything warlike. We purify ourselves with the help of Jesus Christ and through consciousness. The unconscious mind, as discussed in the chapter on the mind, is a receptacle of many impure things. Purifying the unconscious mind is a much bigger job than it may seem. Most of what is in the mind was planted and programmed without us realizing what was happening, which is why we need a powerful technology. M. Catherine Thomas further explains:

> If we are feeding too much, through whatever medium, on the world-mind and its thought-world, which is characterized by enmity and self-seeking, the Natural Mind will be our reality and will run us. We will not have the inner power to abandon ungodliness and to be lifted up in Christ and filled with His love. We must do an energy exchange by chasing darkness with light and consciously choosing the energy that will hum throughout our soul.[7]

 The sacred technology of Kundalini Yoga purifies the subconscious mind (which I believe to be seated in the Heart Center[8]) and strengthens the nervous system, which is the base power. The nervous system and its ethereal counterpart, the nadis, look like a tree branching out from the spine. The nervous system has been likened to a Tree of Life by many people, as it is the system that brings life and energy to the whole body. But as mentioned in the Kundalini chapter, most people never access most of this divine energy.

When the body-mind becomes purified, when the nervous system becomes strong enough to accommodate more energy, and when all the chakras are open and the Kundalini has risen and stays risen and balanced, many amazing things happen.

---

6 M. Catherine Thomas, *Light in the Wilderness: Explorations in the Spiritual Life* (Salt Lake City, UT: Digital Legend Press, 2010), 152.
7 Ibid, 160.
8 See the Mind-Body-Spirit Chapter.

A person becomes awake, born of the Spirit, and Christ-like attributes flow naturally. The impossible becomes possible, and the veil of maya is pulled from our eyes. The façade of our separateness from God is removed, and the world of opposites begins to fall away.[9]

When a person is thus spiritually and physically enlightened, the chakras, to those with spiritual sight, have the appearance of fire. The ancient prophet Daniel describes this phenomenon in his vision of Adam: "I beheld . . . the Ancient of days did sit, whose garment was white as snow, and the hair of his head like the pure wool: his throne was like the fiery flame, and his wheels as burning fire" (Daniel 7:9).

This powerful energy flowing through the nervous system gives life to the tree of life and the flaming sword within us. We become joint-heirs with Christ. Achieving this state is possible in this life and much faster than your previous experiences may have taught you. As you will read in The Body And The Temple chapter, it is essential that we do all we can to merit this awakening (which comes by grace) while still in our physical bodies.

Nephi gave us the path to the tree. The path is straight and narrow (obedience, the spine). And he gave us a guide (the iron rod, or the Word of God.)[10] The Word chapter explores how sacred, highly vibrating keywords or mantras fit into this picture and how they work in conjunction with the gospel knowledge you already have.

MY FLAMING SWORD

A few years into my journey with Kundalini Yoga, I had several devastating life events happen around the same time. Most were beyond my understanding, but my reaction was not what it might have been a few years earlier. I went immediately into a neutral, meditative mind. All was darkness around me, but I stayed in the light of God's love and prayed to "see things as they really are." Things got darker and heavier. I went deeper. For twelve days I hung by a fingernail over the canyon of doom. I clung to faith and hope.

Then one night, in the middle of the night, I heard the word of the Lord tell me that because I had struggled with a dark presence that had possessed my body for many years, he would now cleanse me from it.[11] After twelve days of fervent prayer, twelve years of unexplained torment were over. The next night, in the middle of the night, I felt a burning sensation going up my spine and out the branches of the nervous system in a tree-like pattern across my back. It felt like marbles made of fire were trying to squeeze through

9 The scriptures say there must be "an opposition in all things" (2 Nephi 2:11). The prophets were, of course, speaking in the context of the world of maya. Opposition is not needed in the higher realms. Once a person has achieved the level of purity that qualifies him or her to stand in the presence of God, the need for opposition begins to diminish, along with its effect on the body/mind. We know from Biblical and extracanonical sources that the bodies of the extremely pure are changed (e.g., St. John, the three Nephites, Enoch, and others) so that they are no longer subject to opposition in all things. It is my opinion that after this change, eternal progression occurs by harnessing the same principles of polarity, but only the purest forms of polarity, such as the male and female polarity, which is used to create spirits and worlds—hence the importance of eternal marriage. I discuss this further in The Body and the Temple.

10 1 Nephi 11; see also 2 Nephi 9:41.

11 You can learn more about dark spirits and interference on page 180.

tiny nerve-sized canals. At first, I was afraid it was darkness trying to get in again. Then, I was inspired to sit up straight and do Breath of Fire.[12] In less than a minute, the energy quickly moved through the rest of the nervous system without pain. It felt like my nervous system had just recalibrated and rebooted. I felt great for days after.

For many years I had been adding more and more light to myself, but only after casting out the devil was my Kundalini finally able to flow completely freely through my already-strong nervous system. It was amazing. Keeping it up was an interesting battle during that dark time in my life, but I endured. Shortly thereafter I began to experience an outpouring of spiritual gifts and visions. Many nights I felt Christ come personally to heal me or be with me. One night, I discerned with my spiritual senses that God wanted to give me something: a flaming sword. I didn't understand it then, but I accepted it. He commanded me to wear it on my back and not to use it unless instructed. I imagined placing it, like an arrow, in the quiver of my spine.

Only recently have I come to understand the implications of this symbolic vision. Though I am not yet perfect, I have been given *access*. I had the impression that this experience may have been the transition from growing "grace *for* grace," which implies an exchange, to growing "grace *to* grace," implying steady incremental growth that is *given*. Each day, as I choose to partake of the fruit, more cells in my body are changed.

---

12 Instructions on how to do Breath of Fire are on page 278.

My Deal With God | Bailey Cotant

I first got introduced to Kundalini Yoga when i was serving a mission for The Church of Jesus Christ of Latter-day Saints. The events that took place to get me to Kundalini Yoga and the events that took place after were all inspired, spiritual, challenging, and quite amazing.

As I was spending a significant amount of time studying as a missionary I found myself constantly being drawn to the idea of meditation. I had never explored much into the world of meditation but I was feeling very strongly it was something I needed to know more about. I began asking around in situations where I felt impressed to do so. I asked a dear friend of mine some questions and she had amazing answers. She said she learned much of what she was teaching me from the blog Progressive Prophetess. She showed me one of the posts and I felt with every particle of my being the truth radiating off the page. That next Monday when I was able to email my mom I told her she must check out the blog and learn all that she could about Kundalini Yoga.

So my mom did. And I learned a couple short meditations and practiced as often as I could while being a missionary and having many tasks to accomplish. One of my leaders told me he felt inspired that I come up with a five minute activity for my zone of missionaries. So I even got to teach my zone and district of missionaries about the meditations, and we meditated together. The room was full of joy and the missionaries responses were all positive! It was nerve racking and a little scary as these things were not typically practiced at what we call zone meeting. But I felt inspired so I did it! So then God suggested I start looking into teaching yoga when I returned home. So with much help from Felice and my mom, I got signed up for a level one teacher training. Although at this point I didn't know all that much about it, just that I felt the truth and divinity of it all.

Upon my arrival home from my mission I learned some things I was completely unaware of. God's hand directed me straight to Kundalini Yoga. It was Him. He wanted me to learn and understand this technology. I believe this because I soon found out the effect it had on my family. This technology quite literally saved my mother, and in fact changed her life.

My family has gone through years of abuse—abuse of all different kinds. And I understood that there was nothing any human could do to fix the broken parts of my family. So I made an agreement with God that if I went and served a mission, He would take care of my family. I believed that all things that were unfair about life could be made right through the Atonement of Jesus Christ. So I went and I served Him for eighteen months. And He directed me straight to Kundalini Yoga. It has changed my family. It has changed me. It is in fact LIFE CHANGING. This technology is such a blessing to my family. I'm not sure I could ever put it into words. But I believe that it is of God, and I have a firm testimony of its divinity.

Neither
shall they say,
Lo here! or, lo there!
for, behold,
the kingdom of God
is within you.

— Luke 17:21

Yogic Anatomy

Yogic Anatomy

Our existence is multi-leveled and complex. It is both physical, spiritual, finite, and infinite. Yogic teachings about anatomy therefore are meant to help us understand all levels and avoid "a lower-dimensional definition of what it is to be human." The ancients understood that each of us can consciously link to God, and that this flow happens through the temple body, through channels that are both physical and metaphysical, or beyond physical.

Jesus Christ taught that the Kingdom of God is within each of us (Luke 17:21). If striving to understand the mysteries of godliness, we need not look here or there, as the scripture says, but a serious study of the Kingdom of God begins by looking inward. Within each of us is a multi-dimensional universe with depths upon depths of spiritual treasure, truths, power, gifts, and more. On the following pages you will find the basic concepts of yogic and ethereal anatomy. When exploring the subtle realms, this is a good place to start.

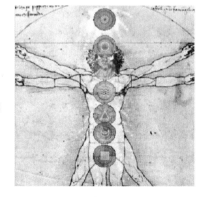

In the next chapter, I have invited Katy Willis RN (Siri Dharma Kaur) to provide basic information about functional western anatomy and Kundalini Yoga's influence on these systems. As you deepen your Kundalini Yoga and Meditation practice, and as you study the Holy Scriptures, you can return again and again to both of these sections and find that there is more to discover each time.

YOGIC ANATOMY QUICK REFERENCE GUIDE

Prana:
: The subtle life force; the first unit of energy. Prana regards the movement and coding of these life energies through the body and mind. Prana has healing powers; most healing comes from moving prana around in the body. Some call prana the light of Christ.

Apana:
: The eliminating force of the body.

Kundalini:
: Your divine creative potential; the energy of the soul itself.

Nadis:
: Channels of flow for the prana. Of the seventy-two thousand nadis, seventy-two are vital. Three of the seventy-two are essential for understanding Kundalini Yoga: shushmana, ida, and pingala.

Shushmana:
: Also called the silver cord. Shushmana is the central nadi and begins at the base of the spine, where the three nadis (ida, pingala, and shushmana) meet. Shushmana travels a straight path up the spine to the top of the head (the Crown Chakra).

Ida:
: The nadi that ends at the left nostril. Ida is the cooling, soothing, mind-expanding energy of the moon.

Pingala:
: The nadi that ends in the right nostril. Pingala brings in the stimulating, energizing, heating energy of the sun.

Chakras:
: Swirling vortexes of energy within the body that correspond to different organs and different psychological states and emotions.

Navel Point:
: Located two inches below the navel. The Navel Point, a center of energy transformation, is the starting point of the seventy-two thousand nadis.

Nervous System:
: The base power, it controls most of the other systems in the body via nerves. The nervous system and the glandular system work together, with the hypothalamus as an intermediary, to repattern the brain.

Pineal Gland:
: The master gland deep in the center of the brain that is related to your intelligence and connection with God.

Pituitary Gland:
: Another master gland, located behind the forehead inside the sphenoid sinus. This gland secretes all the hormones that make you happy and healthy. It works in conjunction with the pineal gland, like a Urim and Thummim. The pituitary gland is associated with intuition and seeing with the spiritual eye.

Tattvas:
: The five tattvas are the elements we are made of: earth, water, fire, air, and ether. If the tattvas are not filtered through the light of consciousness, they are expressed as greed, lust, anger, attachment, and pride. They cannot be eliminated, but their energy can be channelled in positive ways.

Ten Bodies:
: The yogic anatomy includes ten bodies: Soul Body, Negative Mind, Positive Mind, Neutral Mind, Physical Body, Arcline, Aura, Pranic Body, Subtle Body, and Radiant Body. The eleventh body is the Sound Current, which embodies all.

Chakra Basics

Though chakras are discussed separately here for ease and clarity, it is important to remember that the chakras are part of an interdependent system. All of the chakras influence the others in a beautiful dance of color and light and element.

Root Chakra

The first chakra is located at the base of the spine. It is represented by the color red and is associated with the earth and our most basic needs and instincts for survival. The Root Chakra is the home of automatic thoughts and behaviors. It represents elimination through the large intestines and anus.

    The Root Chakra connects us to the earth and, when balanced, grounds us. We are secure, stable, and appropriately loyal. When this chakra is unbalanced, a person will be concerned with only physical survival. They will form unhealthy attachments and give in to unhealthy, instinctual habits and compulsions.[1] The Atonement of Jesus Christ, our most basic need for survival, our grounding influence, helps us eliminate unhealthy habits and root or plant new healthy habits, and our world is reshaped. When we're grounded, we trust ourselves, others, and the world.

Sacral Chakra

The second chakra is associated with the color orange and the flexibility of water. It is the center of feeling, desire, and creation; it is our vision of the world. It is appropriately

---

1 Yogi Bhajan, *The Aquarian Teacher: KRI International Kundalini Yoga Teacher Training Level 1 Yoga Manual* (Santa Cruz, NM: Kundalini Research Institute, 2007), 188.

located in the pelvis near the reproductive organs. Sacred procreative powers allow us to create children and birth them into this world, which brings love and joy into our homes. The Sacral Chakra also helps us create and give birth in all aspects of life, whether it be a book, a garden, or a smile. All are creations.

A weak Sacral Chakra is characterized by little passion for life and opinions about it. An overactive second chakra is characterized by an obsession with the sexual and with fulfilling passions regardless of boundaries. A balanced Sacral Chakra allows us to find the balance in polarity and opposition.[2] Opposition existed even in the Garden of Eden. Adam and Eve were commanded, first, to not eat the fruit of the Tree of Life and, second, to multiply and replenish the earth, in other words, to create children. Eve realized that to organize or create posterity and fulfill God's commandment, she must transgress and step across or through a formal commandment. In doing so, her vision was opened. She found the balance, not to regress but to step forward, become like Father and Mother, and receive the ability to create with Adam.[3] When your second chakra is balanced, you will have a balance of passions, motivations, and opinions. This balance prepares the way for the compassion of the Heart Chakra.

Solar Plexus Chakra

The third chakra is represented by the color yellow and the element of fire. This chakra is located between the diaphragm and the navel point. It is the energy center of the body and provides the motivation we need to support action and follow through. It is associated with the stomach, liver, and kidneys. The stomach receives energy, and the liver metabolizes fat and protein into useable energy. The kidneys filter waste products and coordinate the body's chemical balance. The third chakra is also associated with the adrenal glands, which produce fight-or-flight (action) hormones.

The solar plexus gives us our sense of self. A balanced third chakra helps us realize and visualize our personal missions and then formulate and coordinate energy into conscious action to complete our mission. When the Solar Plexus Chakra is unbalanced, a person is insecure and looks to outside sources for self-worth. They lack the energy to act on ideas and good intentions.[4]

Heart Chakra

The fourth chakra is symbolized by the color green. The Heart Chakra is located in the center of the chest, over the heart and lungs, and is associated with the immune system.

---

2 Ibid., 189–190.
3 Dallin H. Oaks, "The Great Plan of Happiness," *Ensign*, November 1993, 73.
4 Bhajan, *The Aquarian Teacher*, 191.

Accordingly, the Heart Chakra represents love, and the chakra's element is air. Like air, love spreads and awakens compassion. The Heart Chakra is the center of the chakras and brings the upper and lower chakras into balance. This chakra integrates the spiritual with the physical.[5]

Yogi Bhajan said the Heart Chakra is the immune system of self. When the fourth chakra is in balance, it discerns "if something is foreign and needs to be examined, and when something is a part of you, and it can be let in."[6] Balance of the Heart Chakra allows us to see ourselves and others as children of God. We are conscious of our feelings and can direct them to the higher good. When the Heart Chakra is imbalanced, a person shuts feelings and others out, or may have too much sympathy. They may use people to fill their expectations and become dependent. A balanced Heart Chakra leads us to righteous judgment, appropriate mercy, and forgiveness, which is why it is sometimes called the Christ chakra.

Throat Chakra

The fifth chakra is represented by the color blue and the elements of sound and ether. Ether is the void of the the universe that allows matter to exist. The Throat Chakra is associated with the mouth, thyroid, and hypothalamus. The thyroid is located in the throat area and regulates metabolism and autoimmunity. The hypothalamus is located in the center of the brain and is responsible for many autonomic functions (e.g., regulating breathing and body temperature) and essentially creating homeostasis in the body.[7]

The Throat Chakra represents the power to speak and create. It is the power of placing something at the beginning of creation. This idea is evident in many verses of scripture. In the New Testament, John says, "In the beginning was the Word" (John 1:1). In the Book of Mormon, the prophet Alma refers to planting the word, like a seed, in your heart in order to create a fruitful tree (Alma 32–33). Nephi says that by the Holy Ghost men can "speak with the tongue of angels" (2 Nephi 32:2).

When the Throat Chakra is balanced, we are able to convey ourselves to the world, speaking honestly and exemplifying the truth. We are decisive and creative. When the Throat Chakra is out of balance, a person may choose not to make decisions, may be afraid to speak, or may talk excessively.[8]

---

5 Ibid., 192.
6 Ibid., 193.
7 Ibid.
8 Ibid.

Third Eye Chakra

The sixth chakra is symbolized by the color indigo and is associated with intuition, integrity, and integration. It is not associated with an element, but rather, with inner light, and having one's eye single to God: "Therefore when thine eye is single, thy whole body also is full of light" (Luke 11:34). The Third Eye Chakra is located between the eyebrows, right in front of the pituitary gland. As such, this chakra corresponds with the pituitary gland, which controls the endocrine systems of the body as well as the limbic system of the brain. The pituitary gland commands the secretion of hormones that transmit messages, memories, and emotions to the body; thus, the pituitary connects the mind and body.[9]

The Third Eye Chakra, when properly vibrated, has an active relationship with the pineal gland, which is associated with the seventh chakra and is associated with cosmic sound and the voice of the Holy Spirit. The sixth chakra is called the Third Eye because it is associated with seeing and perceiving beyond the two physical eyes. When the pineal and pituitary glands work together, they essentially form a Urim and Thummim within the body. *Urim and Thummim* is a Hebrew term that means "Lights and Perfections." It is "an instrument prepared of God to assist man in obtaining revelation from the Lord and in translating languages."[10]

When the Third Eye Chakra is balanced, our bodies and minds function as one for the good of all. We see beyond the physical and act with eternal perspective, as Eve did in the Garden of Eden. We reason with the heart and the mind, and we have the ability to integrate all truth into one great whole. When the sixth chakra is imbalanced, a person may experience inner turbulence. Signs that the sixth chakra is imbalanced include memory problems, difficulty concentrating, and the inability to recognize patterns of knowledge and wisdom.[11]

Crown Chakra

The seventh chakra is represented by the color violet and is associated with transcendence. It is sometimes called the Tenth Gate. Its vibration is cosmic sound or the voice of the Holy Spirit. The Crown Chakra is located at the top of the head, directly over the pineal gland.[12] The pineal gland is the master gland; if you can influence this gland, you can influence the entire body and its DNA. Some healers believe the Crown Chakra is the seat of the "intelligences"[13] of which we were made. The pineal gland is like the sun,

---

9 Ibid., 194.

10 See Bible Dictionary, s.v. "Urim and Thummim," accessed March 18, 2014, http://lds.org/scriptures/bd/urim-and-thummim.

11 Bhajan, *The Aquarian Teacher*, 194.

12 Ibid.

13 Doctrine and Covenants 93:29. See also Abraham 3:22.

which keeps the entire solar system alive. Though the seventh chakra is associated with sound, this chakra is also very connected with light and the Third Eye because of the pineal gland. This gland regulates the hormone melatonin, which controls the wake/sleep cycle and the circadian rhythm, based on the amount of light present. In other words, the pineal gland is a light receptor.[14]

When the Crown Chakra is balanced, we accept our nobility as children of God. We easily let go of our incorrect perceptions and accept God's perceptions. We surrender our physical limitations and abilities to the glory of God. We humbly bow before God and become His servants. We overcome the temptation of power, and we literally receive the Light. When this chakra is unbalanced, a person may be allured by the temptation of power and glory. They may feel intellectual and elite, or they may seek for power and affluence for the wrong reasons.[15]

Aura

Yogi Bhajan taught that the Aura is the eighth chakra. The eighth chakra is represented by radiant white light. It is our radiance. This chakra symbolizes being one with the Universe/God. The Aura is the convergence and balance of all the chakral energies. This chakra is not associated with any element, only with the sense of being. It is "I AM." When balanced, the Aura is symmetrical and filters the negative and accentuates the sweetness of life. When this chakra is out of balance, a person is vulnerable to pathogens and mental and physical weakness.[16]

---

14 Bhajan, *The Aquarian Teacher*, 194.
15 Ibid.
16 Ibid., 195.

CHAKRA QUICK REFERENCE GUIDE

Chakra	Sanskrit Name	Color	Location	Physical Areas Governed	Balance	Imbalance
1 Root Chakra	Muladhara	Red	Base of the spine	Anus, colon, rectum	Grounded, secure	Threatened, addicted
2 Sacral Chakra	Svadhisthana	Orange	Lower abdomen to the navel	Sex organs, hips, lower back	Creative, flexible	Hypersexual, apathetic
3 Solar Plexus Chakra	Manipura	Yellow	Between the navel and diaphragm	Adrenals, liver, stomach, kidneys	Confident, motivated	Powerless, frustrated
4 Heart Chakra	Anahata	Green/ Pink	Center of the chest	Heart, lungs, thymus	Compassionate, awake	Dependent, isolated
5 Throat Chakra	Visuddhu	Blue	Throat area	Thyroid, hypothalamus	Truthful, decisive	Self-conscious, slanderous
6 Third Eye Chakra	Anja	Indigo	Between the eyebrows	Brain, eyes, pituitary gland	Intuitive, integrated mind/body	Unfocused, self-doubting
7 Crown Chakra	Sahasrara	Violet	Top of the head	Pineal gland	Humble, seeking the best	Power hungry, skeptical
8 Aura		White	Surrounds the body	Biomagnetic field	Spiritual gifts, fully present	Vulnerable to mental and physical disease

The Nadis

The *nadis* are energy conduits that bring vital energy (*prana*) through the body. The nadis are similar to acupuncture meridians, but while there are only twelve meridians, there are seventy-two thousand nadis. They connect the chakras and branch out to the entire body. The nadis may be considered an ethereal counterpart to the nervous system, with its expansive web of nerves, and the nadis do influence and work in conjunction with the nerves. For example, in *Meditation as Medicine*, the authors write:

> The nadis appear to physically affect the nature and quality of nerve transmission from the brain and spinal cord to the outlying peripheral nerves. Therefore, energy blockage among the nadis seems to be associated with pathological changes in the nervous system, and with the closely associated endocrine and immune systems. For example, a decreased flow of energy through the nadis to the throat chakra might result in decreased energy to the thyroid. The physical manifestation of this might be hypothyroidism.[17]

For centuries, healers and yogis—and even early LDS writers, like Parley P. Pratt[18]—have known about this inner spiritual nerve network and its influence. However, there has not been any solid evidence of the nadis' existence until recently. Now, through sophisticated technology, it is possible to detect the fluid-like flow of energy

---

17 Dharma Singh Khalsa and Cameron Stauth, *Meditation as Medicine: Activate the Power of Your Natural Healing Force* (New York: Fireside, 2001), 23.
18 Parley P Pratt, *Key to the Science of Theology*, 9th ed. (1965), 100, 110. Pratt writes about the spiritual fluid, that it contains healing powers, and that it is transferable to parts of the body and to others via the nerves.

48

moving along the channels of the body.[19]

As discussed in the Prana chapter, this flow of energy is the Light of Christ. This energy flow has profound healing effects on the body and can even be directed toward others. The pranic body depends on the nadis to aid in this healing flow.

Of the seventy-two thousand nadis, seventy-two are major *surs*, or zones, through which the nadis flow. Three are of particular importance: *shushmana, ida,* and *pingala.* The shushmana is the nadi that runs up the central spinal channel. This nadi is the straight and narrow path of the spine through which the Kundalini rises. The ida and pingala coil in a serpentine fashion from the base of the spine and end at the left and right nostril, with the ida on the left and the pingala on the right.[20] The ida activates the feminine, cooling, calming force, and the pingala activates the masculine, warming, energizing force.

---

19 Khalsa and Stauth, *Meditation as Medicine*, 23.
20 Yogi Bhajan, *The Aquarian Teacher: KRI International Teacher Training Manual, Level 1* (Santa Cruz, NM: Kundalini Research Institute, 2007), 175.

The Five Tattvas

The tattvas are the basic elements of which we are made. The human body is a microcosm of the entire cosmos; therefore, everything the universe is made of is found in the human body: earth, water, fire, air, and ether. Each element gives the body vital energy, but if the energy inspired by the five tattvas is not filtered through the light of consciousness, a person will manifest the most base aspects of the tattvas: greed, lust, anger, attachment, and pride (negative ego). Yogi Bhajan said, "If you are made of mud, how can you get rid of mud? If you are made of earth, how can you get rid of earth? Nobody can get rid of the five elements of which he is composed. All he can do is channel their projections. . . . You can divert this energy to positive ends."[21] When we examine, discipline, and drink the five tattvas through the cup of meditation and consciousness, they can occur in their highest form, including love, steadfastness, service, and grace.

Below are examples of diverting the tattvas to positive ends:

Greed: Earth (*Pritvi tattva*)—Instead of being greedy to possess things, you can be greedy to possess a higher vibration (seeking more holiness) or to be a noble teacher and spread truth to all people.[22]

Lust: Water (*Apas tattva*)—Instead of being lustful to exploit bodies, you can be lustful to live like God and serve others.[23]

Anger: Fire (*Agni tattva*)—Anger is a destroying emotion; it has great power. Rather than being angry at others, you can channel this power to destroy your own weaknesses.[24]

---

21 Bhajan, *The Aquarian Teacher*, 210.
22 See Mosiah 4:15; 3 Nephi 12:48; 3 Nephi 27:27.
23 See 1 John 2:16; Mormon 9:28.
24 See 2 Nephi 4:27–29; Ether 12:27.

Attachment: Air (*Vayu tattva*)—Instead of being attached to earthly possessions or possessive of people, you can be attached to God and the divine path.[25]

Pride/negative ego: Ether (*Akasha tattva*)—Instead of being an egomaniac, you can have pride and gratitude that God made you. Identify with the Infinite.[26]

Each tattva is associated with one of the first five chakras and has an energy function. The sixth through eighth chakras are beyond the elements and associated with light. Each tattva is also associated with one of the five senses and one of the fingers or the thumb. Meditations like Kirtan Kriya or Ganputi Kriya that use the fingers and the thumb, as well as the five primal sounds, balance the energy of the tattvas.

An imbalance in one of the tattvas can cause a great deal of disruption, pain, and emotional distress. For example, Jennifer was a perpetual love junkie. She would be crying over a breakup one week and then high in love the next. She would often swear off dating, but it only lasted a few days. She was so attached to not being alone, and the pattern had gone on so long, that it was causing many other problems in her life. When she undertook a daily practice of Kirtan Kriya for my forty-day meditation challenge, she found for the first time in her life that she was okay being alone. She didn't go on a date or even think about dating for the whole forty days, and she also began to release her excessive materialism. On day thirty she said to me, "I think I am having a spiritual awakening. Is that normal?"

I explained that it was her True Self being revealed. This self is normal in the heavenly realms, but on this earthly plane, it is an exceptional transformation to witness.

---

25 See Matthew 19:29; Luke 12:15.
26 See Psalm 8:3–5; Psalm 82:6; Isaiah 2:11; Ephesians 2:10.

The Ten Bodies

While most people understand that humans have at least three bodies (physical, mental, and spiritual), the ancients understood that we actually have ten: one physical body, three mental bodies, and six energetic bodies. The scriptures corroborate this understanding:

> And if your eye be single to my glory, your *whole bodies* shall be filled with light, and there shall be no darkness in you. Therefore, sanctify yourselves that *your minds* become single to God, and the days will come that you shall see him; for he will unveil his face unto you, and it shall be in his own time, and in his own way, and according to his own will. (Doctrine and Covenants 88:67–68; italics added)

Below is a brief introduction to the Ten Bodies, plus the all-encompassing eleventh body, and their play in the soul's journey. Each body has specific gifts that manifest when the body is strong; certain liabilities and deficiencies appear when the body is weak. A person's total caliber is determined by the balance of the Ten Bodies. It is important to develop the capacity to know which body is out of balance and then use the appropriate technology to strengthen it. It is said that the root of all disease exists in one of the spiritual or energetic bodies before it manifests openly. Therefore, balancing the Ten Bodies is a key to becoming healthier as well.[27]

1. **Soul Body:** Your soul is the divine aspect of yourself—your higher self, as some would say. When this body is strong, you live by your heart. Inspiration flows freely from the heart, and you come from a place of humility and creativity. You are connected and comfortable in the flow of God's love and use it to create beauty in your life. If this body is weak, a person may come from the head and not the heart.

---

27 Yogi Bhajan, *The Aquarian Teacher: KRI International Teacher Training Manual, Level 1* (Santa Cruz, NM: Kundalini Research Institute, 2007), 200.

They may have trouble accessing their intuition. They may wonder about their life purpose or feel stuck.

KEY TO BALANCING: Raise the Kundalini. Open the heart.[28]

2. **Negative Mind:** The protective Negative Mind sees the negative in every situation. It is an important player in life on a polarity planet. The Negative Mind helps you determine whether there is danger or a need for discernment. The Negative Mind points out every potential obstacle and instills a longing to belong. In this longing's highest expression, it can lead you to connect very deeply with your divinity. If it is underdeveloped, this longing can lead one to be overinfluenced by others and into self-destructive relationships.

    KEY TO BALANCING: Value your discipline. Develop conscious relationships of integrity. If overdeveloped, strengthen the Positive Mind.[29]

3. **Positive Mind:** The expansive Positive Mind sees the positive in every situation. The Positive Mind is open to all possibilities, allows resources in, and allows you to use your power easily and humbly. It is your enthusiasm, optimism, and sense of humor. If this mind is weak, it will become overpowered by the Negative Mind, leading to depression, intolerance, anger, and fear of using power.

    KEY TO BALANCING: Strengthen the Navel Point. Increase your self-esteem. Use positive affirmations. If the Positive Mind is overdeveloped, a person may not see danger and may get blindsided often. If this is the case, strengthen the Negative Mind.[30]

4. **Neutral Mind:** The Neutral Mind is the Meditative Mind. It is the heart of Christ consciousness. This mind evaluates all the input from your Negative Mind, Positive Mind, and all the other bodies, giving you guidance within nine seconds. This mind has a very intuitive vantage point and allows access to your soul and higher wisdom. If this body is weak, a person may have a hard time making decisions, may feel victimized by life, or may have a difficult time seeing beyond the polarities of life on Earth.

    KEY TO BALANCING: Meditate. Tune into the larger, eternal perspective.

5. **Physical Body:** This body is the temple where all the other bodies play their parts. It is the Kingdom of God on earth. It gives you the ability to sacrifice—to make sacred.

---

28 Ibid., 201.
29 Ibid.
30 Ibid.

It gives you the ability to balance all parts of your life and to progress. If this body is strong, it represents the teacher, who can explain abstractions to anyone in simple terms. If this body is weak, a person is likely to be angry, jealous, greedy, competitive, or ungrateful. Weakness may also cause a person to fear being a teacher or to have trouble expressing themself.

KEY TO BALANCING: Exercise regularly. Teach.[31]

6. **Arcline:** Your Arcline is a halo that circles the head from ear to ear across the hairline and brow. It is the foundation of your Aura and your radiance. Women have a second arcline from nipple to nipple, across the heart. The Arcline is your power to project through prayer. This body is like the headlights that guide your soul's journey. The Arcline gives you the ability to focus, to meditate, and to achieve your goals with integrity. The Arcline is associated with the pituitary gland and regulates the nervous system and glandular balance, thus protecting the Heart Center. The Arcline is not subject to this world but is governed by a higher realm. The Arcline is the balance point between two worlds. When it is strong, you have a powerful ability to manifest. It is also a protective power that helps you deal with the stresses of life without shutting down your heart. If this body is weak, a person may lack the ability to focus or manifest. They may not be able to use their intuition to protect themselves. They may be overprotective and easily influenced, and they may have glandular imbalances, which can lead to mood irregularity.

KEY TO BALANCING: Awaken the pituitary gland or the Third Eye Point.[32]

7. **Auric Body:** The Auric Body is the electromagnetic field around your body that can extend for up to nine feet. It is your protection, your shield, and the container into which you can develop your life force and self-esteem and realize your existence beyond your physical boundaries. The Aura can attract or repel negativity and illness. It is also the field where the past and the future are played out. This body holds past memories, which can create ties that hold a person back. When this body is weak, they may be paranoid, negative, and ill, and lack self trust. A healthy, strong Aura can prevent sickness.

KEY TO BALANCING: Meditate. Wear white clothing made of natural fibers.[33]

8. **Pranic Body:** Though prana, the life force, is infinite, your ability to access it is finite. Through your breath, your pranic body brings life force and energy into your system.

---

31 Ibid., 202.
32 Ibid.
33 Ibid.

Prana resurrects your consciousness. As you master prana, you begin to master life. With enough prana, you will feel fearless, alive, and one with creation. If this body is weak, a person is likely to be fearful and defensive. All disease starts with the Pranic Body. A person with a weak eighth body may have chronic fatigue symptoms and low-level anxiety, and may try to get energy from food or stimulants.

KEY TO BALANCING: All pranayam.[34]

9. **Subtle Body:** The Subtle Body helps you see beyond the immediate reality to the higher realms and the other worlds around us. When this body is strong, nothing seems like a mystery; the mysteries of God are more and more easily grasped. You feel calm and peaceful and are able to easily assess situations with clarity and insight that might seem unfathomable to others. A person with a weak Subtle Body is likely to be gullible or naive, have unintentionally crude behavior, and have a restless inability to go with the flow.

KEY TO BALANCING: Complete any meditation or kriya for one thousand days.[35]

10. **Radiant Body:** The Radiant Body gives you radiance. It is your inner royalty and nobility. It reunites you with the light, and where there is light, there can be no darkness. The Radiant Body makes you courageous in the face of any obstacle. Your magnetic presence commands the respect of all who know you. A strong Radiant Body neutralizes all negativity within a nine-foot space of your physical body and can promote harmony across a twenty-five-mile radius. If this body is weak, a person may be afraid of attention and recognition or afraid of conflict. They may feel ineffective in their ability to come through in situations.

KEY TO BALANCING: Commitment.[36]

11. **The Sound Current/Parallel Unisonness:** The eleventh body represents the Sound Current (the Word), "the wellspring of Infinity from which all mantras originate."[37] Yogi Bhajan said, "When the God in you and the human in you are in parallel unisonness, you are an 11. You have no duality. You have divine vision, and the truth flows from you. You don't have to find anything outside of you. The jewels are all in you—you are rich inside, you have satisfaction and contentment."[38] You are your own spiritual master. You can see all the choices in every option and always choose God.

---

34 Ibid.
35 Ibid., 203.
36 Ibid.
37 Ibid.
38 Ibid.

You see God in all and can direct all other Ten Bodies at will. If this body is weak, a person is likely to be selfish, misuse spiritual power, become negative, become a fanatic, and lack compassion.

KEY TO BALANCING: Mantra, mantra, mantra.

A regular practice of Kundalini Yoga, with its balanced kriyas, is a great way to balance all Ten Bodies at once.

And Then She Woke Up | Jessica Jostes

Meditation for me was my way out of a dark place. For fourteen years, I had been dealing with a difficult relationship in which I held on to a lot of anger and feelings of inadequacy. I had read *The Gift of Giving Life* during my last pregnancy, and one day I felt inspired to find Felice's new blog. I did and came across her anger series. I felt like I had nothing to lose, so I started meditating that day. The first day I could not make it through three minutes of the anger meditation before I sat and was overcome with emotion. I felt a huge release. The next day I tried for a little longer, and the same thing happened. I kept with it for a few more days until I was able to do it for the whole three minutes.

During the first few days, amazing things happened in my life. As I let go of the anger, I felt myself being lifted out of my dark place. As I came out, I was reminded how much my Heavenly Father loved me, and I felt His love all around me. I fasted and prayed for my broken heart to be healed. One Sunday at church, my bishop came and told me that he felt inspired for me to read a conference talk called "Balm of Gilead." He didn't know who gave it or when it was given, but he knew I was suppose to read it. I came home, and before I broke my fast I read the talk. It was given in 1977, two years before I was born. It was exactly what I needed to read, and the words penetrated my heart deeply. I closed my fast with much gratitude and physically felt my heart being healed. Adding meditation to my scripture study, fasting, and prayer took my relationship with my Heavenly Father to a new place.

I have continued to meditate every day and have felt myself change. I feel like I had been in a deep sleep my entire life and that meditation woke me up. My eyes see more clearly, my ears listen more sharply, my sense of smell is stronger, and my heart is more open. Open to God. Open to inspiration and open to love, and this has changed my life.

God's Hand | Debi Youngs

I have included the Prosperity Meditation in my daily sadhana for the last eight weeks. Looking back, I can see that my life has changed drastically since I began. My husband was offered a job in another state that will provide more money as well as potential for growth and greater job satisfaction. His new job has allowed me to quit my job, at least for now, and stay at home with my children, something I have prayed for and wanted for a long time.

We are in the process of finding a home, packing our things, and preparing to move. We've gotten rid of so much stuff, which feels so liberating. We've taken our children out of all extracurricular activities for the time being and perhaps permanently. It feels like we are letting go of the things that were distracting and holding us back and making room and time for things that are better, like spending more time together as a family.

The most noticeable change, however, since beginning the Prosperity Meditation has been my ability to see God's hand in my family's lives. My faith is increasing daily, and I know He will provide for us as we follow His counsel. Moving our family is certainly a leap of faith because I have never lived outside of the small city where I grew up.

Along with increased faith, I have felt increased gratitude and have been able to see how the Lord has always guided my life and continues to do so. These are not the changes I was expecting when I began the Prosperity Meditation. What a blessing it is to be guided and directed daily by God, whose wisdom, knowledge, and love are without limits.

Your body,
whatever its natural gifts,
is a magnificent
creation of God. It is a
tabernacle of flesh—a temple
for your spirit.
A study of your body
attests to its divine design.

— Russel M. Nelson

"WE ARE CHILDREN OF GOD," *ENSIGN*, OCTOBER 1998

Western Anatomy

and Kundalini Yoga

Western Anatomy and Kundalini Yoga

by Katy Willis, RN

The topic of Western anatomy and Kundalini Yoga resonates with my journey. Trained as an registered nurse, I perceived alternative medicine and holistic therapy to be a hoax. They appeared to be based on mysticism or magic. In my mind at the time, I could not see a logical explanation as to how such an approach could be healing. Therefore, I did not feel such practices were worth pursuing—until events in my life brought me to a need for healing that couldn't be had solely with the resources at my disposal.

As I began down what I felt was a strange and alternative path, I began to experience healing and transformation. These effects left me completely baffled. How could it be so "simple"? How were these technologies doing what they were doing? I am not the type of person who settles for a whatever-works mentality. I want to break it down and understand it inside and out. I want to know *why*.

My education in anatomy and physiology, or how the body works, became a springboard for me. Rather than a hindrance, as in the past, my knowledge propelled me

forward as I began to learn how the body works *in connection* with the mind and spirit. I have come to understand that many alternative healing and transformation modalities follow laws and principles. (If you are interested in measurable studies performed on aspects of Kundalini Yoga and Meditation, I recommend the book *Meditation as Medicine.*[1])

I urge you to consider approaching your sadhana practice with an open mind. Be consistent in your practice. Before you can make a final judgment call on whether Kundalini Yoga is for you, you must practice for at least forty consecutive days with a serious and committed attitude.

---

1 Dharma Singh Khalsa and Cameron Stauth, *Meditation as Medicine: Activate the Power of Your Natural Healing Force* (New York: Fireside, 2001).

The body is an amazing temple. Below, I will provide a general overview of the body systems. As you have already learned in the Yogic Anatomy chapter, each of these systems corresponds with something non-physical as well (e.g., a chakra, one of the Ten Bodies, a nadi, an emotion, etc.). I will also discuss how Kundalini Yoga can increase efficiency and improve the functions of the physical body. May you be able to join with me in exclaiming "Wahe Guru!" as I give a brief overview of the wonder of the body, its intricate design, and how beautifully it functions!

Circulatory System

This system includes the heart and blood vessels. The circulatory system brings blood, oxygen, and other nutrients to and from the heart, as well as brings wastes to the appropriate organs for excretion. Kundalini Yoga strengthens the heart, improves blood flow, and increases blood volume.[2]

Lymphatic System

The lymphatic system includes the lymph ducts and nodes, tonsils, spleen, bone marrow, and thymus. This system helps return fluid in the tissues to the circulatory system. This system also assists with fighting infection by producing and holding white blood cells and by collecting and killing bacteria. Kundalini Yoga improves the circulation in this system, decreases the demands on this system by improving the function of other organs involved in detoxifying, and increases immunity.[3]

Respiratory System

The organs and structures in this system include the lungs and alveoli sacs, ribs, diaphragm, voice box, nose, and air passages. This system brings oxygen into the body through inhaling and removes wastes through exhaling. The heart rate and brain waves are affected by controlled breathing. The breath also pumps cerebrospinal fluid and lymphatic fluid. The respiratory system is the only system in the body that can be controlled but is also automatic. Because of the dual nature of this system, it is consciously directed by the sympathetic and parasympathetic nervous systems. Kundalini Yoga balances both of these systems, leading to relaxation. Kundalini Yoga and Meditation activates the pituitary gland, improves the excretion of toxins, decreases depression, increases the pH level of blood, and brings in more oxygen for the body.[4]

---

2 Yogi Bhajan, The *Aquarian Teacher: KRI International Kundalini Yoga Teacher Training Level I* (Santa Cruz, NM: Kundalini Research Institute, 2007), 158.
3 Ibid., 159.
4 Ibid., 160.

Digestive System
The digestive system includes the mouth, stomach, liver, gallbladder, pancreas, small and large intestines, and rectum. This system breaks down food into nutrients the body can use. Kundalini Yoga can improve digestion, metabolism, and elimination. It also balances the liver.[5]

Endocrine System
The organs and components in this system include the pineal and pituitary glands, hypothalamus, gonads (ovaries for females; testes for males), thyroid and parathyroid, adrenals, thymus, and pancreas. This system is responsible for producing hormones. Hormones manage the growth, maintenance, and development of our bodies. Hormones are also essential to the functions of the nervous system. Kundalini Yoga helps by stimulating the Kundalini energy to balance the glands. Kundalini Yoga and Meditation can also activate the pituitary and pineal glands as well as the hypothalamus.[6]

Nervous System
The nervous system includes neurons, the central and peripheral nervous systems, the spinal cord, and the brain. Nerves carry messages to and from each other; the nervous system creates more connections with greater use and loses connections with disuse. Nerves help muscles contract, organs to function, and the brain to sense and respond. The hypothalamus is the link between the nervous system and the glands of the endocrine system. Most other systems of the body are controlled directly by the nervous system or indirectly by the nervous system working through the endocrine system. Kundalini Yoga can help energy move through specific nerve pathways, balances the sympathetic and parasympathetic nervous systems, increases the connection and generation of new brain cells, decreases stress, and decreases pain.[7]

Musculoskeletal System
Included in this system are bones, muscles, joints, ligaments, and tendons. This system assists in body movement. Increased movement leads to more oxygen to cells. Less-considered functions include generating heat and increasing the heart rate. Kundalini Yoga uses this system to strengthen the nervous system. The musculoskeletal system balances the muscles, releases tension, and relaxes specific muscle groups. Relaxed muscle groups leads to relaxed organs. This system also increases blood circulation and improves the joints.[8]

---

5 Ibid., 162.
6 Ibid., 164.
7 Ibid., 166.
8 Ibid., 168.

Spinal Biomechanics

Spinal biomechanics regards the vertebrae of the spinal column. The vertebrae hold and protect the nervous system and also allow for movement. Kundalini Yoga can help with disks (the cushions between vertebrae) and can also improve the circulation of cerebrospinal fluid.[9]

Immune System

The immune system includes bone marrow, the spleen, glands, the lymphatic system, and white blood cells. This system defends against viruses, bacteria, and other microorganisms, as well as chemicals and cancer cells. Mental and emotional stress can weaken this system. Kundalini Yoga can cleanse the body. Sound vibration can stimulate the hypothalamus to improve the functions of this system.[10]

Genito-Urinary System

The genito-urinary system includes the kidneys, bladder, ureters, and urethra, as well as the prostate and testes in males and the uterus and ovaries in females. The genital and urinary systems are discussed together because problems in one can create problems in the other. These systems also share nerve and anatomy pathways. The urinary system helps to remove waste from the body. The kidneys also help in producing bone marrow and red blood cells, along with regulating blood pressure through balancing water. Kundalini Yoga can increase blood flow to the kidneys, which are the most important organ responsible for eliminating toxins, this increased blood flow supports both physical and emotional purification.[11]

The way that Kundalini Yoga works with the body systems is truly amazing, and this short summary is only the beginning. To read more about physical and subtle anatomy and Kundalini Yoga, please see the Resources Section.

---

9 Ibid., 170.
10 Ibid., 171.
11 Ibid., 172.

Relieving My Morning Sickness | Katy Willis

A few years ago, I had a life experience that shook me to the very core. It was the most difficult and stretching experience I have gone through. Despite the bitterness, it didn't take me long to recognize that it was for my highest and best purpose. With that insight and trust, I was blessed to easily be able to forgive the individual who had hurt me so deeply. I didn't realize at the time that I had skipped an important step in the process.

About eighteen months later, I was doing a session on myself. I am trained in Theta Healing energy work. I realized that I had not allowed myself to feel anger toward the individual and that anger had become trapped in my liver. Because I was unwilling to feel it and release it, I had literally stuffed the anger there instead. It had been trapped until I began to release the anger daily with energy healing, as well as the meditation for releasing anger and negativity. But I could only release a little bit each day. Naturally, there was quite a bit of anger I had not given myself permission to feel previously. Sometimes changes have been instant; other changes have required time to adjust and process.

I also became pregnant during this time. Morning sickness had been a big issue in past pregnancies. I had made many changes for this pregnancy and only had mild, but very manageable, nausea, until six weeks into the pregnancy. I was suddenly slammed with horrible morning sickness and began vomiting. I tried everything I knew to do to curb it but could not get it under control. I prayed to know why I had it. My answer was a reminder about my liver. My liver was sluggish already from the trapped anger, and the additional demand on the liver with higher hormone levels was more than it could keep up with.

My husband gave me a blessing. In it he reminded me that I had new resources at my fingertips and to use them. I had been added to the Kundalini Yoga Facebook support group, so I asked for anything to help in the situation. When Felice saw my post, she gave me the choice between the kriya for releasing inner anger and one for the liver. The first one felt right. That night, I did the kriya. It was so healing! Because of my pregnancy, there was quite a bit I needed to modify with the breathing and positions. I was amazed that even with modifications, it worked! As I lay there accepting the changes, tears cascaded down my cheeks. I had been unable to release this trapped anger any other way, and it was finally gone.

I still ended up needing an IV and medication because of dehydration, but my morning sickness went away. It was as if my body needed to hit the reset button to be able to catch up with all of the changes. I am grateful for this technology and awareness of it! In this case, I didn't just put a Band-Aid on things and treat the symptoms. My morning sickness was there to alert me that something needed to be addressed, and Kundalini Yoga gave me the tools to be able to take care of it fully.

Meditation Is My Medication | Lisa Underwood

In 2010, I was diagnosed with bipolar disorder and psychosis. I started medication right away and felt more stable in a few weeks. In time, I incorporated other tools to create a holistic bipolar health plan. Kundalini Yoga and Meditation is one of those tools. In November 2012, I began Felice's forty-day meditation webinar. She guided me through forty days of meditation and helped me build a strong foundation of meditation.

Through this building, my life's purposes have been clarified. I'm more loving, more confident, and more in tune with what God wants for me and my family. Meditation gave my husband and me the courage and confidence to confront challenges and make changes. We were able to recognize bipolar triggers and eliminate them.

In April 2013, I took a more advanced class with Felice in which we did yoga kriyas and long meditations, and it was even more empowering. Felice was inspired to suggest Ganputi Kriya followed by a meditation for bipolar resolution as my daily meditation. At the time, with my psychiatrist's guidance, I was slowly scaling down one of my medications. After a week of the new meditation, I had a medication review, and my psychiatrist approved of me stopping the medication altogether. At my next medication review a month later, he told me I could stop taking an antipsychotic medication. In two months, including four weeks of Ganputi Kriya, I went from taking four medications to taking two medications!

Meditation is my medication. It changes your brain and your life!

I have given
them the words
thou gavest me.

— John 17:8

The Word

The Word

One of my early and fondest childhood memories is of sitting on my grandparents' front steps on Anacapa Avenue in old Ventura, California, with a yellow legal pad on my lap and the dictionary at my side. My mother had written a list of evenly spaced words on the lines down the pad. When I found each new word in the worn blue dictionary, I would carefully copy the definition onto the yellow paper.

This activity was as much fun for me as it was for my two younger brothers to crawl around the front lawn acting like rhinos and fighting with swords made of sticks. I loved words as much as my grandmother loved food. We lived next door to my grandparents, but my brothers and I roamed back and forth as if it were one house.

An exotic fruit had recently appeared at one of our houses, and no one was sure what to do with it. But the fruit's strange shape and mysterious pit could not dissuade my grandmother. She would eventually learn every nuance of the mango.

Mango. I felt the word hover around my lips like a kiss. Then I tried the new and consonant-rich word *choreographer*. But what could compare to the beguiling beauty of words like *melancholy* and *nonchalant*.

My grandmother was probably at that very moment standing over the sink with her sleeves rolled up, letting the mango juice drip down her arms as she "just went for it." If my grandmother were to write a definition for *mango*, it would read, "kind of like a peach, but tropical."

For the next several years my mother, who was busy with three younger children, used the dictionary as free babysitting as often as she could get away with it. I never got suspicious.

For the next twenty years, I spent every opportunity I could learning about and playing with words. I didn't know what drove this desire or the pleasure it brought me. Perhaps it was the same force that moved my grandmother to nourish. Perhaps Mozart also did not understand his compulsion to compose music. I believe some things are preassigned.

After about 10,000 hours of practice, I had established myself as a *writer*, and then my path turned unexpectedly toward *healer* and then *teacher*, in which I was again using words and stories. As I healed myself and others, I began to understand the true meaning of *the Word*.

Much can be said about the power of words, but if we are to get right to the heart of the matter, we should start at the beginning with the famous line of scripture from the Gospel of St. John, which is actually a quote from the Vedas: "In the beginning was the Word, and the Word was with God and the Word was God."

Though Christian church doctrine for centuries has interpreted the Word to be a reference to Jesus himself, Paramahansa Yogananda comments, "That was not the understanding originally intended by Saint John in this passage. . . . The term *Merma* (Word) is used to describe God's activity in the world."[1]

The prophet Joseph Smith's inspired translation of this passage in John gives even more clarity: "In the beginning was the gospel preached through the Son. And the gospel was the word, and *the word was with the Son*, and the Son was with God and the Son was of God (Joseph Smith Translation, John 1:1, italics added).

While many great teachers and prophets continue to refer to Jesus as the Word, it is important to understand the distinction noted above. Jesus was powerful because the Word, or gospel, was *with* Him. And He was *with* God and *of* God. Through this power He created all things: "All things were made by him; and without him was not anything made which was made" (Joseph Smith Translation, John 1:3).

Everything in our known universe was created with the power of divinely spoken words: "God said, Let there be light: and there was light" (Genesis 1:3). As sons and daughters of God, our true nature is divine; thus, our words have immense power. That is why mantras are not only powerful but essential.

The word *mantra* has two parts: *man*, which means "mind," and *tra*, which means "tune the vibration." Therefore, a *mantra* is a tool that tunes the vibration of the mind. All sound is, of course, vibration. Our ears, if they are working well, create sound with this vibration, but even when a tree falls in the woods where there are no ears to hear, there is still vibration. Everything has a vibratory frequency. Every object, particle, thought form, and word on this page has its own vibration. All of these vibrations travel through us, and even in the vacuum of space, there are vibrations that our ears would hear as sound.

High-vibration, sacred sound currents affect not only the mind but the whole body. The yogis of old knew that when you repeat the patterns of sound and thought, which make up these sacred *shabds* (sounds/mantras), those sounds counter the direction and intensity of the habitual thoughts based in ego. The shabd provokes a release of the stored subconscious patterns of thinking and feeling. If a person flooded with these feelings and thoughts persists in repeating the shabd, then the new pattern will establish itself. "Your

---

1 Paramahansa Yogananda, *The Yoga of Jesus* (Los Angeles, CA: Self-Realization Fellowship, 2007), 22.

mind clears and you awaken dormant inner capacities or enhance existing ones."[2] Author M. Catherine Thomas says,

> Man is designed to reach for and grasp and fill himself deliberately with Truth and Light and thus to be quickened with the same energies as the Gods in their Heaven. For this purpose the energetic *Word* of God is provided, it having a quickening or vibratory effect on the human mind as it causes the mind to expand.[3]

The Word also has a profound effect on the neurological and endocrine systems as well as other systems in the body. The words we vibrate with our voices have direct, powerful effects on the brain. When mantras are chanted out loud, the tongue strikes the upper palate. This process vibrates the pituitary gland and hypothalamus, which are located near the roof of the mouth. When the right frequency vibrates these glands, a kind of magic occurs: The vibration causes the pituitary gland to secrete and the pineal gland to radiate, which can cause a person to feel bliss, happiness, joy, and even rebirth.

> When a man works by faith he works by mental exertion instead of physical force. It is by words, instead of exerting his physical powers, with which every being works when he works by faith. God said, 'Let there be light: and there was light.' . . . And the Saviour says: "If you have faith as a grain of mustard seed, say to this mountain, 'Remove,' and it will remove; or say to that sycamore tree, 'Be ye plucked up, and planted in the midst of the sea,' and it shall obey you." *Faith, then, works by words; and with these its mightiest works have been, and will be, performed.*
>
> —Joseph Smith, *Lectures on Faith*, Lecture 7 (Salt Lake City, UT: Deseret Book, 2009), Kindle edition.

It should not be surprising that in order to experience Infinity, the actual chemistry of the brain must change, just as Moses and other prophets had to be changed, or transfigured, before they came into God's presence. Having an experience of God, therefore, has both spiritual and physiological components. Chanting expert Dr. Robert Gass says, "Sound is a remarkable bridge between the two worlds, a bridge between spirit

---

2 Yogi Bhajan, *The Aquarian Teacher: KRI International Kundalini Yoga Teacher Training Level I Yoga Manual* (Santa Cruz, NM: Kundalini Research Institute, 2007), 71

3 M. Catherine Thomas, *Light in the Wilderness: Explorations in the Spiritual Life* (Salt Lake City, UT: Digital Legend Press, 2010), 61.

and matter."[4] Indeed, it was God's word that brought spirit and matter together: "And I, God, said: Let there be light; and there was light . . . and this I did by the word of my power, and it was done as I spake" (Moses 2:3, 5).

All of our physiology is affected by sound. In order to have the greatest impact on our minds and bodies, we must attempt to resonate in harmony with the highest and best frequency of all, and that is God's. John A. Widtsoe, in his book *Joseph Smith as Scientist*, said, "Can anyone refuse to believe that man, highly organized as he is can 'tune' himself to be in harmony with the forces of the universe?"[5] We attune ourselves with God through mantras. M. Catherine Thomas writes,

> Everything in the Cosmos is playing music based on its particular configuration and vibration. The spheres are full of music. The elements of our physical world play the music given them by their Creator, but . . . we shall see that Man can choose to a degree the energy by which he will vibrate and the music that he will play.[6]

As implied, not all languages vibrate equally. English, the language of this book, is a lower-vibrating language. The ancients had a pure language, which God has promised to return to His people someday.[7] But until then, to make the greatest impact on our minds we use mantras in one of several ancient languages that are based on the Science of Naad. *Naad* means communication. Here is an explanation of the Science of Naad:

> The most profound changes take place in our consciousnesses on a deeper level. . . . [8] "Naad means harmony, a process of harmony through which the 'Aad,' the infinity can be experienced. Naad is the basic sound current for all languages through all times. The sound comes from one common source called the sound current. It is the universal code behind language and therefore behind communication."[9]

Though there are a few English mantras that work well, English is a symbolic language, which means that if you say the word "love," you have to know what love means. Whereas, in Gurmukhi, the language of most Kundalini mantras, if you say the word that translates as "love," you *feel* love. The patterns of the sacred Sound Current, existed from before the beginning of creation. The patterns are simple, primal sounds that are the tides and rhythms of the creative pulse of the universe. (See more on page 86 about the gong.)

---

4 Dharma Singh Khalsa and Cameron Stauth, *Meditation as Medicine: Activate the Power of Your Natural Healing Force* (New York: Fireside, 2001), 112.
5 John A. Widtsoe, *Joseph Smith as Scientist* (Layton, UT: Eborn Books, 1990), 125.
6 Thomas, *Light in the Wilderness*, 39.
7 Zephaniah 3:9.
8 Shakti Parwha Kaur Khalsa, *Kundalini Yoga: The Flow of Eternal Power* (New York, NY: Dorling Kindersley, 2001), 38.
9 Quoted in Shakti Parwha's Kundalini Yoga: *The Flow of Eternal Power*. Original source: Gurucharan Singh Khalsa, excerpt from "Naad Yoga."

The word *shabd* means "sound" as well as "to cut off the ego." *Guru* means "teacher" or literally "that which brings light to the darkness." So the Shabd Guru[10] consists of sounds that teach, and bring light to the darkness. When we chant mantras from the Shabd Guru, which are believed to be in Naad, we shut off the ego so that we can be humble and resonate in harmony with the ultimate Word or vibration, which is *with* Christ, who is *with* and *of* God.[11]

Yogi Bhajan compared the technology of mantra to a phone number: "Mantra is your heart-line telephone. You are dialing in and you are reaching God."[12] In the ancient temples of God, similar technology was used to come into His presence. In Facsimile 2 from the papyrus scroll that is now known as the Book of Abraham, Figure 7 is explained as "God sitting on his throne, revealing through the heavens the *grand Keywords* of the priesthood" (emphasis added). These keywords are sacred and powerful uses of the technology of the Word. This technology is still used in sacred ordinances in temples today.

As you study the list of top mantras and their translations on page 88, you may notice several characteristics they share. Good mantras combine the Infinite and the finite (God and Me, Me and God are one), and all mantras are some form of praising God.

While the Christian canon may not use the word *mantra*, there are hundreds of scriptures that advise God's people to praise Him or His name. Here are just a few examples:

- Psalm 47:6: "Sing praises to God, sing praises: sing praises unto our King, sing praises."

- Doctrine and Covenants 136:28: "If thou art merry, praise the Lord with singing, with music, with dancing, and with a prayer of praise and thanksgiving."

- Alma 26:8: "Blessed be the name of our God; let us sing to his praise, yea, let us give thanks to his holy name, for he doth work righteousness forever."

There are just as many hundreds of scriptures wherein the ancient writers do just this, they praise God in mantra, repeated over and over again. The first of these scriptural mantras I discovered is in Revelation 4:8. St. John the Divine sees four interesting "beasts" before the throne of God that "rest not day and night, saying, Holy, holy, holy, Lord God Almighty, which was, and is, and is to come."

Though this verse does not use the word *chant*, the beasts repeat the phrase day and night. That is what one does with mantras. Mantras are something that we repeat and repeat—not just once in a while, but all the time. The yogis call this *jap*. *Jap* means meditate, but it implies repetition. We repeat until the mantra becomes part of us and

---

10 The Word and the Sound Current are all used interchangeably in this chapter. The Shabd Guru is a collection of writings compiled in a book that the Sikhs look to as their living Guru. It is believed to be in Naad.

11 Joseph Smith Translation, John 1:1.

12 Khalsa, *Kundalini Yoga*, 37.

we become part of it. This is the same idea as the word *remember*. *Remember* is the most commonly used imperative in the scriptures (used 405 times in the LDS canon).[13] Remembering is one of the things we covenant to do each time we take the sacrament. Here are some great examples of *jap* from the scriptures:

- Ether 6:9: "And they did sing praises unto the Lord; yea, the brother of Jared did sing praises unto the Lord, and he did thank and praise the Lord all the day long; and when the night came, *they did not cease to praise the Lord*" (emphasis added).

- Alma 26:14: "Yea, we have reason to praise him forever."

- Alma 26:16: "Behold, *who can glory too much in the Lord?* Yea, who can say too much of his great power, and of his mercy, and of his long-suffering towards the children of men? Behold, I say unto you, I cannot say the smallest part which I feel" (emphasis added).

- 1 Nephi 18:16: "Nevertheless, I did look unto my God, and I did praise him all the day long; and I did not murmur against the Lord because of mine afflictions." (Nephi is tied to the mast of ship and his brothers are planning to kill him, yet he praises God.)

- 2 Chronicles 20:21: "And when [Jehoshaphat] had consulted with the people, he appointed singers unto the Lord, and that should praise the beauty of holiness, as they went out before the army, and to say, Praise the Lord; for his mercy endureth for ever." (The people of Judah do not have to fight. All they do is sing this mantra, and the opposing armies kill each other until there are no enemies left.)

The likely reason for the prolific use of *remember* is that God knew mortality would be full of distractions. He knew, and the prophets knew, that the Word had great power to deliver God's children and keep them from sleepwalking through life. The Book of Mormon prophet Alma the Younger asks his people several times if they have sufficiently remembered God's mercy toward their ancestors: "Behold he changed their hearts; yea, he awakened them out of a deep sleep, and they awoke unto God. Behold, they were in the midst of darkness; nevertheless, their souls were illuminated by the light of everlasting word" (Alma 5:7).

I love how Alma uses *light* to describe sound. For any who have the perception that light is more powerful than sound, or that they are different, that scripture should settle the issue. Everything proceeds from the Word, and the Word has great awakening and en*light*ening power.

---

13 The LDS canon includes the Hebrew Bible, the New Testament, the Book of Mormon, the Doctrine and Covenants, and the Pearl of Great Price.

Krista's Immediate Response to the Sound Current

In my experience teaching this sacred science, I have witnessed many people have immediate reactions to the Sound Current. Not long ago, on the eleventh day of the New Moon, I held a meditation gathering for friends. We needed at least eleven people in order to do a special meditation. We were short a few people and prayed that people would somehow show up. One of the participants went outside to look for a lost guest and while outside saw a passerby, whom she invited to come in and meditate. That is how 21-year-old Krista joined us. We were thrilled to have her. She was wearing a t-shirt with a black spider painted on it, and her hair was untamed and wild. She looked like a nice girl, but I could see that she struggled with awkwardness and probably other issues.

After some brief instruction, we chanted the tune-in mantra three times, followed by the protection mantra. After we tuned in, quiet Krista blurted out, "This is totally taking away my anxiety."

She seemed surprised. I agree that on the surface, chanting mantras in an unknown language with a group of strangers would normally seem like a great recipe for anxiety. Yet in just a few minutes, she felt it all flow out of her. I let her know that her feeling of calm was a normal side effect of the Sound Current and that with regular practice, she could enjoy every day without anxiety.

Kimberly's Immediate Response the the Sound Current

In January 2014, I received an e-mail from Kimberly. Kimberly had some experience with yoga and meditation but never with Kundalini Yoga. Kimberly had suffered from depression and anxiety her entire life and sought many techniques to heal from her trauma and abuse. She had been praying fervently for months and attending the temple to petition God for a solution to her pain. She was almost to the point of giving up when she found one of my meditation videos on YouTube.

This meditation, for managing fears (explained on page 270), requires that the mantra Chattra Chakkra Vartee be played in the background in order for the meditation to be effective. Kimberly completed the three-minute meditation with the video, and as she did, she felt her fears falling away from her. She wept. In her mind, she heard the words, *This is your answer.* She e-mailed me and asked me what on earth this experience was and how a mantra in a strange language could have such power. She wanted to learn everything she could. She started an intense training and daily sadhana practice the next day and within forty days everyone was noticing the difference. She then went on to do a teacher training and is now teaching others.

THE STRAIT AND NARROW PATH AND THE IRON ROD

Throughout this book I have compared the strait and narrow path to the central spinal channel (shushmana). Here is an interesting tidbit about that channel: "If you can vibrate the shushmana then you can vibrate all three surs (ida and pingala and shushmana), which will vibrate all seventy-two major nadis and you can adjust the entire system."[1] The nadis (see page 48) are like the branches of the ethereal nervous system, which is essentially the tree of life within you. It brings life (prana/Light of Christ) to the whole body. "It is for this reason that when we chant and we use the power of shabd, we consciously locate that shabd in the central channel so that we can vibrate the seventy-two major meridians."[2]

Shabd (as explained on page 72) is equivalent to "the Word." From Nephi's vision of the Tree of Life, we learn that the rod of iron represents "the word of God." It would seem then, that with the Kingdom of God within you, the strait and narrow path of the spine and the Word have an intimate relationship in bringing you to the tree of life.

---

1 Yogi Bhajan, The Aquarian Teacher: KRI International Kundalini Yoga Teacher Training Level I Yoga Manual (Santa Cruz, NM: Kundalini Research Institute, 2007), 175.
2 Ibid.

One Reader's Response

Lani, whose healing experience with the Siri Giatri Mantra (Ra Ma Da Sa) is on page 101, forwarded the following e-mail to me from a blog reader:

Thank you for the link to that mantra. I listened to it that day, and my toddler was singing it and kept saying "gain" (again) when it would end. I shared it with my husband that night, and he bought the whole album from the link you shared to iTunes. He listened to it on his two-hour drive home last weekend, and said it made him feel wonderful! Like some of the feelings he has had during the very most sacred times of his life—when he was in a coma, and likely had a near death experience (though he can't remember it), and also when our baby girl died. So, I really wanted to thank you. I have been looking for and praying for more spiritual experiences—more revelation, more inspiration, more visions and dreams. I'm hoping this might be a way to help me with that.

I receive e-mails like this every day, and I rejoice in God.

THE NAME OF GOD

After reading the stories above, you may wonder, as Kimberly did, how simple words and sounds can have such a powerful effect. St. John gives us a powerful clue:

But as many as received him, to them gave he power to become the sons of God, *even to them that believe on his nam*e: which were born, not of blood, nor of the will of the flesh, nor of the will of man, but of God. (John 1:12–13, emphasis added)

As a writer, I notice the structure of language, and in the passage above, the third clause seems redundant. If a person receives Christ, doesn't that mean the person believes on His name? It is my experience that God is not redundant, and seeming redundancies often indicate multiple layers of meaning if the reader will search them out.

The word *name* is associated with, and inseparably linked with, the Word, or sound current. Every book of scripture admonishes God's people hundreds of times[14] to call upon, praise, glorify, and believe on "the name of the Lord," "Jesus's name," "God's name," "His holy name," and so forth. Why wouldn't these ancient writers just tell us to call on the Lord, receive the Lord, or praise Him? John adds that *power* was given to them that *believed on His name.* It would seem from this scripture and hundreds more that the names of God are an important key in worshiping Him and becoming like Him (i.e., the children of God and born of God).[15]

Jesus also sets the example by repeatedly exalting His Father's name. In fact, Jesus states in in 3 Nephi 9:15 that His life is for that purpose: "I am in the Father, and the Father in me; and in me hath the Father glorified his name."

Another common pleading of the ancients is that we should each retain *His name written in our hearts.* As you will read in the a later chapter, *heart* may also be symbolic of the subconscious mind as well as the central point of transformation, where body and spirit exchange information.

To have such writing in our inward parts, or to take upon us the name of Christ—which members of the LDS church covenant to do every Sunday when participating in the

Sometimes people ask me if mantras qualify as vain repetitions. I consider mantras to be the opposite. In the scriptures, vain repetitions are associated with "much speaking" (Matthew 6:7) and "multiplying many words" (3 Nephi 19:24). Another key to vain repetitions is vanity. Mantras are simple, basic sounds and phrases, and they will do little for your vanity. In fact, many people will think you are crazy. Yogi Bhajan says, "We repeat and repeat so it becomes part of us, we become part of it. We who practice this are not insane. We look insane to those who are insane. Please understand that."[1]

1 Yogi Bhajan, PhD and Gurucharan Singh Khalsa, PhD, *The Master's Touch: On Being a Sacred Teacher for the New Age* (Santa Cruz, NM: Kundalini Research Institute, 1997), 207.

---

14 More than three hundred variations can be found in the LDS canon.
15 Power is associated with the ordinances of the temple, which you can read more about in the "Temple and the Body" chapter.

ordinance of the sacrament—requires some serious technology. Paramhansa Yogananda says, "When the mere mention of His name sets the soul afire with love for God, it will start the devotee on his way to liberation."[16] What kind of technology can set our souls afire with devotion and write on our hearts? The sacred sound current.

The mantras from the Shabd Guru are filled with the names of God or a string of His names, as well as attributes and praises to those attributes. As described above, science has shown how these mantras have powerful psychological and physiological effects that change a person's brain, as well as one's subconscious mind, body, and spiritual organs. Yet science can't explain *why*. But scripture can. There is power in *the name*: "honor, power and glory be rendered to his holy name, both now and ever" (Doctrine and Covenants 20:36). From the very beginning, humans have praised the name of God: "And Adam and Eve blessed the name of God, and they made all things known unto their sons and their daughters" (Moses 5:12).

It is evident from the scriptural record that God has many names. I once started what was to be an exhaustive list of all the names of God I could find. I still find new ones. It seems that God has no limit to His names or His power, as His name and His power are linked.

The ancients understood this truth, and they knew how to call on and praise which name for what purpose. For example, the mantra for prosperity calls on/praises the generating aspect of God (see page 94). The mantra for healing calls on the all-powerful aspects of God (see page 96). Other mantras use names that represent other attributes, such as Liberator, Sustainer, and Infinite (see pages 92).

We can learn much about this concept by studying the names of deity used by modern-day LDS prophets in special prayers, such as temple dedicatory prayers. Below are three examples:

From the Provo, Utah, Temple Dedication, 1972

O God, the Eternal Father, the Creator of heaven and earth and all things that in them are; thou Man of Holiness who hast created us thy children in thine own image and likeness and endowed us with power and agency to follow thee; thou who knowest all things and hast all power, all might, and all dominion; thou who created the universe and ruleth with justice and equity and mercy over all the works of thy hands, hallowed be thy great and holy name!

We come before thee in the name of thine Only Begotten Son, even the Son of Man, in whose sacred name thou hast ordained that we shall have access to thee, the Lord.[17]

---

16 Yogananda, *The Yoga of Jesus*, 29.
17 "Provo Temple Dedicatory Prayer," accessed March 14, 2014, http://www.lds.org/ensign/1972/04/provo-temple-dedicatory-prayer.

From the Ogden, Utah, Temple Dedication, 1972

Our Father who art in heaven, even the God of our fathers, who keepeth covenants and showest mercy; thou Almighty Elohim who liveth and reigneth, from everlasting to everlasting; thou Man of Holiness and Man of Counsel who hast created us in thine own image and likeness and commanded us to worship thee in spirit and in truth; thou who knoweth all things and hast all power, all might, and all dominion—hallowed be thy great and holy name!

We come before thee in the name of thine Only Begotten Son, even him through whom salvation cometh; him whom thou hast appointed to be our Advocate with thee.[18]

From the Bountiful, Utah, Temple Dedication, 1995

O God, our Eternal Father, Thou great Elohim, Creator of the heavens, the earth, and all things thereon. . . . We pray to Thee, our Father, in the name of Thy Beloved Son, Thine Only Begotten, even our Redeemer and our Savior, Jesus Christ, the Lord.[19]

OTHER IMPORTANT EFFECTS OF CHANTING MANTRAS FROM THE SHABD GURU[1]

- Improves immune function via the hypothalamic-pituitary axis
- Increases brain-hemisphere balance
- Sends ethereal energy through the nadis
- Quiets inner dialog
- Helps potentiate the proper replication of DNA

---

1 Khalsa and Stauth, *Meditation as Medicine.*

The above examples praise several of God's names and call upon many of His attributes, which are also considered names for our purposes. Each prayer also mentions the name of the Savior, in whose name we are taught to always pray to the Lord (see 3 Nephi 18:21).

There is power in using the Lord's names in the appropriate ways, and there is condemnation in using the names inappropriately (think of the third commandment). It is in the name of Christ that we baptize, that we cast out devils, and that we can work miracles such as commanding the weather and commanding mountains and trees.[20] It is through faith in His name that we may be glorified.[21] Glorified! And it is through Him, and His name that we can have a fulness of joy: "Hitherto have ye asked nothing in my name. Ask and ye shall receive that your joy may be full" (John 16:24).

---

18 "Ogden Temple Dedicatory Prayer," accessed March 14, 2014, http://www.lds.org/ensign/1972/03/ogden-temple-dedicatory-prayer.

19 "News of the Church: Bountiful Utah Temple Dedicated," accessed March 14, 2014, http://www.lds.org/ensign/1995/03/news-of-the-church.

20 See Mark 16:17. See also Doctrine and Covenants 45:8.

21 Doctrine and Covenants 3:20.

EVIDENCE OF MANTRA MEDITATION IN THE SCRIPTURES

In ancient scripture, the words *prayer* and *meditation* were often used interchangeably. In fact, the word in Naad that is translated "I call upon" (*namo/nameh*) is also translated as "I bow to," demonstrating that anciently, praise (meditation) was inextricably linked to all petitions to God (prayer). Only in modern times have these two words come to mean different things, which may cause some confusion unless you know how to look deeper. President David O. Mckay, a modern prophet and champion of meditation, points out many examples of meditation in the life of Jesus:

> As soon as he was baptized . . . Jesus [went] to what is now known as the mount of temptation. I like to think of it as the mount of meditation where, during the forty days of fasting, he communed with himself and his Father, and contemplated upon the responsibility of his great mission. . . . Christ also meditated in solitude before he gave the beautiful Sermon on the Mount. . . . Again, after Jesus had fed the five thousand he told the Twelve to dismiss the multitude, but Jesus went to the mountain for solitude. . . . Meditation! Prayer![22]

We find even more evidence of the use of mantra meditation in the account of Christ's visit to the Americas in the Book of Mormon. As described above, mantra meditation with the primal sounds of the Sound Current can change your brain cells, purify the subconscious, and awaken the soul to a state of bliss. In the following example, we witness exactly this as a group of people, through the power of the Word, are quite literally and visibly changed to receive Christ in their image.

It begins during Christ's visit to the America's, the crowning event in the Book of Mormon. The people who had survived the three days of earthquakes and destruction after His death had gathered to the temple to marvel at the changes in the land. At this point, Christ comes to them in glory. Christ is happy to see that people who assembled there were much more faithful than the people at Jerusalem had been, and the entire visit is full of miracles. After ordaining twelve disciples, Jesus prayed with them and then went a little ways off to pray for them to the Father.

> And it came to pass that when Jesus had thus prayed unto the Father, he came unto his disciples, and behold they did still continue, without ceasing, to pray unto him; and *they did not multiply many words, for it was given unto them what they should pray,* and they were filled with desire. (3 Nephi 19:24, emphasis added)

The words of this scripture are very interesting: the phrase "it was given unto them

---

22 The Church of Jesus Christ of Latter-day Saints, *Teachings of the Presidents of the Church: David O. McKay* (Salt Lake City, UT: The Church of Jesus Christ of Latter-day Saints, 2003), 32.

what they should pray" sounds like they were given a mantra. And the phrase "*they did not multiply many words*" suggests that they may have been repeating what they were given, because they had been praying for some time and had to fill the time with something, if not many words, then perhaps a repetition of the same words. Sounds like a mantra.

When Christ returned and saw them still praying *without ceasing,* he blessed them and they were changed:

> And it came to pass that Jesus blessed them as they did pray unto him; and his countenance did smile upon them, and the light of his countenance did shine upon them, and behold they were as white as the countenance and also the garments of Jesus; and behold the whiteness thereof did exceed all the whiteness, yea, even there could be nothing upon earth so white as the whiteness thereof. And Jesus said unto them: Pray on; nevertheless they did not cease to pray (3 Nephi 19:25–26).

Jesus again prayed in private and thanked the Father for purifying the people. He then said a special prayer for the people those disciples would one day teach, that any who "believe on their words" would be purified in the same way, as if Jesus Christ were shining on them personally.[23] The purification that the twelve disciples (and later their people) experienced enabled them to establish one of the few known Zion societies, lasting for two hundred years.

The second time Jesus rejoined the multitude, they were still praying "steadfastly, without ceasing." He smiled on them again, and they seemed to become even brighter. It is not surprising to me that they didn't show any desire to stop praying. Mantra meditation for a long period has the power to take you beyond time and space. My experience tells me that the members of the multitude were probably feeling the ecstatic bliss of being purified and being one with God. This feeling may be what is meant by the statement "and they were filled with desire." This is the experience of Wahe Guru!

I have loved this chapter in the Book of Mormon for years, even before I understood anything about meditation, because I was obsessed with the last few verses, which suggest an ineffable experience:

> And tongue cannot speak the words which he prayed, neither can be written by man the words which he prayed. And their hearts were open and they did understand in their hearts the words which he prayed. Nevertheless, so great and marvelous were the words which he prayed that they cannot be written, neither can they be uttered by man. (3 Nephi 19:32, 34)

Not having words to describe something was unfathomable to me. I had spent most of my life crafting with words. And yet I could not stop thinking about what the Nephites'

---

23 3 Nephi 19:28–29.

experience must have been like, an experience of words that was beyond words. It is not surprising that my journey led me to find out for myself one day. And now, Wahe Guru! I am filled with desire.

WHAT IS THE RELATION BETWEEN THE SOUND CURRENT AND THE SIKHS?

Yogi Bhajan was the first master of Kundalini Yoga to teach this ancient yogic science openly to everyone. "In addition to being a Kundalini Yoga master, he was also a Sikh. In his teachings, he often intermingled the science of Kundalini Yoga with stories from Sikh history. In addition, he would explain Sikh Dharma through a deep yogic perspective."[1]

Many practitioners of Kundalini Yoga wonder what the relationship is between Kundalini Yoga and Sikh Dharma. Ek Ong Kaar Kaur Khalsa explains: "There are some people who claim there is no relationship between yoga and Sikhism. However, Yogi Bhajan talked about it very differently." She states that part of understanding includes "recognizing the interplay between the ancient yogic teachings that predate Sikh Dharma by thousands of years, and the Sound Current of the *shabad* that the Sikh Masters manifested through their teaching."[2]

To recognize this interplay, we must go back to the first Sikh Guru: Guru Nanak, born in 1469. Yogi Bhajan says, "Guru Nanak was a very good yogi, trained by very good yogis. He had a very great friendship with yogis. . . . Birds of a feather flock together. All his life, Guru Nanak flocked together with the yogis."[3]

Born into a Hindu family, at a young age Nanak questioned the caste system and empty rituals; he began to be a seeker of truth. He studied far and wide for truth and consciousness, and eventually ended up with the yogis. He practiced yoga until he attained a very high state of elevation and then had a three-day visionary experience from which he emerged with the technology of the Shabd Guru.[4]

Eck Ong Kaar Kaur Khalsa explains the importance of the revealed (or in my view,

restored) Sound Current, which Guru Nanak and the nine gurus who followed were able to hear and transmit.

> The ancient teachings of yoga have tremendous power and merit. But it is through the *Shabd*, the Sound Current, that an average, every day person can be awakened to the same state of consciousness which was formerly reserved for the ascetics. This is why in Kundalini Yoga, every exercise includes the Sound Current. If no mantra is given, we still inhale "*Sat*" and exhale "*Naam*" with an exercise. As we open our centers through the practice of Kundalini Yoga, the Sound Current of the *Shabd* helps move and clear the blocks faster. It takes us to an ever more refined state of consciousness.[5]

This might be a good time to quote Elder Orson F. Whitney's talk at the LDS church's ninety-first general conference:

> God has been using not merely his covenant people, but other people of the world as well, to carry out a work that is too demanding for the limited numbers of Latter-day Saints to accomplish. God and great men and women . . . who have thought profoundly . . . have been inspired by God under many circumstances to deliver dimensions of light and truth . . . [including] Zarathustra, Buatama Buddha, Lao Tzu, Muhammed, and Guru Nanak."[6]

---

1 3HO Foundation, "Kundalini Yoga and Sikh Dharma," accessed March 10, 2014, http://www.3ho.org/kundalini-yoga/kundalini-yoga-sikh-dharma.
2 3HO Foundation, "Guru Nanak and the Yogis," accessed March 8, 2014, http://www.3ho.org/kundalini-yoga/kundalini-yoga-sikh-dharma/guru-nanak-and-yogis.
3 Yogi Bhajan, "Lecture," August 19, 1979.
4 Ibid.
5 3HO Foundation, "Guru Nanak and the Yogis."
6 Orson F. Whitney, Conference Report, April 1921, 32–33.

A New Song

Psalm 40:3 reads, "And he hath put a new song in my mouth, even praise unto our God: many shall see it, and [stand in awe], and shall trust in the Lord." Over and over the scriptures declare that Zion is home to those who sing "songs of everlasting joy" (Doctrine and Covenants 45:71). Zion's people are a singing people, and God's praises fill their mouths. The story of the Jaredites crossing the ocean to the Promised Land illustrates the power of such songs:

> And it came to pass that they were many times buried in the depths of the sea, because of the mountain waves which broke upon them, and also the great and terrible tempests which were caused by the fierceness of the wind. . . . And they did sing praises unto the Lord; yea, the brother of Jared did sing praises unto the Lord, and he did thank and praise the Lord all the day long; and when the night came, they did not cease to praise the Lord. . . . And when they had set their feet upon the shores of the promised land they bowed themselves down upon the face of the land, and did humble themselves before the Lord, and did shed tears of joy before the Lord, because of the multitude of his tender mercies over them. (Ether 6:6–12)

It took 344 days for the Jaredites to reach the Promised Land. They sang without ceasing for 344 days, and I have a hunch that it wasn't just because they liked singing. That voyage had the potential to be a frightening one as the waves beat incessantly upon the vessels, but there's no doubt that singing helped bring peace to the Jaredites' hearts and minds.

When you use your *voice* as a sound instrument, powerful things happen inside of you, such as the following:

- Your heart rate decreases.

- Your blood pressure decreases.

- Your stress/fear hormones decrease.

- Your body enhances the release of endorphins.[24]

Research indicates that singing or chanting phrases that facilitate six breaths per minute (breathing at ten-second intervals) produces the most favorable psychological and physiological effects.[25]

Singing with a group brings even more benefits. A recent study conducted in Turkey found that singing in a choir is associated with reduced anxiety levels.[26] When individuals sing in a group setting, they become unified through the music's harmony and rhythm, and they also become unified within their bodies. Research shows that when people sing together, their heart rates synchronize.[27] Perhaps this synchronization is one reason that Zion's people sing: "The Lord called his people Zion, because they were of one heart and one mind" (Moses 7:18). Singing makes many hearts as one. According to a team of Swedish researchers, "this synchronicity can produce a sense of calm that is similar to the effects of yoga."[28] It is interesting to note that structured, slow chants "were found to induce a stronger synchrony in the singers' heartbeats."[29]

May we join with the Psalmist who wrote: "I will sing unto the Lord as long as I live: I will sing praise to my God while I have my being. My meditation of him shall be sweet: I will be glad in the Lord" (Psalm 104:33–34).

---

24 Dharma Singh Khalsa and Cameron Stauth, *Meditation as Medicine: Activate the Power of Your Natural Healing Force* (New York: Fireside, 2001), 114.

25 Luciano Bernardi, Peter Sleight, Gabriele Bandinelli, Simone Cencetti, Lamberto Fattorini, Johanna Wdowczyc-Szulc, and Alfonso Lagi, "Effect of Rosary Prayer and Yoga Mantras on Autonomic Cardiovascular Rhythms: Comparative Study," *BMJ* 323, no. 7327: 1446–1449, accessed March 24, 2014, http://www.ncbi.nlm.nih.gov/pmc/articles/PMC61046.

26 "Choir Singing Could Help Reduce Anxiety, Study Finds," *Huffington Post*, April 28, 2013. http://www.huffingtonpost.com/2013/04/28/choir-singing-anxiety-_n_3147861.html.

27 Chris Palmer, "Choir Singers Synchronize Heartbeats," *Scientist*, July 10, 2013. http://www.the-scientist.com/?articles.view/articleNo/36412/title/Choir-Singers-Synchronize-Heartbeats.

28 Claire Groden, "Many Hearts, One Beat: Singing Syncs Up Heart Rates," *Time*, July 10, 2013. http://healthland.time.com/2013/07/10/many-hearts-one-beat-singing-synchs-up-heart-rates.

29 Palmer, "Choir Singers Synchronize Heartbeats."

The Name Written in Our Hearts

I say unto you, I would that ye should remember to retain the name written always in your hearts, that ye are not found on the left hand of God.—Mosiah 5:12

Some people wonder what is the value of consecutive meditation days. One Kundalini Yoga teacher, Guru Singh, explained that it is not actually about days but about heart beats.[30] Each blood cell in the body has iron in it, which is the reason blood is red.[31] Iron is a substance that can be written on electromagnetically—that is how the old technology of cassette tapes worked.

Blood cells are made within the bone marrow, primarily in the flat bones of the skull, sternum, and pelvis.[32] With each beat of the heart, an electromagnetic signal is produced, the strongest signal in the body and measurable from outside the body.[33] A message is recorded on the million or so new blood cells that have been produced: your attitude, who you are mentally and physically, who you think you are. A million different messages are imprinted onto the blood cells via the iron from which the cells are primarily composed.[34]

Guru Singh asserts that the lengths of Kundalini Meditations are not picked randomly. The length of each is related to the approximate frequency of the heartbeat and, therefore, how many heartbeats will occur during the meditation. The number of heartbeats relates to how many blood cells will be affected by the vibrations and imprinted by the message during the meditation. The reason forty consecutive days of meditation is important is

---

30 Guru Singh, "40-Day Sadhana," YouTube video posted October 14, 2008, http://www.youtube.com/watch?v=BxcimeKrfpU.

31 University of Cambridge, "Why Is Blood Red?" September 30, 2006, http://www.thenakedscientists.com/HTML/questions/question/1312.

32 Puget Sound Blood Center, "Introduction to Hematology," accessed March 24, 2014. http://www.psbc.org/hematology/02_how.htm.

33 Esoteric Metaphysical and Spiritual Database, "The Heart Has Its Own 'Brain' and Consciousness," August 20, 2012, http://www.in5d.com/heart-has-brain-and-consciousness.html.

34 Puget Sound Blood Center, "Introduction to Hematology," accessed March 24, 2014. http://www.psbc.org/hematology/02_how.htm

that blood cells live for around one hundred twenty days. If you are repeating the same meditation every day, forty days is about the point at which the new population of blood cells, written with your new message, can begin to overpower the old message. The new cells will hold a new attitude and consciousness. Of course, if you keep going to one hundred twenty days, you'll see even more results, but the full power and value of Kundalini Yoga meditation is best seen after a trial of forty consecutive days.

The Gong:
The Original Sound Current

Among the tools the yogi has to merge the finite with the infinite the gong reigns supreme. . . . The gong is a beautiful reinforced vibration. It is an inter-vibratory system. It is like a multitude of strings, like playing a million strings.[35]—Harijiwan Khalsa

If you attend Kundalini Yoga classes often enough, or watch enough videos, there is a good chance you'll experience gong playing. If you have never experienced gong meditation before, it is a sublime experience. There are many reasons why this is so. The gong affects the body and its meridians, releasing blocks, reducing tension, and stimulating circulation. The result is a reorganization of the emotional energy and feelings that are tied to the body structure.[36]

The vibrations that come from good gong playing are very similar to the vibrations you would hear from a recording of the vibrations found in deep space. The sound is the reverberation of the generating, organizing, and creative forces that keep the whole of creation together—the original Sound Current (the Word), which was used to create the universe. The gong takes us into the Sound Current, where we can "resonate with pleasure, joy and bliss."[37]

The gong is also an amplification device; it amplifies the energy field of the player and the mantra that the player is mentally reciting. Listening to the sound of the gong provokes emotions and thoughts from the subconscious, which puts the entire nervous system under pressure to adjust and heal itself,[38] which can be momentarily uncomfortable, but eventually sends you into the deepest meditation possible. The sound will carry

---

35 Harijiwan Khalsa, "The Gong," accessed March 24, 2014, http://www.harijiwan.com/gong.
36 Yogi Bhajan, *KRI International Teacher Training Manual, Level 1*, 4th ed. (Santa Cruz, NM: Kundalini Research Institute, 2007), 137.
37 Harijiwan Khalsa, "The Gong," accessed March 24, 2014, http://www.harijiwan.com/gong.
38 Sometimes this process can bring up fear or discomfort, but if you don't run away, the gong will wash these subconscious thought structures away.

you beyond all fears. The sound penetrates into every atom of your body and aids in replenishing the parasympathetic nervous system (which is ruled by sound). This process balances the sympathetic nervous system, which can often be overstimulated due to stresses in the body.[39]

The vibrations of the gong are able to completely wash away negative thought structures that are being transmitted by the subconscious and the Negative Mind. Listening to the gong can magnify and expand thoughts of self-love and other positive thoughts and feelings. Listening can bring a deep state of relaxation, allowing the body to heal and revive in order to be productive and efficient. Gong vibrations can set your whole system into a path of vibrating and attracting positive things. Harijiwan Khalsa says that regularly "listening to the gong will re-pattern your magnetic field, open you to the vastness of your own psyche, and release you from all that prevents you from living a life of complete and utter happiness."[40] He asserts that good gong playing[41] is "a gift of God, Heaven on Earth."[42]

---

39 Yogi Bhajan, *KRI International Teacher Training Manual, Level 1*, 120.
40 Harijiwan Khalsa, "The Gong."
41 Bad gong playing can be damaging. It is inadvisable to play the gong without proper training.
42 Harijiwan Khalsa, "Gong Basics," YouTube video posted January 2, 2011, http://www.youtube.com/watch?v=vpU2noreEyc.

Commonly Used Kundalini Mantras and Their Meanings

On the following pages I have included some of the highest and most commonly used mantras. I have included their common names and easy spellings as well as phonetic spellings to help you pronounce them. I have also included translations, comments, and scriptural references that I have found helpful to anchor the mantras in a gospel context. This short list includes most of the mantras you will find in the manual section of this book. You may learn more about these and other mantras through the Mantrapedia database at http://www.spiritvoyage.com/mantras. You can also listen and purchase music there. As you read the mantras, you may notice that even reading them is powerful. But as mantras are experiential, I invite you to go a step further and allow the sounds to form in your mouth and vibrate through you.

You are welcome to play or chant any of these mantras at any or all times. However, before beginning any kundalini yoga kriya or meditation, always tune in the Adi Mantra: Ong Namo Guru Dev Namo (instructions on page 190), and when you are finished, always tune out with a long Sat Nam.

ONG NAMO
Ong Namo, Guroo Dev Namo

I bow to/I call upon the Divine Teacher who is also within me.

This mantra is called the Adi Mantra. Adi means "first" or "primal." Technically it links the chanter to the Golden Chain of teachers who have brought you this opportunity. It allows the chanter to relate instantly to the divine teacher within. This mantra is used to tune in before Kundalini Yoga classes and before your personal meditation practice. The Adi Mantra centers the teacher and the students in their highest selves and allows the divine teacher to guide us and work through us. In the *Shabd Guru*, the words for "I bow to" and "I call upon" are the same, indicating there is no distinction between prayer and praise. *Namo* also relates to a person's identity, thereby blending Infinite and finite into the Self.[43]

> "And the glory which thou gavest me I have given them; that they may be one, even as we are one" (John 17:22).

AAD GURAY NAMEH
Aad Guray Nameh, Jugaad Guray Nameh, Sat Guray Nameh, Siri Guroo Dayv-ay Nameh

I bow to/call upon the primal (first, original) guru.
I bow to/call upon the truth that has existed throughout the ages.
I bow to/call upon True Wisdom.
I bow to/call upon the Great Divine Wisdom.

This is called the Mangala Charn mantra. If you choose to, after the Adi Mantra you may chant this mantra three times. This mantra puts a circle of protective light around a person. It clears clouds of doubt and opens one to higher guidance.[44] Yogi Bhajan taught that this mantra should always be recited at least three times in a row.[45]

> "I will go before your face. I will be on your right hand and on your left, and my Spirit shall be in your hearts, and mine angels round about you, to bear you up" (Doctrine and Covenants 84:88).

---

43 Yogi Bhajan, *The Aquarian Teacher: KRI International Teacher Training Manual, Level 1* (Santa Cruz, NM: Kundalini Research Institute, 2007), 86.
44 Ibid., 82.
45 *Mantrapedia*, s.v. "Aad Guray Nameh," accessed July 18, 2014, www.spiritvoyage.com/mantras.

AAP SAHAEE HOA
Aap Sahaee Hoa Sachaa Daa Sachaa Doaa, Har, Har, Har

You, Divine One, have become my refuge. True is Your support, Great Creative Infinite.

This mantra neutralizes negativity from around you, helps one walk into the unknown without fear, and gives protection and mental balance.[46] It also calls on the generating aspect of God (Har), which makes it a prosperity mantra as well.

"I will say of the Lord, He is my refuge and my fortress: my God; in him will I trust" (Psalm 91:2).

ADI SHAKTI
Adi Shakti, Adi Shakti, Adi Shakti, Namo, Namo
Sarab Shakti, Sarab Shakti, Sarab Shakti, Namo, Namo
Prithum Bhagawati, Prithum Bhagawati, Prithum Bhagawati, Namo, Namo
Kundalini, Maata Shakti, Maata Shakti, Namo, Namo

Namo: *I bow to, I call upon.*
Adi Shakti: *Primal (first, original) power.*
Sarab Shakti: *All power.*
Prithum Bhagawati: *Which creates through God.*
Kundalini: *Divine energy.*
Maata Shakti: *Divine female energy.*

This mantra connects us with our Divine Mother and the feminine power in the universe. It will help you be free of insecurities that block action.[47]

"When he prepared the heavens, I was there: when he set a compass upon the face of the depth: When he established the clouds above: when he strengthened the fountains of the deep: When he gave to the sea his decree, that the waters should not pass his commandment: when he appointed the foundations of the earth: Then I was by him, as one brought up with him: and I was daily his delight, rejoicing always before him; rejoicing in the habitable part of his earth; and my delights were the sons of men. Now therefore hearken unto me, O ye children: for blessed are they that keep my ways" (Proverbs 8:27-32).[48]

---

46 Bhajan, *The Aquarian Teacher*, 82.
47 Ibid.
48 Some scholars believe the verses in Proverbs 8 that refer to "wisdom" are actually referring to the Divine Mother (see Kevin L. Barney, "How to Worship Our Mother in Heaven (Without Getting Excommunicated)," *Dialogue: A Journal of Modern Thought*, Vol. 41, No. 4, 121–146).

ANG SANG WAHE GURU
Ung Sung Wah-Hay Guroo

The ecstasy of God is in me and vibrates in every cell of my being.

"This mantra expresses a universal truth. Repeating it creates a thought, which gradually guides the psyche to adjust itself. It re-connects every fragmented projection of the psyche, each separated part of the body, and synchronizes the finite sense of self to the Infinite Oneness. This act of rejoining the separated parts is the quintessential act of healing. Under attack, under war, under the pressures of fear, this meditation keeps us together, conscious, and ready to act. It brings the inner peacefulness that comes only from the touch and scope of spirit."
—A Commentary by Gurucharan Singh, KRI Director of Training[49]

"Ye must bow down before him, and worship him with all your might, mind, and strength, and your whole soul" (2 Nephi 25:29).

ARDAS BHAEE
Ardas Bhaee, Amardaas Guroo
Amar Daas Guroo, Ardaas Bhayee
Amar Daas Guroo, Ardaas Bhayee
Ardas Bhaee, Amardaas Guroo
Raam Daas Guroo, Raam Daas Guroo
Raam Daas Guroo, Sachee Sahee

Guru Amar Das: The energy of grace and hope when there is no hope.
Guru Ram Das: The energy of humility, healing, miracles, and blessings.
Sachee Sahee: This is the prayer to answer all prayers. The miracle is complete.

This mantra is known as a mantra for miracles. It will help release a difficult situation. It is a prayer that ensures all prayers will be answered. If you sing it, your mind, body, and soul will combine, and without having to say what you want, every need will be provided and life will be adjusted.[50]

"For behold, I am God; and I am a God of miracles; and I will show unto the world that I am the same yesterday, today, and forever" (2 Nephi 27:33).

---

49 *Mantrapedia*, s.v. "Ang Sang Wahe Guru," accessed July 18, 2014, www.spiritvoyage.com/mantras.
50 Bhajan, *The Aquarian Teacher*, 82.

EK ONG KAAR SAT NAM SIRI WAHE GURU
Eck Ong Kaar Sat Naam Siri Wah-Hay Guroo

Eck Ong Kaar: The Creator and the Creation are One.
Sat Nam: Truth is my identity, this is my true identity.
Siri Wahe Guru: The ecstasy of the experience of this wisdom is beyond all words and brings indescribable bliss.

This mantra has eight parts, which correspond to the body's eight major chakras. It was the first mantra Yogi Bhajan taught during his first year in the United States. This mantra is "very powerful for awakening the Kundalini energy and suspending the mind in bliss." It creates "a responsive interrelationship between you and the universal creative energy."[51]

"Ye are all one in Christ Jesus" (Galatians 3:28).

GOBINDAY MUKUNDAY
Gobinday Mukunday Udaaray Apaaray Hariang Kariang Nirnamay Akamay

Sustainer, Liberator, Enlightener, Infinite, Destroyer, Creator, Nameless,[52] Desireless[53]

This mantra calls on eight different names or aspects of God. This mantra can eliminate blocks and errors of the past. According to Yogi Bhajan, "Besides helping cleanse the subconscious mind, it balances the hemispheres of the brain, bringing compassion and patience to the one who meditates on it."[54] It has the power to purify one's magnetic field, making it easier to relax and meditate.

"Cast thy burden upon the Lord, and he shall sustain thee" (Psalm 55:22).

"Verily, verily, I say unto you, I will impart unto you of my Spirit, which shall enlighten your mind, which shall fill your soul with joy" (Doctrine and Covenants 11:13).

---

51 Ibid., 84
52 See Revelation 2:17.
53 It is difficult to translate the word *Akamay*. The use of the word *desireless* here means "without attachment to worldly things."
54 Bhajan, *The Aquarian Teacher*, 84.

GOD AND ME, ME AND GOD ARE ONE

Though it is not good grammar, it is a good mantra. This affirmation was given by Yogi Bhajan. Its purpose is to remember that God is within every one of us. The ultimate empowerment is finding the divine within.[55]

> "And the glory which thou gavest me I have given them; that they may be one, even as we are one" (Galatians 3:28).

GURU GURU WAHE GURU
Guru Guru Wahe Guru, Guru Ram Das Guru

Guru: Teacher or guide that brings one from the darkness to the light
Wahe: Exclamation of ecstasy and joy for that which one has gained through experience of God
Ram Das: God's humble servant

This mantra is known for its healing qualities and for conferring humility on the one who chants it. It will rescue you in the midst of danger and trial. Chanting this mantra projects the mind to the infinite, the source of all knowledge and ecstasy. It also gives you a finite guiding relationship on a practical level.

This mantra was given to Yogi Bhajan by Guru Ram Das in his astral body.[56] Guru Ram Das was the fourth Sikh guru. He was known for healing, miracles, and service. He is called the patron saint of Kundalini Yoga because he was Yogi Bhajan's astral teacher.[57] When chanting "Guru Ram Das," some people praise this guru, but the highest level of truth I have discovered about this mantra is that it tunes us into the energy represented in the *name*. That energy is of the ultimate *humble servant* of God, Jesus Christ, who did the will of his Father in all things.

> "Behold, I am Jesus Christ the Son of God. I created the heavens and the earth, and all things that in them are. I was with the Father from the beginning. I am in the Father, and the Father in me; and in me hath the Father glorified his name." (3 Nephi 9:15).

---

55 *Matrapedia*, s.v. "God and Me, Me and God Are One," accessed July 18, 2014, www.spiritvoyage.com/mantras.
56 Bhajan, *The Aquarian Teacher*, 84.
57 Guru Dharam S. Khalsa and Darryl O'Keeffe, *The Kundalini Yoga Experience:Bringing Body, Mind, and Spirit Together* (New York, NY: Fireside, 2002), 136.

HAR
Har (Pronounced with a rolled *R*. Sounds like Hud.)

Creative Infinity.

Har is the name for the generating aspect of God.[58] This mantra is often used for prosperity meditations. It is a mantra for life on earth and earthly needs.

"Save now, I beseech thee, O Lord: O Lord, I beseech thee, send now prosperity" (Psalm 118:25).

HUMEE HUM BRAHM HUM
Hummee Humm Bruhm Humm

We are we, we are God.

"This mantra literally means we are the spirit of God. . . . It fixes the identity to its true reality."[59] It creates a rhythm between parts and whole. The energetic form and flow of these sounds work on the heart center, navel center, and throat and brow centers together. This mantra allows you to experience the Self and be fully present in your mind and body.[60]

"I have said, Ye are gods; and all of you are children of the most High" (Psalm 82:6).

I AM, I AM

The first *I AM* is you, and the second *I AM* is the divine—blending finite and Infinite, reminding the meditator of his or her own Infinite nature.[61]

"Hearken and listen to the voice of him who is from all eternity to all eternity, the Great I Am, even Jesus Christ" (Doctrine and Covenants 39:1)

58 Bhajan, *The Aquarian Teacher*, 84.
59 Ibid., 85.
60 Gurucharan Singh Khalsa, http://www.yogachicago.com/sep11/gurucharan.shtml, accessed December 15, 2014.
61 *Matrapedia*, s.v. "I Am, I Am," accessed July 18, 2014, www.spiritvoyage.com/mantras.

MUL MANTRA

Ek Ong Kaar, Sat Naam, Kartaa Purkh, Neer bo Neer vair, Akaal Moorat, Ajoonee, Saibhang Guru Prasaad, Jap! Aad Such, Jugaad Such, Heh Bhee Such, Naanak Hosee Bhee Such

Ek Ong Kar: God is One, I am One with all beings.
Sat Naam: I am truth, truth is my identity.
Kartaa Purkh: God is the Doer.
Nirbhao Nirvair: Fearless and all-loving is He.
Akaal Moorat: God transcends time, is without death or change.
Ajoonee: God is without beginning.
Saibhang: God is self-illuminating.
Guru Prasaad: God is the compassionate guru.
Jap: Meditate!
Aad Such, Jugaad Such: True in the beginning, True through all the ages.
Hai Bhee Such: True here and now.
Nanak Hosee Bhee Such: Nanak (composer of the mantra/poem) says God will forever be true.

Mul Mantra is known as the Ballad of Enlightenment. It was given by Guru Nanak, a great yogi, healer, and founder of the Sikh Dharma. The mantra is a compass that points toward God. The entire mantra points toward God and describes the God-in-human conciousness. Guru Nanak says that we only sin when we forget our Infinity—when we forget in our essence, in our being and our vibration, the reality of God and guru in our soul. This mantra creates a comfortable and happy way to meditate that is perfectly balanced and keeps us in the flow of life and in contact with the perception of the soul at each moment. Mul Mantra is a complete technology in itself. To chant this mantra, to go into its inner depths, is to remain in contact with our own Godhood. It is to be entranced by the soul. Chanting Mul Mantra over time can alleviate depression and can take a person to a state of alignment with divine truth.[62]

"Behold, I am the Lord God Almighty, and Endless is my name; for I am without beginning of days or end of years" (Moses 1:3).

---

62 Bhajan, *The Aquarian Teacher*, 81.

RA MA DA SA
Raa Maa Daa Saa Saa Say So Hung

Ra: Sun
Ma: Moon
Da: Earth
Sa: Infinity
Sa Say: Totality of Infinity
So Hung: I am Thou

Ra Ma Da Sa will attune the self to the universe. It is a powerful healing mantra. These sounds directly stimulate the kundalini for healing.[63] This mantra is one of the most precious, sought-after gems. Read the full commentary about this mantra on page 258.

> "This is the light of Christ. As also he is in the *sun*, and the light of the sun, and the power thereof by which it was made. As also he is in the *moon*, and is the light of the moon, and the power thereof by which it was made; as also the light of the stars, and the power thereof by which they were made; and the *earth* also, and the power thereof, even the earth upon which you stand. And the light which shineth, which giveth you light, is through him who enlighteneth your eyes, which is the same light that quickeneth your understandings; which light proceedeth forth from the presence of God to *fill the immensity of space*—the light which is in all things, which giveth life to all things, which is the law by which all things are governed, even the *power of God*" (Doctrine and Covenants 88:7–13, emphasis added).

SA RE SA SA (ANTAR NAAD MANTRA)
Saa Ray Saa Saa, Saa Ray Saa Saa, Saa Ray Saa Saa, Saa Rung
Har Ray Har Har, Har Ray Har Har, Har Ray Har Har, Har Rung

Sa is the Infinite, God. It is the element of ether that is the origin or beginning and is through all things. Har is the the creative power of God manifested through the tangible and personal. Woven together, these sounds blend the finite and Infinite and project together with the sound of "Ung," or Totality.[64]

This mantra is called the Antar Naad, meaning the first mantra or base of all mantras. It enhances communication and gives your words power. Adversity melts before this mantra.[65] Learn more about this mantra in the commentary on page 252.

> "I can do all things through Christ which strengtheneth me" (Philippians 4:13).

---

63 Ibid., 86.
64 Ibid.
65 Ibid., 86.

SAT NAM (BIJ MANTRA)
Sut Naam

I am truth, truth is my identity.

Sat Nam is probably the most widely used mantra in the practice of Kundalini Yoga. *Sat* means truth. *Naam* means identity, acknowledging your own divine identity. Sat Naam is a *bij* (seed) mantra. The seed contains all the knowledge of the fully grown tree. Chanting this mantra allows the seed to grow, awakening the soul and giving you your destiny. This mantra also balances the five elements (tattvas).[66]

"Now, we will compare the word unto a seed. Now, if ye give place, that a seed may be planted in your heart, behold, if it be a true seed, or a good seed, if ye do not cast it out by your unbelief, that ye will resist the Spirit of the Lord, behold, it will begin to swell within your breasts; and when you feel these swelling motions, ye will begin to say within yourselves—It must needs be that this is a good seed, or that the word is good, for it beginneth to enlarge my soul; yea, it beginneth to enlighten my understanding, yea, it beginneth to be delicious to me" (Alma 32:28).

As a greeting, *Sat Nam* means "I see the Truth in you; I see your truest self." Saying this phrase to another person not only acknowledges their true self but calls that self forward to respond.[67]

"And that all their salutations may be in the name of the Lord" (Doctrine and Covenants 109:19).

SA TA NA MA
Saa Taa Naa Maa

Birth, life/growth, death/change, rebirth.

This mantra expresses the five primal sounds of the Universe ("Sss," "Mmm," "Ttt," "Nnn," and "Aaa"). This mantra is the internal energy or Naad form of the mantra Sat Naam and is used to raise intuition, balance the brain, and create a destiny where there was none. This mantra describes the cycle of life and creation.[68] This mantra also bears record of Christ's miraculous life: His birth, His life, His sacrifice, and resurrection.

"I am Alpha and Omega, the beginning and the end, the first and the last" (Revelation 22:13).

---

66 Ibid.
67 Yogi Bhajan, "Gurdwara," lecture, May 3, 1992, Hamburg, Germany, www.Libraryofteachings.com, accessed August 7, 2014.
68 Bhajan, *The Aquarian Teacher*, 87.

WAHE GURU
Wah-Hay Guroo

I am in ecstasy when I experience the indescribable wisdom of God.

Wahe Guru is the Mantra of Ecstasy. It is the mantra that most effectively stimulates the Third Eye/pituitary gland. This mantra expresses complete and ecstatic awe for the greatness of God. *Wah* is an expression of wow and should be said quickly. *Hay* is the longer syllable and means "I have gained." When saying this mantra, focus on the joy and ecstasy you have received by experiencing the nature of the divine. *Guru* means "the One who brings us from darkness to light."[69] A person can interpret this thing or person who is a bringer of light in any way they choose, based on their own personal and religious comfort, but for those who know Christ as the light of the world, it's an obvious expression of praising Him and His Father who sent him.

"Then will I go up unto the altar of God, unto God my exceeding joy: yea, upon the harp will I praise thee, O God my God" (Psalm 43:4).

---

[69] Dharma Singh Khalsa and Cameron Stauth, *Meditation as Medicine: Activate the Power of Your Natural Healing Force* (New York: Fireside, 2001), 122–123.

Daily Dose of Wellness | Michelle Larsen

My meditation journey began when I was desperately searching for a way to calm my crazy mind. My mind wasn't always crazy but I went through a "breaking open" period that began with feelings we needed to adopt a child. I was busily caring for my five children when through a series of direct revelations from God I was led to adopt four siblings from Ethiopia. The adoption process was blessed and we had many miracles and "heaven meets earth" moments that carried us through that time. However, the crazy mind and severe anxiety came after the children came home.

Trying to love four new children that didn't speak English or like any food I fixed and had tantrums and nightmares was overwhelming. I suddenly had nine children between the ages of 4 and 16. It was a crisis every minute and my nerves were frayed. My senses and abilities were overloaded with doubt, dread, and fear. I wasn't myself. I had never felt anxiety before and it became debilitating. Friends of mine who were on anti-anxiety medication urged me to look into that so I could function again and rest from all the negativity that was flooding my senses. Being a holistic person, I knew there was another way.

I started researching and came across Felice's blog. The Spirit immediately told me that she would lead me to some relief. I watched a few videos and it all looked a little "kooky" to me. But, I went ahead and tried her 40-day meditation challenge. I felt a lot of resistance to meditating in the Kundalini way. I was looking for relaxation, not more stimulation. I soon realized that it was my subconscious causing my anxiety and Kundalini meditation was scrubbing out that subconscious.

The first few tries of Kirtan Kriya were wonderful, and the mantras kept my mind from wandering and kept me from falling asleep like I did in normal meditation. Then after just a few days, I started noticing some serious anger coming out of nowhere. I felt enraged and resentful that God had asked me to go through these difficult days and to do this to my family. It became too intense and I stopped meditating many months to ease up on the "subconscious cleansing."

Fast-forward a year or so and as I prayed and learned to trust God again, I started getting strong impressions to pick back up the daily Kundalini meditation practice. It was time to "wake up" and start cleaning my mind again. This time as I noticed those same feelings starting to surface, I recognized them and let them flow away. As I kept up the practice, it only took about a week before I noticed that the majority of negativity, resentment, anger, and distrust was now gone. It wasn't squelched down for the time being, but it was truly gone.

Part of waking up is a bit painful—but my pain was teaching me. I kept going and little by little pain was replaced with joy and my mind felt free from negativity. Countless gifts and blessings have now come to me quite effortlessly. The greatest gift has been the immense love I feel towards all my children. I am more able to see others how God sees them—all by my ability to tap into that higher vibration through meditation. Another gift has been the ability to control my thoughts. Part of life is negativity and darkness but now when it comes I call upon that "meditation vibration" in my mind and am able to first recognize it for what it and then dispel it.

Meditation has increased my patience, love, and understanding of myself as well. I look back how far I've come these past three years and my heart swells with gratitude for this nutty method of meditation. My prayers are more personal and scripture study and journal writing have become revelatory—not just once in a while, but regularly.

My meditation story hasn't been one particular sensational experience, but rather slow, incremental change. The change that has come has been on a cellular level that is difficult to describe. The overall change though is so profound to me that I am now committed to making meditation a lifetime practice for myself. Kundalini meditation began as my medication and now is my "daily dose" of wellness that I couldn't do without.

Healing My Daughter's Pre-Birth Wounds | Lani Axman

In early 2013, I discovered that my youngest daughter had come to this earth carrying wounds from a previous womb experience. She had been aborted by another mother. As a result of her prebirth trauma, my daughter spent much of her toddlerhood in a state of distress, anger, sadness, and angst. Once I understood why, I felt compelled to do whatever I could to help her heal.

In June 2013, I attended a meditation retreat taught by Felice. While there, I learned the meditation Ra Ma Da Sa. I learned that this particular meditation is a powerful healing prayer. We chanted the mantra at the retreat, and it was so beautiful that it penetrated every inch of my body and sent my spirit soaring.

The complete mantra is "Raa Maa Daa Saa Saa Say So Hung." It means *Sun, Moon, Earth, Infinity, Totality of Infinity, I am thou*. Or, as I like to say, it's basically a very condensed version of Doctrine and Covenants 88:7–13:

> This is the light of Christ. As also he is in the sun, and the light of the sun, and the power thereof by which it was made. As also he is in the moon, and is the light of the moon, and the power thereof by which it was made; as also the light of the stars, and the power thereof by which they were made; and the earth also, and the power thereof, even the earth upon which you stand. And the light which shineth, which giveth you light, is through him who enlighteneth your eyes, which is the same light that quickeneth your understandings; which light proceedeth forth from the presence of God to fill the immensity of space—the light which is in all things, which giveth life to all things, which is the law by which all things are governed, even the power of God."

All healing comes from Christ, and His light infuses and gives life to everyone and everything in the universe. After returning home after our summer trip to Utah, I decided that I wanted to do forty days of Ra Ma Da Sa with the intention of helping my daughter heal from her prebirth wounds. So I did. And it was life changing.

Before I tell you more, I want to explain some more background. I learned when my daughter was born that she was likely originally sharing my womb with a twin. Since then, I have received line upon line more and more information about her twin, my unborn son. I feel he is a powerful healer-soul; his name is Elijah, and he very much wants to come to our family, in part because he is very close with my daughter and his presence will help her (and me).

Four days into my forty days of Ra Ma Da Sa, I had a powerful vision type of experience while meditating. It was early in the morning, and my daughter was still asleep on my bed.

As I chanted on her behalf, I envisioned where she was and sent my love to her. Then I saw (in my mind) my unborn son, Elijah, appear at her side. He lay down by her. And then, suddenly, it was like her spirit was in pieces floating around her body. Elijah started gathering all the pieces of her spirit in the palm of his hand.

A few moments later, the Savior appeared at the foot of the bed, and Elijah handed all the pieces of her spirit to Christ. In the palms of His hands, the pieces fused together in white light. Elijah gathered more and more pieces and continued handing them to Christ, and in His hands they continued to glow and combine.

At the end of the meditation, I kept feeling the urge to cup my hands to receive her spirit. Finally I did. I held her recombined spirit in my palms. Then I put my hands to my chest and put her spirit into my heart. I told her, "You can be whole now, Baby." And I filled my heart with love for her. Then I moved my hands from my chest, outstretched in front of me, and set her free.

The next day, my daughter was awake while I meditated. When I started Ra Ma Da Sa, she sat on my lap and grabbed my arms to wrap them around her. So I sat with my arms around her, singing until she got up.

A little bit later she came back in with her baby doll. At first my daughter pushed her doll toward me and put its arms around my neck. Then she sat down in my lap with the baby on her lap and told me to hold the baby. So I continued Ra Ma Da Sa with my hands holding her arms and both of our arms around the baby.

At that moment it seemed so clear that she was presenting the baby doll as her inner child—the spirit who had experienced prenatal and premortal traumas. And we were cradling that part of her in our arms while I prayed for her in song. It was only one of many beautiful, tender moments we shared during that time.

There were many days, however, when my daughter's behavior seemed worse than ever. Her anger, neediness, screaming, and obvious emotional pain weighed heavily on me, and I wondered, *If this meditation is supposed to be helping her, then why does she seem worse than ever?* But I carried on, telling myself that it was stirring things up for her.

For forty days I prayed in song for my daughter's healing. And slowly, bit by bit, it came. Gradually, her energy shifted. The angst that had been so much a part of her presence dissolved little by little until it was just *gone*. She was, quite literally, a *new child*. But it wasn't just her. We were all new. My husband and I especially saw that in seeking healing for her, we also found healing for ourselves and our relationships with her. For the first time since she had been conceived, my husband felt an intense love for her, unlike anything he had felt for her before. It brought him nearly to tears when he told me about it, and he doesn't cry.

Once freed from her pain, we watched my daughter soar. While she hadn't been very verbal before, she suddenly began speaking in sentences. She blossomed socially, becoming a much more chatty and talkative companion. Where I used to feel weighed down by the pain radiating from her, I now could feel her peace and joy. Faraway family members who visited couldn't believe the change in her. She was free!

Another mother who is raising a former-castaway asked me last year:

> When I discovered that my daughter had been aborted, it made sense to me why she is the way she is and the love I needed to show her. But I was thinking, why would her soul need healing if she was in heaven in Christ's presence? Wouldn't you think being in His presence would heal those wounds?

Her question led to lots of pondering and seeking. The following is the answer that came to me: In many near-death experience accounts, we see that individuals are given a choice of whether to return to their bodies or remain in heaven. I believe this emphasis on freedom of choice is a universal principle in God's plan. As I pondered the aborted children waiting in heaven, the impression that came to me was that some of them *are* completely healed by divine love. But I felt impressed that it was all governed by *choice*. Some of those children choose to receive complete healing of their previous womb trauma. Their pain and sadness are completely swept away.

However, I believe the aborted are also given another option: to retain a portion of their memory of the experience and their pain upon returning to Earth. I feel that some of these children accept a mission to bring to light the reality of their existence and the truth about the trauma experienced by the aborted. They retain their scars just as Christ chose to retain His scars—as a testament to the world. They take up this bitter cup in order to share their truth so that future souls can perhaps be saved the anguish they have suffered.

When all of these impressions washed over me, I was in awe of these courageous souls. I began to weep as I looked down at my own daughter, recognizing the immense greatness of her soul, willing to carry such a painful burden so that others might know the truth. What strength! What love!

What a privilege to have been chosen to bear her, love her, and play a small part in helping her heal. I pray her experience and mine will aid others in their own paths to healing.

This is the light of
Christ…which proceedeth
forth from the presence
of God to fill the
immensity of space.

— D&C 88: 7, 12

Prana

Prana

It is said that our first breath sets the tone for our life. I came into the world fighting and angry at the authority that was pulling me from my mother's womb. In my baby pictures, I still have the marks on the side of my head from the forceps. True to the saying, an emotional theme was set in my life for a few decades.

When I started my Kundalini Yoga and Meditation journey in earnest, I found myself at a rebirthing class, where I was told we were going to do a meditation to clear any pain or trauma from our own births and then we would each retake our first breath.

I dropped into a deep state of self-hypnosis and saw myself in the womb. I also saw through my mother's eyes and all her love and hopes for me. I prepared for the birth as I chanted and meditated, and then came the breathing. We breathed for a long time, slowly and deeply across the tongue.

I was not sure which breath would be the first breath of my rebirth, but I could feel it approaching. I was in the birth canal. I could feel a pressure building. Inexplicably, I started laughing and crying. A blissful feeling was rising up my spine, and my legs went tingly. It was more amazing than any kind of bodily ecstasy I had ever felt. The bliss was almost too much to bear, but I allowed it to flow all through me as I wept joyful, laughing, ecstatic tears. I was told afterward that my experience was not uncommon for people who practiced Kundalini Yoga. I was hooked.

Though I was never really sure which breath was my new first breath, there was no question that I had been reborn, and it was an ecstatic rebirth. From that day on, my life began to transform. That simple breath full of joy and excitement set a new direction for my life. The biggest change that everyone soon noticed was in my voice and the power of my words.

Indeed, the breath and the Word are intimately related. In the heavenly realms, first came the Word, followed by its servant, the breath of life, *prana*. In the earthly realms, however, the breath comes first. Then, as everyone anxiously awaits, comes the first sound—or yell, in some cases—the sound that signifies we are alive and here to stay.

I am here to stay—however, only temporarily—as long as God gives me breath. It is said that the breath is the kiss of God. It is the spark that animates the body and the glue that holds spirit and body together. The account in the book of Abraham of the creation of man is interesting because we learn that even though both body and spirit were joined, they did not become alive until God breathed the breath of life into Adam: "[God] formed man from the dust of the ground, and took his spirit (that is, the man's spirit), and put it into him; and breathed into his nostrils the breath of life, and man became a living soul" (Abraham 5:7).

According to ancient masters, "Prana is a mystical force that is found in all living physical entities, but which is non-physical. It is in the air without being air. It is in water without being water. It is in food without being food."[1] The ancients said that wherever there is life in the universe, there is prana. Without prana, all would be dead, lifeless matter. The word *prana* is derived from the Sanskrit word signifying absolute energy, divine energy, or as I know it, the Light of Christ.[2]

The scriptures say that the Light of Christ "proceedeth forth from the presence of God to fill the immensity of space" and is "the light which is in all things, which giveth life to all things, which is the law by which all things are governed."[3] Though prana fills the immensity of space and is in all things, humans have a special relationship with prana because of our intellectual capabilities, which empower us to receive and transfer prana. Consequently, we can choose to fill ourselves with more prana,[4] and we can also "send" prana to others for healing purposes.

As I have stated elsewhere in this book, most people sleepwalk through life, giving away their agency to subconscious thought forms until they are powerless, emotional zombies.

Kundalini Yoga teaches that as prana enters the body, it awakens our divine energy. The purpose of Kundalini Yoga is to raise this energy back to God, where it can blend with Infinite energy and then circulate back through us, creating amazing outcomes: awakening, healing, rebirth, and other benefits shared by contributors to this book. In order to raise that energy, however, we need enough prana.

There are many ways of taking in prana to the body, but the number one way is through the air, through our breath. The close association between breath and spirituality is evident in many languages. In English, the word *inspiration* means "to breath in." The Greek word for *breath* means "soul." The Hebrew word for *breath* means "spirit of God." Many yogis believe that the length of one's life is not predetermined in years but in a pre-fixed number of breaths. Therefore, by lengthening the breath, we can lengthen our lives.

---

1 Dharma Singh Khalsa and Cameron Stauth, *Meditation as Medicine: Activate the Power of Your Natural Healing Force* (New York: Fireside, 2001), 55.

2 The Light of Christ should not be confused with the Holy Ghost (the Holy Spirit). The Light of Christ influences people for good and prepares them to receive the Holy Ghost.

3 Doctrine and Covenants 88:12–13; see also Doctrine and Covenants 88:6–11.

4 In the scriptures, the Light of Christ is sometimes called the Spirit of the Lord, the Spirit of God, the Spirit of Christ, or the Light of Life. For the purpose of this book, I will use the terms *prana* and *the Light of Christ*.

The prana we take in with our regular breathing can be a source of great energy, vitality, and nourishment to the body and spirit. Yet according to Dr. Dharma Singh Khalsa and Cameron Stauth, one-third of people don't breathe deep enough to sustain normal health.[5]

PRANAYAM

The magic of the breath is that it is the only system in the body that can be controlled consciously or unconsciously.[6] You can choose to breathe, or you can let the respiratory system breathe you. By choosing to consciously control what is normally an unconscious process, you can change unconscious patterns. As the scriptures teach us, living unconsciously is like sleepwalking. I believe it is safe to assume from all the uses of the word *awaken* in the scriptures that the ancients were concerned about this sleepwalking condition. One of their techniques for combating it was *pranayam*.

Pranayam is the use of breathing techniques to control the movement of prana. Kundalini Yoga includes a wide range of pranayam techniques to manage and affect different energy states of emotion, consciousness, and health.[7] Even a slight change in this *pran*, or "seed energy," can change your entire world. Mastering the breath is therefore fundamental to mastering life.

I love how answers to some of the deepest mysteries and most complex problems in life are often embedded in very simple things. If you want to change your mental or emotional state, change your breath. That's what I taught Janice. Here is her story:

> I noticed that I was always super grumpy and irritated when I got home from work. I realized it was from having a difficult time transitioning from work mode to homemaker/mother mode. In a meditation class, I learned that alternate nostril breath was really helpful in transitioning and changing states. So I started to use this tool to help me be happy with my family. After driving home from work, I take a minute to do my breathing routine. I also take a minute to visualize how I want to act when I am home with my children. I say a few affirmations like "I am joyfully choosing to serve my family," etc., and then go inside to greet my family. It is amazing what a difference this has made. I really am happy and joyful when I remember to take one minute to do this. It makes my home a much happier place.

---

5 Khalsa and Stauth, *Meditation as Medicine*, 55.

6 Some people distinguish between the subconscious and the unconscious minds; however, for simplicity, they are used interchangeably in this book.

7 Yogi Bhajan, *The Aquarian Teacher: KRI International Teacher Training Manual, Level 1* (Santa Cruz, NM: Kundalini Research Institute, 2007), 90.

Janice has also taught this deep mystery of life to her children:

> When my children are arguing, fighting, talking back, or otherwise choosing bad behavior, I have them play the breath game. Each child gets to make up a new way to breathe as quickly as they can. If they protest, I make one up for them or just breathe consciously myself. They come up with some pretty silly breaths. It immediately creates a shift and change. All negativity vanishes in an instant, in just one breath. It is truly amazing how quickly and effectively that one simple change (the breath) can change everything else.

Janice's children are blessed to have this opportunity to examine and break the habit of ignoring the breath. This simple breathing exercise, learned while they are young, will give them the power to creatively direct their lives, their relationships, and their potential.

The manual section of this book describes several pranayams that are fundamental to the practice of Kundalini Yoga. All of them are fairly simple, but not necessarily easy, depending on your currently established patterns. Learning to breath correctly is arguably one of the most important things for a student of Kundalini Yoga to master.

When Bonnie (see page 177) was beginning her Kundalini Yoga and Meditation journey, she learned that she was a paradoxical breather. In other words, she was breathing backward and pulling her navel in on the inhale. It took her many days of conscious practice to correct this pattern. One day I received a message from her that said, "I woke up feeling happy today, which hasn't happened in a long time. I know it has something to do with breathing correctly."

A few years ago, my friend Lani went through a horrible five-month battle with anxiety and depression. When she started getting sick, she told me that she couldn't breathe. Breathing problems are common among those who suffer from anxiety. For Lani, the problem was partially tied to suppressed grief about losing a beloved grandmother. As she learned and practiced several breathing techniques, her constant gasping for air decreased and her anxiety and depression diminished. As she began to breathe correctly (in combination with other treatments), she was able to heal from the inside out and open her heart to feel and release the grief. She is much better now, but whenever she feels panic setting in, she stops whatever she is doing (or thinking) and begins conscious breathing techniques—breathing out the panic and restoring peace.

QUICK REFERENCE GUIDE TO PRANA

- Prana comes in on the air but is not air.[1]
- In LDS terminology, prana is the Light of Christ.[2]
- We can obtain more prana, and we can direct it.[3]
- As prana enters the body, it awakens the Kundalini energy—the divine, purifying, healing, enlightening energy.[4]
- Though prana comes in with the air, it doesn't necessarily go to the lungs. Prana circulates through the nadis and can be directed to different areas. For some people, when they have a lot of prana at the Third Eye Point and they meditate with closed eyes, they see purple.[5]
- The spiritual importance of breathing is evident in the English language: Inspiration means "to breath in"; the Greek word for breath (pneuma) also means "soul." The Hebrew word for breath also means "spirit of God."[6]
- Life is a series of breaths. Some say life is a fixed number of breaths: you can lengthen your life by slowing down your breath.[7]
- The body can store the Pranic energy, thereby adding vitality.[8]
- Prana is not physical and is not limited to space or touch. People who have mastered prana have a heightened ability to heal others with touch, as well as with the mental powers of intuition, precognition, and telepathy and distance healing.[9]
- Insufficient prana results in malaise and a decrease in spiritual sensitivity.[10]
- We must cultivate and command the breath before we can command words and emotions.[11]
- Prana gives the Word power.[12]

Physiology of Breath

- Every cell is dependent on oxygen.[13]
- Without enough oxygen, cell function declines, causing pain and disease. If brain cells do not receive enough oxygen, emotional distress results.[14]
- Abundant oxygen results in high energy and a good mood.[15]
- Breathing, which involves the diaphragm and the lungs, also increases blood circulation.
- One of most common problems resulting from shallow breathing is poor digestion. (The intestines have been likened to the second brain.)[16]
- Regular conscious breathing tones the nervous system.[17]
- Regular deep breathing directly cleanses the lungs of toxic debris.[18]
- Breathing has a powerful effect on mood. The mind follows the breath, and the body follows the mind, so change your breathing to change your mood.[19]
- Controlling the breath is an effective method of decreasing pain, anger, and fear.[20]
- Conscious breathing shifts the body out of fight-or-flight mode, which can destroy the body over time.[21]

- Conscious breathing can reprogram the autonomic nervous system, which is the body's first defense against illness.[22]

- One-third of people do not breathe well enough to sustain normal health.[23]

---

1 Khalsa and Stauth, *Meditation as Medicine,* 55.
2 Doctrine and Covenants 88:12–13.
3 Khalsa and Stauth, *Meditation as Medicine,* 56.
4 Ibid.
5 Ibid., 57.
6 Ibid., 59.
7 Ibid.
8 Ibid., 57.
9 Ibid.
10 Ibid.
11 Bhajan, *The Aquarian Teacher,* 90.
12 Ibid.
13 Khalsa and Stauth, *Meditation as Medicine,* 60.
14 Ibid.
15 Ibid.
16 Ibid., 60–61.
17 Ibid., 60.
18 Ibid.
19 Ibid.
20 Ibid., 60–62.
21 Ibid., 62.
22 Ibid.
23 Ibid. 55

Life Support | Allie Duzette

I was not always awake.

I feel as though I was always very spiritual—I have had beautiful experiences with the Spirit since I was very, very young—but it wasn't until recently that my body caught up with my spirit. And when that happened, everything changed.

I woke up.

I had recently birthed my first child, and my husband and I had chosen to practice so-called "attachment parenting." This style of parenting involves a lot of breastfeeding and a lot of babywearing. My son was born at 10 and a half pounds. So babywearing and breastfeeding started off hard and got harder—mostly on my back.

One day I was looking at myself in the mirror, and I realized that my shoulders were practically touching my ears. I remember feeling surprised, and wondering what would happen if I relaxed them. It took a mighty effort, but with a giant inhale and then an even more gigantic exhale, I forced my shoulders down, down into the space where they should have been.

The effect only lasted until I took my next breath, and I watched as my shoulders immediately returned to their former position. As I stared at myself, I realized I couldn't remember a time that my shoulders weren't in a state of tension.

That was the day I made the conscious decision to breathe—to breathe relaxation into my shoulders every single day. I didn't want that tension there, and I didn't know what else to do but breathe it out.

Looking back, this was probably the one single thing that set the stage for my spiritual awakening. Deep breaths infuse the body with prana, with life force, and strong, mindful exhalation ejects toxins from the body—toxins both physical and spiritual.

At the time, I didn't see the connection, but now looking back, it is so clear: as I began to breathe more mindfully, my soul started to change. Backlogged trauma and emotions began to clear. In their place, I was left with calm and peace.

Eventually, my shoulders took their rightful place once again, for the first time in maybe a decade or maybe two. The first time I saw my best friend after that day, she commented on how much longer my neck looked. "It looks good," she said.

I had studied breathing for years. In my youth I worked as a singer, and I took lessons and practiced very diligently. I would sing at the National Cathedral, the White House, the Kennedy Center for the Performing Arts. My teacher would have me practice inhaling and exhaling and holding my breath every day. I had to learn how to project the breath in the form of sound, loud enough that my voice could fill a room without a microphone. I had to learn to breathe from the diaphragm instead of the chest; I had to learn how to create sound from even dwindling breath that yearns to be exhaled all at once. I had to learn to master my lungs enough to sing even when I ached to inhale or exhale; I had to control my volume and the depth of the sound escaping my lips.

In singing, everything comes down to breath support. I had known that for years and I had practiced it diligently in the context of music. But what I didn't realize was that everything in life comes down to breath support. As Dharma Singh Khalsa, MD writes in his book *Meditation as Medicine*, breath is life, and life is but a series of breaths. Logically I had always known this—logically, we all know it—but it wasn't until I began to practice it that I realized how exceptionally true this is.

A few months into my awakening, I was led to the Progressive Prophetess blog, and I signed up for the 40-day introductory meditation class. During the class, Nam Joti Kaur explained that most people do not even breathe deeply enough for normal health.

I was shocked, and then decided to take matters into my own hands. I prayed that night for God's help in breathing deeply enough for optimal health. The next day, I couldn't stop gasping for air! Each breath felt like it could be my last, I breathed with such desperation. I needed more air. More and more and more. I think I breathed more often and more deeply that day than I had ever breathed in my entire life prior. But it was worth it. I noticed that in my more highly oxygenated and life-force-infused state, I was more easily able to handle the small things: the screaming children, the burned dinner, the sharp remarks from others. My increase in breath control led to an overall increase in self-control. And self-control is one of the most important things we can learn on this earth.

The prophet Brigham Young taught that eternal life is contingent on our self-control:

"The [body] must be brought in subjection to the spirit perfectly, or your bodies cannot be raised to inherit eternal life. . . . Seek diligently, until you bring all into subjection to the law of Christ."[1]

As we learn to control the breath, we learn to control the self. Breath support is nothing more than life support.

---

1 *Teachings of Presidents of the Church: Brigham Young* (Salt Lake City: The Church of Jesus Christ of Latter-day Saints, 1997), 204.

Even as he
ascends to your height
and caresses your
tenderest branches that
quiver in the sun,
so shall he descend
to your roots
and shake them in their
clinging to the earth.

— **Kahlil Gibran,** The Prophet
NEW YORK: KNOPF, 1923, 11

The
Holy Trinity
of Mind, Body,
and Spirit

The Holy Trinity of Mind, Body, and Spirit

Knowledge of the mind-body connection has existed for eons. Thousands of years ago, humans left drawings on cave walls depicting shamanism—the oldest known tradition that used visualized images for healing. In the fourth century before Christ, the Greek philosopher Socrates commented, "There is no illness of the body apart from the mind."[1] There is also ample scientific documentation on the mind-body connection, beginning with the simple and ubiquitous "placebo effect" and moving on to more in-depth studies on meditation, the mind, and physical health. I will reference some of these studies later.

We can also find examples of the mind-body connection throughout the scriptures. In the Old Testament we read, "A merry heart doeth good like a medicine: but a broken spirit drieth the bones" (Proverbs 17:22). In the Book of Mormon, we learn of a man named Zeezrom, who "lay sick at Sidom, with a burning fever, which was caused by the great tribulations of his mind on account of his wickedness" (Alma 15:3). And in the New Testament, we read that at the Garden of Gethsemane, where Jesus Christ took upon himself the sins and sorrows of the world, he suffered such great physical agony that "his sweat was as it were great drops of blood falling down to the ground" (Luke 22:44).

The restored gospel of Jesus Christ also teaches there is an intimate link between body, mind, and spirit. For example, in the revelations containing the Lord's law of health, God has promised blessings of physical health and also blessings of the mind and spirit (see Doctrine and Covenants 89:19–21). Jesus Christ also taught of the importance and link between these bodies, especially when it comes to worship and service:

> Thou shalt love the Lord thy God with all thy heart, and with all thy soul, and with all thy mind, and with all thy strength: this is the first commandment (Mark 12:30).

---

1 Socrates, *The Writings of Plato*.

Therefore, O ye that embark in the service of God, see that ye serve him with all your heart, might, mind and strength, that ye may stand blameless before God at the last day (Doctrine and Covenants 4:2).

My belief is that our spirits are pure and perfect, and as Truman G. Madsen taught, "our bodies can either be an impediment or an enhancer"[2] to the divine potential coiled within us. Though the physical body may be the "strength" referred to in the scriptures, the physical body is a servant to the mind.[3]

As a hypnotherapist, I explain the mind to people every day. The very simple explanation is that, from the time of birth until eight years old, your mind is one big receptacle for everything you ever hear, say, see, dream, or experience. Every kind and unkind word spoken to you—it all pours into your mind and forms a collection of knowns. These knowns can be added to throughout your life, but for the first eight years there is almost no barrier to entry. When a child nears eight years old, the mind separates and organizes into the conscious and unconscious mind, and a barrier is formed between the two. The newly formed conscious has many cool features, such as logic, reason, willpower, and decision-making abilities, that were not in fully functioning until eight years old.

Though these new critical-thinking skills are lauded as important keystones of free agency, the critical-thinking part of the mind is not as powerful as we wish to believe. Experts agree that the conscious mind makes up less than 10 percent of the mind. The subconscious, which is already full of subconscious programs by eight years old, makes up

The LDS church recognizes the shift in consciousness by age eight as the ability to choose right from wrong, which is why children are not baptized before the age of eight (SEE DOCTRINE AND COVENANTS 68:27). Younger children are believed to be pure and without sin, but the actual doctrine is that they are not held accountable for their sins until eight years old (their parents are held accountable). The porous nature of the subconscious mind before age eight and the programming that early messages create informs the importance of raising children "in light and truth" (DOCTRINE AND COVENANTS 93:30) from their very early days.

---

2 Truman G. Madsen, "Joseph Smith and The Temple," Lecture 8 in audio series *The Prophet Joseph Smith*.
3 The yogic concept of the Ten Bodies, which includes three mental bodies, The Negative, Positive, and Neutral Minds, is a separate concept from the conscious and subconscious mind.

90 percent or more of the mind. Much of our behavior and patterns, despite our conscious wishes, are a result of subconscious programming that was formed before we reached an age of awareness.[4]

Consequently, though the conscious mind might make a logical decision (e.g., to stop eating chocolate or to make a daily habit of meditation), the subconscious mind, if it does not have any knowns to match this decision, will not cooperate. Thus begins the conscious versus unconscious tug of war. This unfairly stacked tug of war explains much of the resistance to lasting behavioral change. It also explains how easy change can be when the subconscious can be reprogrammed and the 90 percent and the 10 percent are on the same team.

If we were just trying to reprogram patterns from birth to age eight, that would be enough, but to add to the mix, there is also daily subconscious overload that comes with living in the current information age. This overload has created sicknesses unique to our time, most notably stress and stress-related illnesses. Though the mind is a giant receptacle, it has limits to what it can handle. Yogi Bhajan taught that the mind receives 1,000 thoughts per wink of the eye. Yet the mind can only process one of these message units at a time. The other 999 (per wink) go to the subconscious. If we do not have a regular practice of consolidating and cleaning the mind, the subconscious starts to unload into the conscious mind and the body. The consequences are stress, anxiety, depression, the inability to think or to work, and a condition that is much like sleepwalking through life.

When the conscious mind becomes overloaded, the mind may put pain in the body as a cry for help. This communication via the mind-body is often very literal. For example, when Sam's mother-in-law came to visit for three months, he experienced unexplained, severe rectal pain. When questioned in a hypnotherapy session about what was going on at home, he admitted that he thought his mother-in-law was "kind of a pain in the butt." When he made the connection that the pain was related to his emotions about his mother-in-law, the pain instantly went away as he dealt with the emotions.

As another example, Summer has suffered from chronic stomachaches since childhood; the pain was exacerbated by a childhood trauma. She also had experienced anxiety from a young age. She never connected the stomach aches with the anxiety or with an inability to digest what happened to her. As she has used meditation tools, her stomach aches have lessened.

At other times, pain seems to come from outside, such as an attack, bad food, or an accident, but when examined, these "accidents" are often subconsciously created as a way of mind-body communication. As one of my teachers often suggests, nothing happens *to*

---

4 George Kappas, *Professional Hypnotism Manual: Introducing Physical and Emotional Suggestibility and Sexuality* (Kyalami, South Africa: Panarama, 1999).

you; everything happens *through* you. I used to hate that saying because I thought it meant that I was to blame for all my problems, even others' abuses. And in fact, I was more responsible than I wanted to believe, but when I let go of the guilt/blame mentality and started paying attention to the *communication* that was embedded in these patterns, I became more empowered to change them.

For example, for about ten years, every time I broke off a serious relationship, I had a strange accident: I would break or maim one or more of my toes. Each time seemed so accidental (why would I do that on purpose?), but after about six or more toes being injured, I awoke and saw the pattern. I realized that it was a subconscious way of putting pain into my body so I could have a physical indicator of the speed of the healing process. As my toe healed, I would take comfort knowing that emotional healing was also happening and would be complete within six weeks. I eventually faced and dropped the toe-breaking pattern when I found better tools. Others have done the same with the tools in this book.

Nancy came to Kundalini Yoga after she broke her right foot for the second time in one year (her story is on page 13). When I asked her if she had a desire to run from a career or financial situation,[5] she thought I was psychic, but it was only the body communicating loudly.

Donnette shared another interesting insight about the role of the mind as a helper or hindrance in healing: "Last night He opened my mind enough to understand what you were saying; it's all about what you believe. So what came to me was that since I asked to be healed, I was. But I need to clear my mind so that I can believe that I'm healed. So now I believe my healing process and that of my family will be *much faster*! This opens a whole new world! A world of faith, belief, and miracles!"[6]

Though we may not be consciously aware of all that exists within our subconscious mind, we must understand that we can only get out what is inside. It is like the proverb of the orange: If you squeeze an orange, you will not get apple juice. It is often when we are squeezed that we discover what is inside.

So the idea, as the Apostle Paul wrote to the Romans centuries ago, is that transformation comes through the renewing of the mind: "Be ye transformed by the renewing of your mind (Romans 12:2). Yogi Bhajan expressed the same idea:

> The idea is, sit up and meditate. Thoughts come, they hit the floor, and you say, "*Waahay Guroo, Waahay Guroo. . . .*" They hit you. You hit them. You clean it out. You do this so there may be some space left where more garbage can be dumped.[7]

---

5 Problems with the feet or legs sometimes represent a desire to run. The right side of the body is connected to the left brain, which is often associated with career/financial issues.
6 Private communication via text message, March 21, 2014.
7 Harbhajan Singh Khalsa and Yogi Bhajan, *The Master's Touch: On Being a Sacred Teacher for The New Age* (Santa Cruz, NM: Kundalini Research Institute, 1997), 146.

How is this renewal achieved? How is the garbage dumped? Paul gives us the answer: I beseech you therefore, brethren, by the mercies of God, that ye present your bodies a living sacrifice, holy, acceptable unto God, which is your reasonable service (Romans 12:1).

Though the body is a servant to the mind, the deeds done in the body will affect the mind. Using the temple-body to perform sacred acts, both exoteric (baptism, temple ordinances, etc.) and esoteric (meditations, kriyas, fasting, etc.), is the way that we present our bodies as a living sacrifice. Sacrifice means "to make sacred," and only in the physical body is sacrifice possible.

THE SUBCONSCIOUS MIND AND AGENCY

Sometimes people complain to me that subconscious programming robs us of agency. I agree it doesn't seem fair at first glance, but when the records are considered, God has warned us. Though He calls this programming by other names, God warns His people of subconscious programming all throughout the scriptures. Words and phrases such as "the foolish traditions of your fathers," "hard heartedness," "stiff necked," "asleep," and "the natural man" may take on new meaning as you read with an understanding of how the subconscious mind works. You may also take note of the many injunctions, such as "awake," "renew," and "remember."

Knowing the pitfalls of mortal existence, God recognized we wouldn't get through unscathed. So He prepared a way to clean out the subconscious. That way is through the Savior Jesus Christ. Because Jesus Christ lived a mortal life and suffered all the temptations and afflictions of the flesh, He knows how to succor us.[8] One of the lesser-known definitions of *succor* is "to go beneath." By "descending below all things,"[9] Christ was showing us the way to true healing, which happens at a deeper level.

Though the Atonement is the source of all healing and is available to all, I have learned that it is not applied equally, even among the equally good or deserving. I see many who genuinely seek change and healing but receive only small relief, while others receive amazing outpourings of healing and enabling power. I have wondered about this paradox many times, and I realize the reason may be that while we may ask for healing, we may at the same time subconsciously block it. Transformation takes more energy than we have on our own. Those who know how to use certain energetic tools, such as meditation, are able to peel back the layers for Christ—they are able to open their minds and hearts and give Him access:

---

8 See Hebrews 2:18; Alma 7:12; Doctrine and Covenants 62:1.
9 Doctrine and Covenants 88:6.

Behold, he offereth himself a sacrifice for sin, to answer the ends of the law, unto all those who have a broken heart and a contrite spirit; and unto none else can the ends of the law be answered (2 Nephi 2:7).

A broken heart is an open heart. The Latin root of the word *contrite* means "worn down, broken, crumbled."[10] We must wear down, break, and crumble the ego. Do we know how to subdue the ego? It requires energetic power. This power comes through a combination of sacred technology, such as ordinances, fasting, the Sound Current, and Kundalini Yoga kriyas and meditations.

---

10 *Dictionary.com*, s.v., "contrite," accessed March 14, 2014, http://dictionary.reference.com/browse/contrite?s=t.

End Fear Detour | Jennifer Rogers

My journey to meditation and yoga started in 2012, when my family switched to eating a plant-based diet. The less junk we ate, the more I felt the promise found in Doctrine and Covenants 89:19 coming true for me: "And ye shall find wisdom and great treasures of knowledge, even hidden treasures." I stumbled on Felice's blog during my scripture study one day, and the more I read the more I was drawn to meditation. I did several scripture studies on it and found that the scriptures and prophets tell us to take time to meditate. I had always used the words *meditate* and *ponder* interchangeably. I pondered the scriptures and the things of God and therefore thought I was meditating on them but I didn't fully understand what meditation was until I signed up to do the Forty-Day Meditation Challenge.

I started doing Kirtan Kriya and Kundalini Yoga, and within a week my prayers deepened and became more focused. My scripture study was more alive with things I wanted to learn. I was also more open to learn things I hadn't seen before in my scriptures, my church meetings, and the world around me. It was great!

The inspiration I was gaining was wonderful for me. My husband was deployed to the Middle East, and I was home alone with three little girls (ages 5, 3, and 1), and I was pregnant with a fourth child. I had relied very heavily on priesthood blessings from my husband for answers to my questions and prayers, but now he wasn't here to do that for me. Feeling the inspiration from meditating was such a blessing and filled the void that came from the lack of priesthood blessings.

A few weeks into the forty-day challenge, I was assigned to do the meditation for healing addictions and the meditation for releasing anger and negativity, in addition to Kirtan Kriya. With the meditation for releasing anger and negativity, I would often bring up several minutes' worth of anger and frustration about my debilitating fear of driving. I had been in a car accident with my mother and my siblings when I was about twelve years old. Ever since that day, I had had a fear of driving. I didn't want to be responsible for the lives of others on the road or in my car. I never ever wanted to drive. The thought of it made me ill.

I remember being sixteen years old and overhearing my father tell my sister he was going to take me out to learn to drive. I hid under the desk in his office for twenty minutes as he looked for me. This is the only time in my life I remember not coming when called for. I felt guilty for not being obedient, but I didn't want to go.

Later, my parents convinced me that if I wanted to grow up and be a good mother to my children, I needed to be able to take them places. I took driver's ed and passed. I took my driver's license test and passed, but every time I had to get in a car, I felt like I was going to be sick, and I hated it. This fear of driving and being lost and killing or hurting others when I was in a car became part of my personality. I identified myself and others identified me with this antidriving characteristic, but it was not who Heavenly Father wanted me to be.

Everyday as part of the releasing anger and negativity meditation, I would bring up these feelings of being angry that I couldn't go places without panic attacks and all the negative impacts this fear of driving had on my life. Also at this time I had planned to see my parents for Thanksgiving, requiring me to be brave and take my very first road trip ever. I didn't want to spend the holidays alone without my husband, and I felt in my heart that now was the time to try and conquer this fear or at least attempt a trip. I was nervous one minute and confident the next. The more I meditated and planned for this trip, the more flashbacks I would get of our accident when I was young.

I asked Felice about a different meditation or if it was the meditation at all that was bringing on these constant flashbacks. She was surprised to hear that even though I was phobic about driving on freeways I was planning a seventeen-hour drive for my first freeway experience. She blamed/credited meditation for my bravery and said that it would all work out, but since I had a fast-approaching deadline for the drive and was still having traumatic flashbacks, she recommended doing a hypnotherapy session with her. She said that she only had one day open and to pray about it and tell her if I wanted to take it or not. I prayed and prayed and prayed. My husband had already talked to me that morning, so I was not able to counsel with him or ask him what he thought I should do, or even if it was okay to spend a large amount of money on the session. I knew in my heart that I wanted to do it. But I also knew that my husband would feel bad if I made a big decision without talking to him.

I finally asked a neighbor for a priesthood blessing. In it I was counseled to take the session and that my husband would understand. The blessing also said that "Satan will no longer have power over you to keep you from going and doing things; you will be free from the debilitating effects of the accident and be troubled by them no more."

After the session, I felt so much better. I felt more complete and more like who I am meant to be. I made it to my parents' house and back with no problems. I have also driven other places without the feeling of fear or panic. I thought of all the times I had opted not to do something because the drive scared me. I thought of the many opportunities I had lost because I felt like it was something I couldn't do. It was so uplifting to be free from those worries.

I didn't realize how much control Satan had over me by playing on this one fear, this one traumatic event. Now I can go and do. This has also caused me to take a look at other areas of my life that I need to change in order to keep Satan from using them as tools to control me and keep me from my divine potential and eternal destiny. As I read the scriptures, pray, attend the temple, and continue to meditate, I feel stronger and more in control of my own life. I also feel my life being guided by God.

Generational Healing

One of the presuppositions of my work is that everyone is doing the best they can with the resources they have consciously available. This perspective implies our parents and our ancestors did their best, so we shouldn't blame our parents or their choices. Yet, it is useful to know about these choices, because our parents' lives influence ours, through DNA and epigenetic imprinting. *Epigenetic* means "on top of the genes." Traits and tendencies such as an unhealthy love of chocolate and a disposition to anxiety are not technically on the genome map but are handed down by a kind of imprint on top of the genes.[11] The poet Rilke wrote beautifully about these legacies that exist in us:

> Our ancestors could not live to see us. And yet they, who passed away long ago, still continue on in us, as predisposition, as burden upon our fate, as murmuring blood, and as gesture that rises up from the depths of time.[12]

Though our ancestors passed on strengths and gifts, they also passed on accumulated garbage. Here is what gospel scholar Truman G. Madsen says about it:

> And, therefore, as you look back at your seventy or so forebears . . . you might recognize that you have inherited the blood of many generations. And blood may not be a correct word scientifically, but in the scriptures it stands for seed, which means heredity, the inheritance of tendencies, and all of us have them. You have the blood of this generation, from which we must become clean—"clean from the blood of this

---

11 Tim Spector, *Identically Different: Why You Can Change Your Genes* (London: Weidenfeld & Nicolson, 2012), 8. "Just over ten years ago researchers found that the diets of pregnant mothers could alter the behaviour of genes in their children and that these changes could last a lifetime and then be passed on in turn to their children. The genes were literally being switched on or off by a new mechanism we call epigenetics—meaning in Greek 'around the gene'. Contrary to traditional genetic dogma, these changes could be transferred to the next generation. In this case the mothers just happened to be rats, but recent similar findings in humans have created a revolution in our thinking."

12 Rainer Maria Rilke, *Letters to a Young Poet,* trans. Stephen Mitchell (New York: Vintage, 1986), 62.

generation" (Doctrine and Covenants 88:85). If you do, you will be clean from the blood of every generation, because it is compounded and accumulated into now—and that includes the blood of some degeneration.

So perhaps you do have problems that you can blame on your ancestors, and if you forgive that and choose to stand close to the Lord in the process of purifying your life, that will affect your whole family in both directions. You are not alone. There is no way you can gain solitary and neutral ground. You are in it—you are involved. And this, I believe, is one of the profound meanings of the tame and wild olive trees. If you take a wild branch and graft it into a tame one, if the branch is strong enough it will eventually corrupt and spoil the tree all the way to the roots. But if you take a tame branch and graft it into a wild tree, in due time, if that branch is strong enough, it will heal and regenerate to the very roots. You will have then been an instrument in the sanctification even of your forebears.

To be that kind of branch and achieve that kind of transformation backward and forward is perhaps the greatest achievement of this world. But to do it one must be great, one must be linked, bound to the Lord Jesus Christ. One must be mighty. One must be something of a savior. And that is exactly what the Prophet Joseph Smith said we are: "saviors on Mount Zion."[13]

As Madsen states, in order to do this great work—savior work—we need great power. Every aspect of Kundalini Yoga and Meditation works generationally, forward and backward. For example, Kirtan Kriya (page 262) and Ganputi Kriya (page 257) are known for powerful generational healing, as is every complete shabd (mantra). Dr. Gurucharan Singh says, "Each complete shabd adds an inheritance, a spiritual DNA, that establishes your identity and lineage with Infinity—the unknowable unknown, itself."[14] Scientific evidence has also documented that mantras containing primordial sounds can help the DNA replicate more perfectly.[15]

I believe one of the reasons that Kundalini Yoga was restored in our day is to aid the many souls who have come (and will come) to help complete God's saving work. They are willing and able advanced-placement spirits, finishing their premortal lessons on becoming like the Savior. To become like Him, they need to complete saving work within their bodies and minds, as well as in the temples of the Lord. If they succeed, thousands of their progenitors and posterity will rejoice and praise them. As Isaiah 58:12 says, "Thou shalt raise up the foundations of many generations; and thou shalt be called, The *repairer of the breach*, The *restorer of paths to dwell in*" (italics added).

---

13 Truman G. Madsen, *The Temple: Where Heaven Meets Earth* (Salt Lake City, UT: Deseret Book, 2009), 84.
14 Qtd. in Khalsa and Stauth, *Meditation as Medicine*, 120.
15 Ibid., 119.

Healing Circle of Ancestors | Name Withheld

I knew I was supposed to do genealogy work for my family. When I learned about generational healing, I had a strong feeling it was the genealogy work I was to focus on. After praying and getting the answer that this was what I was supposed to do, I went to my family tree. I would look at the names and pray. Then the Spirit would direct me to a name.

I had a very strong feeling that I should do work for my great-grandfather's mother. This surprised me. I also did not know how to go about doing this because my grandfather broke all ties with his father's family. He changed his name and got away from anything to do with them. He was upset that not only his father but is grandparents had abandoned his family. I didn't know how to do this work. Even though I didn't have my great-grandmother's name I felt I was suppose to do work for her.

Then I had an overwhelming feeling to sit in a circle with my great-grandmother and her ex-mother-in-law. I could tell they had had very negative feelings toward each other in this life and wanted to let them go. I sat down in a circle with the two of them and did the meditation Ra Ma Da Sa. The love and power that was present was incredible; the love and forgiveness overwhelming. Not only was this one of the most spiritual experiences I have had, it was eye-opening.

I realized that we never know what the other person is going through. We never know their story. It helped me understand the scripture where Christ tells us "Love your enemies, do good to them which hate you, bless them that curse you, and pray for them which despitefully use you. And unto him that smiteth thee on the one cheek offer also the other" (Luke 6:27–29). That night during that meditation, there was pure love between two women who had every reason to hold a grudge and be offended.

I will forever be grateful for that experience and the lessons I learned while meditating with the spirits of two amazing women. God is love, and if we allow Him, He will change our hearts and open our understanding. With the help of our Savior, we can develop the pure love of Christ. We can let go of pain, anger, hatred, and any feelings or emotions that are not of God. That night I felt the power of God and His healing power through meditation.

Breaking The Chains | Sarah Cooksley

Abuse and neglect are patterns of behaviour that have long threads travelling through my family lines. My mother did her best to help me and my siblings overcome difficult circumstances and emotional abuse from our father, but she was never given the right tools to handle things in the most efficient way. She has done the best she could, and for that I am grateful.

I feel that meditation has helped me to change habits and deeply ingrained thought patterns in my life. Meditation has also given me greater insight into my mother. I know that she volunteered to bear the brunt of the pain and heartache of abuse and neglect so that she could be the catalyst for change in our family. She was able to save her children from being brought up in a dysfunctional home through her divorce and, eventually, in moving her small family to a different country.

My path toward Kundalini Yoga was put into motion many years before I found this technology. Preparations began when I was a young teenager, during family counselling sessions and tentative attempts to meditate on my own without any instruction or guidance.

Now, many years later, my children are being raised by a mother who knows herself better than ever before. They meditate with me and have seen the difference in our family life. I think I can safely say that the chain of abuse has been broken; the chain that stretched back through several generations of my ancestors no longer binds me.

The Width and Depth of the Heart

Blessed are the pure in heart for they shall see God.—Matthew 5:8

No discussion of the body, mind, and spirit is complete without discussing the heart. The word *heart* is used more than fifteen hundred times in the scriptures. From the many diverse uses of the word, it is evident the heart is more than a mere physical organ. According to my scriptural research, the heart has the following functions (and more):

- The heart can have thoughts, intentions, wisdom, and understanding (see Proverbs 2:2; 23:15; Mosiah 5).

- The heart is a center for transformation and healing (see Alma 5:7, 14).

- The heart is also a center of communication and a dwelling place of the Spirit (see Doctrine and Covenants 8:2).

- The heart can feel (see 2 Nephi 9:52; Doctrine and Covenants 98:1; 100:12; 110:6; 128:22).

- The heart can be written on (see Mosiah 5:12).

- The heart can be open or closed, hard or soft (see 1 Nephi 15:3; Mosiah 2:9; Alma 24:8).

- It is evident from the repetitive admonition to "love the Lord thy God with all thine heart" (Deuteronomy 6:5) that the heart is vast and that it may be partitioned off by some (see Mark 12:30; Matthew 22:37; Luke 10:27; and many others).

- God has told us to purify our hearts that we may stand in His presence and be like Him (Matthew 5:8; Doctrine and Covenants 88:74).

To purify our hearts, we need to give our hearts to God, and in order to do so, we need spiritual technology. For example, fasting and prayer (regularly) are the spiritual technology identified in the following scripture:

> Nevertheless they did fast and pray oft, and did wax stronger and stronger in their humility, and firmer and firmer in the faith of Christ, unto the filling their souls with joy and consolation, yea, even to the purifying and the sanctification of their hearts, which sanctification cometh because of their yielding their hearts unto God. (Helaman 3:35)

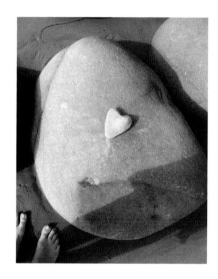

When Christ came and fulfilled the law of Moses, blood sacrifice was no longer necessary; in its place, He required a sacrifice of a broken heart and a contrite spirit: "And whoso cometh unto me with a broken heart and a contrite spirit, him will I baptize with fire and with the Holy Ghost" (3 Nephi 9:20).

Elder Jeffrey R. Holland says, "Think of the heart as the figurative center of our faith, the poetic location of our loyalties and our values."[16] As you come to understand yogic anatomy and the chakras, you will know these words are not merely poetic. The heart is the literal center of the seven cerebrospinal chakras, the place where the lower triangle (earth bound chakras) and the upper triangle (spiritual/heavenly centered chakras) meet and overlap. The heart is the center for transformation and communication between the physical and etheric bodies.

The heart may also be the center of the mind. In the prior age, the mind and the brain were thought to be one and the same; however, the mind is non-physical. Scientists and mind-body experts now realize that the mind does not exist in the brain but throughout the whole body and even outside of the body. The nucleus of the mind may reside in the heart, which is supported by the scriptures.

During the Piscean age the brain was considered king. Its latitude was higher than that of the heart and was therefore considered higher in hierarchy and importance. However, in the 1970s, scientists discovered that the heart has an intricate nervous system of its own. This discovery gave birth to a new branch of science called neurocardiology. It turns out that the body has two brains, with the brain in the head obeying the brain in the heart.[17]

---

16 Jeffrey R. Holland, "Safety for the Soul," *Ensign*, November 2009, http://www.lds.org/general-conference/2009/10/safety-for-the-soul.

17 "Heart-Brain Interactions," Institute of HeartMath, accessed March 24, 2014, http://www.heartmath.org/free-services/articles-of-the-heart/heart-brain-interactions.html.

Compared to the electromagnetic field produced by the brain, the electrical component of the heart's field is about 60 times greater in amplitude, and permeates every cell in the body. The magnetic component is approximately 5,000 times stronger than the brain's magnetic field and can be detected several feet away from the body with sensitive magnetometers.[18]

The heart—or as the yogis call it, the Heart Center—is in fact the essence of You. In your mother's womb, your heart formed first, before the brain and before any other organ. The heart has its own intelligence. It can think and feel and remember.

The scriptures (and the yogic prophecies too) say that in the last days, "all things shall be in commotion; and surely, men's hearts shall fail them; for fear shall come upon all people" (Luke 21:26; see also Doctrine and Covenants 88:91). We are living in these times.

When God asks us to purify our hearts, He is asking us to purify our minds and bodies. The many clichés that exist about the heart can teach us something of its nature. For example, if we are to "get to the heart of the matter" and make a mighty change, we need to look to the heart and use a technology that purifies the mind, body, and spirit.

O all ye that are pure in heart, . . . receive the pleasing word of God, and feast upon his love; for ye may, if your minds are firm, forever.—Jacob 3:2.

---

18 Rollin McCraty, Raymond Trevor Bradley, and Dana Tomasino, "The Resonant Heart," *Frontiers of Consciousness*, February 2005, 15–19.

My Heart Was Failing Me | Chablis Adams

On July 17, 2012 at 4:00 a.m., while sleeping, I was hit with a major, sudden, and unexpected panic attack. I had never experienced anything like it before and thought I was having a heart attack. Embarrassingly, I was transported to the ER via an ambulance and spent an entire day being tested and probed for heart problems, only to be told over the phone by a cardiologist that my heart was healthy, I must've had some anxiety, and I should just go home and rest. I felt like an idiot.

That day began my journey of painful, never-ending anxiety. I suffered every day. Sometimes all day and all night. My heart would race, and I couldn't catch my breath. My chest was sore, and it hurt to breathe. Sometimes the pressure in my chest would be so overwhelming, I couldn't do anything but lay down. I had pulling/straining pains in my upper back, digestion issues, headaches, and exhaustion. I became very depressed.

Kind people who wanted to help would tell me to find things I enjoy and do them often. It was then that I realized that I didn't enjoy anything anymore. I didn't enjoy my kids, even when they were being sweet. I didn't enjoy baths or baking or makeup or making friends. I didn't have any close friends in Atlanta yet. Though the church group is wonderful and I knew I could call several people from church at anytime and receive help, I didn't want to call them. I didn't want to put forth any kind of effort toward socialization.

During these weeks, I would beg my husband, almost on a daily basis it seemed, to give me a priesthood blessing before bed. I would read my scriptures and pour my soul out in prayer. "Help thou my unbelief," I would cry, as I was sure that my Heavenly Father could heal me and stop this madness and that it was just my wavering faith that was in the way. My prayers helped . . . a little. I would sob nightly in conversation with God. Eventually, in exhaustion and with the peace of knowing that my Heavenly Father would take care of me, I would slip into a slumber (often just to be woken up a few hours later with the pounding of my heart).

I knew I needed to see a doctor. It took roughly four weeks before I was seen. When I finally got in to see a doctor, she was very understanding and really wanted to be very helpful. She suggested that I start taking two prescription medications and one over-the-counter medication. I have always been wary of taking medications, so I told the doctor I would have to do some research and think and pray about the medications and get back to her.

That very day I heard from a friend whose brother-in-law had just committed suicide weeks after taking a new antidepressant medication. This was a huge red flag for me, and I saw it as a sign from God that these pills would not help me. I *wanted* to take these pills, and I *wanted* them to help me. But the more I thought about the possibility of them making my situation worse and not better (which is rare, but does happen), the worse my anxiety would get. This was my answer from God about the antidepressants. I knew there was another way I could overcome my anxiety. I just didn't know what it was yet.

I began seeing a therapist weekly. She helped me immensely. On our very first visit, she taught me the importance of breathing, breathing correctly, and paying attention to my breathing. I began breathing down through my belly and diaphragm and focusing on slowing the breath down and pushing the breath deeper. This helped me a ton, but I was still battling anxiety almost daily.

Then one day I stumbled upon Felice's 40 day meditation challenge. It was as if a light turned on inside my soul and I could feel the Holy Ghost telling me inside that this was my answer.

I knew right away that I wanted to be a part of this meditation challenge. The word *meditation* was hitting me so strongly. I had always known that meditation was a good thing

for people to do. I just didn't know how to do it. I had tried before, but just sitting in my room, trying to be quiet was always so confusing. I couldn't do it. I needed someone to teach me how to meditate. This is where Felice came in. I signed up for her weekly webinar class. This was one of the best things I've ever done for myself.

In our first class, Felice quoted Doctrine and Covenants 88:91: "And all things shall be in commotion, and surely men's hearts shall fail them for fear shall come upon all people." This scripture just blew me away because my heart was failing me. I could not function in my daily life because my heart was failing to keep up with the stress going on in my mind. I would venture to say that people's hearts are failing them every day in every way, and some may not even know it. The more I open up about my issues with anxiety, the more I find that everyone is dealing with anxiety on some level.

Felice taught me several different meditations. The one I have done for the last forty days is called Kirtan Kriya. You can google it. Meditation may seem way too weird" or out in left field for some of you. All I can say is that it has changed my life. When I had a few days of resistance or hesitation with the meditation, I would ask Heavenly Father if this was something that was good for me and would help me. I always got the answer, "Yes, this is good for you." I would feel happy and excited to meditate again.

Within three days of starting Kirtan Kriya, I was finding myself falling asleep without having to count my breathing to keep my heart rate down. I can now look back and see how seriously depressed I really was, even though I didn't really think that was part of my problem. I feel happy and so blessed to be a mother to my children. They are no longer a burden to me. In fact, my ability to stay calm and patient when they are acting up has increased tenfold! My follow through with discipline and my ability to communicate with my kids has improved greatly. I feel so much love for them. I feel so much love for other people. Now that my heart is open to God's, I can feel His love flowing out of me to other people. My prayers have changed, and I somehow feel inspired to ask for certain things from God that I never would have asked for before. I have been much more grateful and sincere in my prayers. This all may seem very drastic, and it is! It's only been six weeks.

Do I still struggle with anxiety? A little bit. Basically, I've noticed that when I am tired, I lose the ability to control my thoughts and emotions. So, when I am overly tired, I struggle more. But let me just tell you that even those moments are mild in comparison to my everyday struggles six weeks ago. Meditation works!

This essay was taken from a blog post Chublis wrote 6 weeks after beginning meditation. Two years later, she reported that she is still meditating.

The Power of the Mind and Intention

It is widely known a person's thoughts can speed up or slow down the healing process. This phenomenon has been demonstrated through millions of cases of the placebo effect and the nocebo effect. Though research has given us some understanding, the mind has powers beyond comprehensible thought and beyond current scientific discoveries. The mind can heal, transform matter, change the outcome of events, and even change the order of events in time and space. Below are just a few of the astonishing findings from studies on the power of intention, thought, prayer, and mental focus.

- Study participants were able to slow the growth of yeast growing in 151 of 194 dishes just by directing mental focus toward the yeast. This experiment was repeated sixteen times, and each time the results were similar.[19]

- Neurologists found that when people are open-minded and suspend judgment until both sides of an argument are considered, neurological functioning increases. But cynicism, which implies hostility and distrust toward the other point of view, is so neurologically damaging that it can shorten your life.[20]

- In a study conducted by cardiologist Randolph Byrd, patients who were prayed for by other people (without the patients' knowledge) were five times less likely to need antibiotics or to develop pulmonary edema. Additionally, none of the prayed-for patients needed an artificial breathing apparatus; in contrast twelve patients who were not prayed for did need an an apparatus.[21]

---

19 Dharma Singh Khalsa and Cameron Stauth, *Meditation as Medicine: Activate the Power of Your Natural Healing Force* (New York: Fireside, 2001), 127.
20 Andrew Newberg, *How God Changes Your Brain* (New York: Random House, 2009), 142.
21 *Meditation as Medicine*, 128–129.

- Other studies on prayer show that nondirect prayers work best, meaning that individuals who do not pray for a specific outcome but rather for the highest and best good often receive the best results.[22]

- In a Princeton University study, participants projected their intentions at a machine that generates random numbers, with the goal of influencing the machine to generate a predictable pattern of numbers. The results were astounding: In the majority of the 256,000 trials of the experiment, the participants were able to influence the machine. The Princeton study also included some other fascinating details:

    - The results were better when the subjects bonded with the machines—similar to how people bond with their cars—before trying to exert influence.

    - The study involved not only individuals but also pairs. Among all the subjects, couples in love were the most able to influence the machines.

    - The most astonishing of the results is that subjects were able to influence the machines after the machines had already run, suggesting that the power of the mind is not limited by ordinary constraints of time and space.[23]

This mental power is yet more evidence that man is not merely flesh, but rather a spark of the divine. As divine beings, whatever we create—even mentally—can become reality. The power of the mind is only limited by our own imaginations. This power also applies to negative thoughts and imaginings, which produce negative results and even neurological damage.

For good or for bad, our minds are powerful. And we can make them even more so. According to scientific research,[24] and my own anecdotal studies, advanced meditators have the most developed of mental powers and the most powerful abilities to project through prayer.

---

22 IBID., 131–31.
23 Khalsa and Stauth, *Meditation as Medicine*, 127–128.
24 Newberg, *How God Changes Your Brain*.

The Sun Was Always Shining | Andy Rasmussen

Kundalini Yoga and Meditation are powerful tools for spiritual mastery in this life. For much of my life, I struggled with depression, anxiety, and bipolar disorder. Many of my coping techniques were born of a desperate desire to escape the crushing despair, guilt, and fear that dominated my life. In fact, it wasn't until I began to heal that I became aware of how much my every decision was affected by a hopeless cycle of shame. It shaped my relationships with family, friends, and God. I felt trapped in a consciousness of doubt, grief, and apathy. I often experienced life as hopeless, frightening, or even tragic.

I was born and raised in the Church of Jesus Christ of Latter-day Saints and have always been blessed with a deep testimony of the mission of Jesus Christ. Yet my view of God often settled somewhere between condemning and permitting. But almost never did I experience God as inspiring, merciful, or loving. In fact I often wondered at the expressions of joy and love for the Lord that some members offer. That kind of connection to God was simply outside my experience for thirty-five years. I knew the gospel was true, but I couldn't make it work for me. My spiritual life was decidedly unfulfilling.

Yet eventually I learned to recognize the grace of Christ in my life. God led me to various natural healing modalities that were very helpful. This journey led me to Kundalini Yoga and Meditation As Taught by Yogi Bhajan®. I found Felice's blog that provided a "translation" of this ancient Indian practice into LDS concepts, and I was inspired.

I took her introductory webinar series and later attended an all-day retreat where she taught Christ-centered meditation. It was a sublime experience. I finally had a tool of transformation that not only accessed the Atoning Power of Christ more effectively than traditional psychotherapy or medications, but placed me in command of my life in a way that was totally new to me. No longer did I need to run to a therapist or doctor when I felt anxious or depressed! No longer did I need to obsess about controlling everything and everyone around me in order to maintain my composure! At last I had the power to change, independent of outside forces! For the first time I felt truly free, able to exercise my agency to live life fully. I discovered the sun had always been shining behind the clouds!

The concepts and truths discussed in this book have blessed and opened my life in a way I never imagined. Kundalini Yoga and Meditation have scrubbed the debris from a half-lived life and prepared a space for me to receive the inspiration and abundance of my Redeemer.

Not every day is magnificent, and sometimes this journey of rebirth is surprisingly painful and intense. But every day that I include my Kundalini sadhana in my morning devotional is a better day. Even though I still notice short cycles of mania and depression, they are no longer debilitating. I have been free of psychotropic medications for years, and I live most often (though certainly not always!) in a consciousness of gratitude and willingness. My mind is clearer, and every faculty of reason and understanding is enhanced. Put simply, I am awakening to clearer and cleaner views of life.

Every week is drenched in meaning and purpose; relationships trend toward harmony more often than discord; and the God I worship is loving, wise, and everywhere. I know that I am His son, beloved and blessed and in the similitude of His Only Begotten. And so is everyone I meet.

Everyone's journey is different, and every individual must find his or her own relationship with God, but for me, the science of Kundalini Yoga has given me the freedom and space to experience Christ's joy. And I fully expect to continue to receive and prepare to serve Him as I pursue this path of spiritual discipline.

What?
Know ye not that
your body
is the temple of the
Holy Ghost
which is in you.

— 1 Corinthians 6:19

The Body and the Temple

The Body and the Temple

NECESSITIES FOR EXALTATION

Latter-day Saints who understand even the basic doctrines of the gospel are privileged in that they do not have to wonder about the purpose of life. Prophet Joseph Smith said, "What is the design of the Almighty in making man? It was to exalt him to be as God."[1] From Joseph Smith and from the scriptures it is clear that two things are essential for exaltation: temple ordinances and bodies.

The Prophet Joseph said there were certain ordinances "which God ordained for the salvation of man, to prepare him for, and give him a title to, a celestial glory."[2] In latter-day revelations compiled in the Doctrine and Covenants, God says, "For man is spirit. The elements are eternal, and spirit and element, inseparably connected, receive a fulness of joy; And when separated, man cannot receive a fulness of joy" (Doctrine and Covenants 93:33–34).

Joseph Smith also taught the following:

That which is without body, parts and passions is nothing. There is no other God in heaven but that God who has flesh and bones. John 5:26 reads: "For as the Father hath life in himself; so hath he given to the Son to have life in himself." God the Father took life unto himself exactly as Jesus did.[3]

Because we believe that God himself has a body and because we are in His image and wish to become exalted like Him, then bodies must be an important key. Paul taught that the body is a temple of God. Yet what is not as often quoted is the second part of Paul's declaration: God "does not dwell in unholy temples." The Prophet Alma in the Book of

---

1 *Times and Seasons*, October 15, 1841, 578; see also Moses 1:39.
2 Joseph Fielding Smith, ed., *Teachings of the Prophet Joseph Smith* (Salt Lake City, UT: Deseret Book Company, 1976), 48.
3 Ibid., 181.

Mormon also addresses the importance of maintaining temple-bodies, saying that we will be judged for the deeds done in the body (see Alma 5:15).

SIMILARITIES BETWEEN TEMPLE BODIES AND TEMPLES OF GOD

The word *temple* comes from the Latin word *templum,* which has a meaning similar to *observatory,* a space from where one can contemplate and consider the cosmos.[4] The ancient temples of God were in fact a microcosm of the cosmos and were built to represent human's ascension through the cosmos to the presence of God.[5] The architecture of the body is also designed with ascension in mind, with the Kundalini rising through the lower chakras and eventually to God (see the chapters on Kundalini and the yogic anatomy).

By this point in the book, hopefully you understand that the technology of Kundalini Yoga is all about unlocking the divine within, merging finite and Infinite, and purifying the

> The elements are the tabernacle of God; yea, man is the tabernacle of God, even temples. — Doctrine and Covenants 93:35

mind, heart, and body in order to stand in the presence of God. And I hope you joyfully note this technology complements the ordinances of the temple.

These technologies are not only complementary; they also have similarities and motifs that are impossible to ignore. It is clear from orthodox sources that the Lord has taught a body of esoteric principles called "mysteries" to His patriarchs in every age. Many scholars agree that these mysteries included temple rites and ordinances, as well as *many other things.*[6]

In the temples of the Lord, sacred ordinances are performed. In the Guide to the Scriptures, *ordinances* is defined as "sacred rites and ceremonies. Ordinances consist of acts that have spiritual meanings." I am not the first to suggest that there are also ordinances of a kind that occur in the temple of our bodies. As I explained earlier, the term *ordinance* has a meaning roughly similar to the word *sacrament* in other Christian denominations. Elder Jeffrey R. Holland suggests that human intimacy is such a sacrament. As he explains, "For our purpose here today, a sacrament could be any one of a number of gestures or acts or ordinances that unite us with God and his limitless

---

4 Matthew B. Brown, *The Gate of Heaven: Insight on the Doctrines and Symbols of the Temple* (American Fork, UT: Covenant, 1999), 1.

5 Including the outer courts and inner courts, to the center, or holy of holies (the presence of God). For more about the architectural symbolism of ancient and modern temples, see Brown, *The Gate of Heaven.*

6 Brown, *The Gate of Heaven.*

141

powers."[7] Elder Holland adds that all special moments of union with God are sacramental moments and that we should seek them out as often as possible and appropriate. In doing so, we "gain access to [God's] power."[8]

The implications here are many. The premise of my entire book *The Gift of Giving Life: Rediscovering the Divine Nature of Pregnancy and Birth* was that giving life is a sacrament, as is death. And the premise of this whole book is that creating a daily practice of Kundalini Yoga and Meditation is an act that can unite us with God and His power; therefore, this technology is a sacrament, or inward ordinance.

A HOUSE OF SACRIFICE, A HOUSE OF COVENANTS, A HOUSE OF PRAYER

In biblical times, the temple of Jehovah was a house of sacrifice (see Ezra 6:3, 10). When I was young, I was taught that the definition of *sacrifice* was giving up something good for something better. I suppose these teachers were trying to keep me hooked with the idea of "something better." I later learned that sacrifice actually means "to make sacred."[9]

In Psalm 50:5 we learn that the Lord's people make covenants with Him by sacrifice: "Gather my saints together unto me; those that have made a covenant with me by sacrifice." The sacrifices spoken of involved sacrificial animals (first male without blemish), but since the time of Jesus Christ's Infinite sacrifice, believers have been required to give an inward sacrifice of "a broken heart and contrite spirit" (3 Nephi 9:20).

As illustrated in Psalm 50:5, sacrifice is closely associated with the act of covenant making. The temple of the Lord is a house of covenants. Matthew B. Brown explains the following:

> What type of covenants were entered into in the temple precincts? In 2 Kings 11:17 we read of a covenant entered into by the Israelites "that they should be the Lord's people." The nature of this type of covenant is clarified in Deuteronomy where it is stated that the children of Israel covenanted to walk in the Lord's ways and to obey His commandments, judgements and statutes (see Duet. 29:12–15; 30:1–2, 8–10, 16, 19–20; see also 2 Kings 23:3; 2 Chronicles 15:8–12; 23:16). [10]

Do we not also make covenants privately with God and agree to be obedient to personalized instructions and commandments from Him regarding our stewardships and divine destinies? Can we not renew these covenants each morning through offering prayer

---

7 Jeffrey R. Holland, "Of Souls, Symbols, and Sacraments" (devotional, Brigham Young University, Provo, UT, January 12, 1988), accessed March 21, 2014, http://www.familylifeeducation.org/gilliland/procgroup/Souls.htm.
8 Ibid.
9 Yogi Bhajan, *The Aquarian Teacher: KRI International Kundalini Yoga Teacher Training Level I Yoga Manual* (Santa Cruz, NM: Kundalini Research Institute, 2007), 202.
10 Brown, *The Gate of Heaven*, 124.

and praise as we meditate and chant the name of God in the ambrosial hours (see "The Word" and "Sadhana" chapters, p. 66 and 166).

The Hebrew Bible, the New Testament, and modern prophets refer to the temple as "a house of prayer."[11] It is evident from numerous scriptures that prayer is considered a temple offering, keeping in mind that "prayer," in the scriptural context, means more of what is now considered meditation:

> By him therefore let us offer the sacrifice of praise to God continually, that is, the fruit of our lips giving thanks to his name. But to do good and to communicate forget not: for with such sacrifices God is well pleased. (Hebrews 13:15-16; see also Psalm 119:108)

Latter-day temples are also built with this idea in mind:

> And let the lower part of the inner court be dedicated unto me for your sacrament offering, and for your preaching, and your fasting, and your praying, and the offering up of your most holy desires unto me, saith your Lord. (Doctrine and Covenants 95:16)

Therefore, it stands to reason that the praises to His name offered in the temple of the body are also sacrifices/offerings, in which God is "well pleased." As you learned in the chapter on the Word, when we repeat certain high-vibration mantras (which praise the name of God), we change our bodies by repatterning the brain to allow us to merge with the Infinite. In the temples of God, there are also grand keywords[12] that, through different means, allow us access to the presence of God.

I enjoy reading about the many forms of praise that the ancients, the early Christians, and the early Saints chanted in association with worship in and around temples. It appears that group meditation and chanting praises was a happy and frequent occurrence. Just one example is found in 2 Chronicles. The Levites' job was to stand every morning and evening "to thank and praise the Lord" with one voice:

> Also the Levites which were the singers, all of them . . . being arrayed in white linen, having cymbals and psalteries and harps, stood at the east end of the altar, and with them an hundred and twenty priests sounding with trumpets:

> It came even to pass, as the trumpeters and singers were as one, to make one sound to be heard in praising and thanking the Lord; and when they lifted up their voice with the trumpets and cymbals and instruments of musick, and praised the Lord, saying, For he is good; for his mercy endureth for ever: that then the house was filled with a cloud, even the house of the Lord. (2 Chronicles 5:12–13; see also 1 Chronicles 23:30)

---

11 Isaiah 56:7; Matthew 21:13; Mark 11:17; Luke 19:46; see also Doctrine and Covenants 59:9; 88:119.
12 Abraham, Facsimile 2.

Several other similarities may exist between temples and bodies. First, a temple is a house on which the Lord has placed His holy name. In the chapter on the Word, you learned how His name can be written on a temple body. Second, a temple is a place for the Lord and his Holy Spirit to dwell in. Is your body and your nervous system strong enough to house the Lord Himself? Practicing Kundalini Yoga kriyas and meditations prepares the body to accommodate more energy so that your own divine self can be unlocked, ascend through the body to merge and blend with the Infinite energy, and then descend back into the body.

GESTURES AND ACTS

Anciently, *mudras* (gestures with the hands or arms) were connected with prayer in and out of the temples. In Psalm 134:1–2 we read, "Stand in the house of the Lord. Lift up your hands in the sanctuary and bless [i.e., praise] the Lord." And Psalm 63:4 says, "Thus will I bless thee while I live. I will lift up my hands in thy name." When King Solomon dedicated the Jerusalem temple, "He stood before the altar of the Lord in the presence of all the congregation of Israel, and spread forth his hands toward heaven" (1 Kings 8:22; see also vs. 54). There are many other examples of praying and praising in the temple with uplifted, open, or stretched-out hands.

Though we don't know all the details of the ancient mudras, it is sufficient to note that mudras have interrelated physical and spiritual benefits and that they are used in both technologies. (See Mudras, page 201.) Stretching forth the hands opens the heart (see Ego Eradicator, page 195). This idea is evident in Job 11:13: "Prepare thine heart, and stretch out thine hands towards him."

Due to the number of references to God stretching out His hands or arms to reach out to His children, it would seem that these gestures, when made by humans, are more than symbolic in nature.

PATRIARCHAL PATTERN

The scriptures say that Melchizedek was able to stand in the presence of God because of his faith (Joseph Smith Translation, Genesis 14:25–40). Enoch also walked in the presence of God (Gen 5:22), as did Noah (Gen 6:9) and all the other major patriarchs and dispensation heads. They each reached this level of awakening despite living in times of wickedness and turmoil on the earth.

Standing in the presence of God meant that these men had to have strong nervous systems (see page 33) and pure hearts (see page 120). This indicates that they had a practice that was physical as well as spiritual. They were high priests of both kinds of temples.

There is enough evidence (some of which is presented above) in scriptural accounts, prophetic teachings, scholarly research, and Jewish legendary material to reason that all of the ancient patriarchs[13] were acquainted with the esoteric body of teachings called the Mysteries of God, which included temple rites and perhaps other teachings such as Kundalini Yoga, though the teachings may have been called something different.

Every prophet's role is to bring his people into the presence of God. Enoch was the only one we know of who succeeded, but all the others tried. The scriptures say Moses plainly taught the children of Israel the need for ordinances. He "sought diligently to sanctify his people that they might behold the face of God" (Doctrine and Covenants 84:23). What do you suppose was the nature of the things he taught his people to prepare them for the blessings of the temple?

My answer to this question came the day after I posed it to myself. I came across a Kundalini Yoga kriya about which Yogi Bhajan has said, "Moses instructed the Jews to do this exercise before long journeys to raise their spirits, correct their slave mentality and give them the will to fight and not give in."[14] My belief is that Moses taught them about inward ordinances.

Unfortunately, the Lord's covenant people went far off the path at this point in history. They "hardened their hearts" and "could not endure his presence." So, the Lord took the priesthood ordinances and mysteries out of their midst and gave them a fragmented, carnal version of the law.[15]

JESUS'S MINISTRY

At the time of Jesus's earthly ministry, only fragmented versions of the ordinances were being performed in the temple. The mysteries, both the esoteric teachings and the ordinances of the priesthood, had been taken away or hidden up. As I have discussed earlier, there is evidence and I believe that God inspired Jesus to go to the East, where He could learn the sacred yogic technology that had been preserved there for millennia through a royal, priestly lineage.

When Jesus returned from India, one of His first acts was to find His cousin and set the example for all by receiving the first of the exoteric ordinances: baptism. Afterward, he did many things that are highlighted in the Gospels, as well as many more things that are not written. Though we don't have all the details, there is ample evidence that Jesus taught His closest disciples a body of knowledge called "mysteries."[16]

The word translated as *mystery* is *musterion*, which can mean either a "secret

---

13 Adam, Enoch, Noah, Melchizedek, Abraham, Isaac, Jacob, Moses, and Jesus Christ.

14 The title of the kriya is Emotional and Mental Balance and Prevention of Early Menopause. Originally taught by Yogi Bhajan on July 12, 1977.

15 Joseph Smith Translation, Exodus 34:1–2.

16 1 Corinthians 4:1; see also Matthew 13:11.

teaching" or a "secret rite."[17] Scholar Robin Scroggs says the "wisdom" mentioned in Paul's letter to the Corinthians is esoteric. Scroggs suggests that if you take Paul's words at face value, and there is no evidence not to, "He does have an esoteric wisdom teaching in which he instructs only a few and which the congregation at Corinth seems not even to have heard about."[18] Another scholar shared the following:

> That the more learned of Christians, subsequently to the second century, cultivated, in secret, an obstruse [sic] discipline of a different nature from that which they taught publicly, is well known to everyone. Concerning the argument however, or matter of this secret discipline, its origin, and the causes which gave rise to it, there are infinite disputes.[19]

The orthodox and apocryphal sources relating to these mysteries could go on for hundreds of pages. One historian says there is a cave located on the Mount of Olives and "authentic history informs us that in this very cave the Savior imparted His secret revelations to His disciples."[20] When I read this information, I could not help but think of yogis meditating in caves. Modern revelation gives some insight that these mysteries include the fulness of the temple ordinances, as well as much more.[21]

It is interesting to note that Christ cleansed the temple twice—once at the beginning of His ministry and once at the end. He also took two forty-day sojourns—one at the beginning and one at the end.

After Christ's resurrection, He ministered to His apostles at Jerusalem for forty days. What exactly happened during this forty-day visit? The scriptures say that He spoke to the apostles of "things pertaining to the kingdom of God" (Acts 1:3). This description is interesting when you consider Christ's teaching that "the kingdom of God is within you" (Luke 17:21). Further, Luke 24:45 indicates that He "opened their understanding, that they might understand the scriptures." "Opening their understanding" could refer to their intuition and their Third Eye, as well as to their hearts, which is what He commands us to understand with (see Proverbs 8:5). He also did many other things which are not written (see John 21:25).

It is evident from the quotes above that at least some early Christians practiced the temple ordinances and enjoyed a fulness of the priesthood, but after all of the apostles had died or disappeared, the authority of the priesthood did too. And though Christianity continued to spread, the deeper teachings and "mysteries of Godliness" were lost or badly corrupted. This state of affairs led to a dark age of civilization that would last for almost two centuries.

---

17 Brown, *The Gate of Heaven*, 182.
18 As qtd. in ibid., 197.
19 As qtd. in ibid., 197.
20 As qtd. in ibid., 181.
21 Ibid., 180–184.

THE RESTORATION

Most Mormons, and by now many others, know the story of the Prophet Joseph Smith, and how he had a personal visit from God the Father and Jesus Christ in a grove of trees in upstate New York. Then, through divine revelation and angelic visitation, he restored the gospel of Jesus Christ. As part of the Restoration, priesthood authority and the ordinances of the Lord's temple were also reinstituted. What many forget is that the Restoration didn't happen all at once. As is God's pattern, He gave babes milk and then later he gave them meat, or the deeper doctrines and principles. And He had not yet given all. Bruce R. McConkie notes:

> We are in the process of receiving all that God has spoken by the mouths of all his holy prophets since the world began. Only a small portion has come to us so far; we do not, as yet, begin to know what the ancients knew.[22]

M. Catherine Thomas, a retired professor of ancient scripture, explains:

> We acknowledge that even in the Restored Gospel we do not yet have a fulness. Though there has been restored to us a flood of rich doctrines and a greater access to Truth, much yet remains to be revealed to each of us. The Restoration is still going on, dependent to some degree on our preparation and diligent seeking.[23]

Despite not having a fulness, Joseph was commanded very early on to build a temple. In fact, the early Saints, poverty-stricken though they were, built a temple even before they built a proper meeting house.

Accounts about the Kirtland Temple are interesting to read from a yogic perspective, as they contain many of the previously discussed elements, such as the power of the Word and raised hands. Jeremiah Willey relates in his journal that the First Presidency, the Apostles, and and other leaders "met in solemn assembly and sealed upon us our washings, anointings and blessings with a loud shout of Hosannah to God and the Lamb."[24] Further, "Oliver Cowdery likewise testified that 'Anointing blessings were sealed by uplifted hands and praises to God."[25] There were also spiritual manifestations:

> This eve the Spirit of the Lord rested on the congregation. Many spake in tongues, many prophesied, angels were in our midst and ministered unto some. Cloven tongues,

---

22 As qtd. in M. Catherine Thomas, *Light in the Wilderness: Explorations in the Spiritual Life* (Salt Lake City, UT: Digital Legend Press, 2010), 199.
23 Ibid.
24 As qtd. in Brown, *The Gate of Heaven*, 235.
25 As qtd. in ibid.

like unto fire rested upon those who spake in tongues and prophesied. When they ceased to speak, the tongues ascended. [26]

Despite these awesome outpourings of spirit, the Kirtland Temple seems to have been only a preparatory temple, and the full ordinances were not revealed until later, in Nauvoo. The reason the Lord did not give the early Saints the fulness all at once is because, quite simply, they weren't ready. Elder George A. Smith said the following:

> If the Lord had on that occasion revealed one single sentiment more, or went one step further to reveal more fully the law of redemption, I believe he would have upset the whole of us. The fact was, he dare not, on that very account, reveal to us a single principle further than he had done, for he had tried, over and over again, to do it. He tried at Jerusalem; He tried away back before the flood; He tried in the days of Moses; and he had tried, from time to time, to find a people to whom he could reveal the law of salvation, and he never could fully accomplish it; and he was determined this time to be so careful, and advance the idea so slowly, to communicate them to the children of men with such great caution that, at all hazards, a few of them might be able to understand and obey.[27]

On numerous occasions, Joseph Smith insinuated there was much more that he knew that the Saints were not ready for. He told Brigham Young during the Kirkland period, "If I was to show the Latter-day Saints all the revelations that the Lord has shown unto me, there is scarce a man that would stay with me, they could not bear it."[28] At another time, he said: "Would to God, bretheren [*sic*], I could tell you who I am! Would to God I could tell you what I know! But you would call it blasphemy and want to take my life!"[29]

Isn't this always the case with truth when we are not ready for it? May we use the technologies that we do have to prepare our hearts for more restoration of truth and of our true identities.

SAVIORS ON MOUNT ZION

As stated at the beginning of the chapter, God's purpose in creating humans was to exalt them to be like Him. Jesus Christ, the Savior of the world, opened the way and set the example. In order to become like God, we must be saviors ourselves. We can accomplish this two-fold objective through both types of temples.

---

26 As qtd. in ibid., 237.
27 George A. Smith, in *Journal of Discourses*, 2:214–215.
28 *Millennial Star*, September 1, 1851, 257.
29 Orson F. Whitney, *Life of Heber C. Kimball* (Salt Lake City, UT, 1888), 333.

In the temples of the Lord, we perform saving ordinances by proxy for our ancestral dead. But there is another kind of saving work that we can do for our ancestors, by proxy, in the temple of our bodies. This saving work is sometimes called generational healing, chain breaking, or repairing the breach. One of the things about living in the latter days (or the Aquarian Age) is that there is a lot of temple work to be done. Also, the "blood and sins" of many generations needs to be cleansed from our physical bodies, mental bodies, and energetic bodies (see Generational Healing, page 124).

By purifying our bodies, we not only save ourselves but can heal generations of ancestors who can't, for whatever reason, receive certain kinds of healing blessings without a body. The multitude of stories about ancestors who are coming and requesting both outward and inward saving ordinances emphasizes the importance of doing all we can while in our mortal bodies to elevate and perfect ourselves, so that we may be restorers of "paths to dwell in" (Isaiah 58:12).

THE PRIESTHOOD POLARITY

As Latter-day Saints know, the Melchizedek Priesthood is the power by which the ordinances are administered. Ordinances are essential for eternal life and exaltation, and therefore the priesthood is essential. As we also know, mortal life is essential—without a physical body, there can be no fulness of joy.

While some criticize the patriarchal pattern of the priesthood, it is balanced when you consider the yogic teachings. Yogi Bhajan taught that woman is sixteen times more powerful than man because her Aura is sixteen times more enmeshed so that it can expand to create life. Giving life is the ultimate inward ordinance; life is a critical key. In this world, women are the stewards over giving life. Eve led the way by making a courageous choice. Adam wisely followed her lead.

So while it is women who lead us into life, it is priesthood holders who lead us into eternal life through the ordinances of the holy priesthood. I believe that the power of the Melchizedek Priesthood is the only thing that can elevate a man to the same level of life-giving power as a woman is naturally and unconditionally granted.[30]

As I hinted at in my discussion of the chakras, God (and other exalted or translated beings) are no longer subject to opposition in all things. Yet there are certain natural laws that are eternal. There is a law that says that opposites make the vortex swirl, and this swirling vortex is the most powerful force in nature. Though God is not subject to opposition, there may still be a polarity power at work. In God's case, however, it may be the perfect polarity of the exalted masculine and feminine, joined together.

---

30 Though not all women may have children, women still contain sixteen times the power of men. I'm not sure why this unconditional power is granted to all women when men have to remain faithful to be worthy of the priesthood. It may be interesting to note also that women are given some temple blessings unconditionally, while the same blessings are conditional for men. I cannot cite a source for this, but you can do your own research.

It seems that a righteous woman and a valiant Melchizedek Priesthood holder, both exalted, is the only kind of polarity that can generate the power to create worlds. Therefore, in keeping with the theme of covenants and consciousness, not only is the eternal marriage covenant critical, but it is also critical to master the marriage relationship, what the yogis call "the highest yoga."

This image from an ancient Chinese tomb, which contains both temple and Kundalini symbology, might be instructive. Hugh Nibley included drawings of this depiction of the ancient Chinese gods Fuxi and Nuwa in his book *Temple and Cosmos*, adding the following commentary:

> In the underground tomb of Fan Yen-Shih, d. A.D. 689, two painted silk veils show the First Ancestors of the Chinese, their entwined serpent bodies rotating around the invisible vertical axis mundi. Fu Hsi holds the set-square and plumb bob ... as he rules the four-cornered earth, while his sister-wife Nü-wa holds the compass pointing up, as she rules the circling heavens. The phrase *kuci chü* is used by modern Chinese to signify "the way things should be, the moral standard"; it literally means the compass and the square.[31]

> We see the king and queen embracing at their wedding, the king holding the square on high, the queen a compass. As it is explained, the instruments are taking the measurements of the universe, at the founding of a new world and a new age. Above the couple's head is the sun surrounded by twelve disks, meaning the circle of the year or the navel of the universe.[32]

There is so much to ponder about all of these symbols and about the temple of the Lord's house and also about the temple body. I hope that as you continue to do sacred work in both temples that even more mysteries unfold to you.

As the work of the Lord continues to move forward, more temples will dot the earth and the technology of Kundalini Yoga and Meditation for the temple-body will continue to spread. I believe the spread of this technology is a necessary part of the restoration of all things. For my proof, I have my own growth experiences and personal revelations, along with the witnesses of several hundred students who are growing exponentially in faith and purity.

---

31 Hugh Nibley, *Temple and Cosmos: Beyond This Ignorant Present* (Salt Lake City, UT: Deseret Book, 1992), 115.
32 Ibid., 111–112.

I Fix Broken Things | Name witheld

I love yoga. (My parents did yoga, which I always thought was weird and hippie-ish until I tried it and loved it—funny how that happens.) I had never done Kundalini Yoga and Meditation until I signed up for *The Gift of Giving Life* newsletter and saw that a Christ-centered Kundalini Yoga retreat was going to be held in a few weeks. The newsletter mentioned the need to heal to be prepared for birth (or something along those lines), and I thought it was perfect timing. I was about fourteen weeks along in pregnancy and was just finished with the being sick part of pregnancy. I was struggling with feeling prepared for another baby, and my husband was trying to break a serious addiction at the time.

I thought the retreat would be a wonderful place of healing in preparation to bring a spirit to earth—but I wasn't sure we could afford it. I was the sole breadwinner at the time, while my husband finished his studies. I prayed and tried the Prosperity Meditation. Two days later, I double-checked our account before registering for the retreat, and I saw my husband's old employers had given my husband a bonus. The company told him it wanted to pay him during the summer even though he was no longer working for the company. We were expecting a few hundred dollars but were astounded to see their payment of fifteen hundred! I knew the retreat was where I needed to be.

Once there, I felt such amazing power in the room. The sound of so many (twenty or so) women tuning in together gave me goose bumps. For me, the entire weekend was spent removing fear and adding love in its place. I experienced the scripture "perfect love casteth out all fear" (1 John 4:18). I couldn't make it through the tuning-out song without crying; it was all about love! I indeed felt lifted.

One of the most powerful experiences from the retreat (and there were so many powerful experiences!) was during the Adi Shakti meditation. Felice asked us to draw on the power of our righteous female ancestors before we began, so I decided to focus on my husband's mom, who had passed away when he was a young child. I've always felt very close to her—I felt her presence in the temple when I was getting my endowment shortly before our wedding, and I know she was in attendance at my first daughter's birth.

Even though she isn't my blood relative, I thought she counted as a righteous female ancestor because I was sealed to her son. And because my husband and I were facing a rough road of addiction, I thought she might have some wise counsel for me in my relationship with her son, whom I know she loves dearly. During the meditation, I had a conversation with her. I know it was her. It wasn't a spoken conversation; it was more that our spirits were communing. She expressed love—deep love for my husband and for me. She promised to do all she could on her side of the veil to help her son, and I agreed to do all I could on my side. It was powerful.

I felt so much strength knowing that the woman who brought him into this world was "rallying the troops" on her side of things. I didn't feel so powerless, so alone anymore.

During the retreat, we also had a workshop on journaling, and one task was to write a prayer for someone. I wrote my prayer for my husband. One part reads, "Please guide him to the tools to escape the grasp of this addiction and the influence of evil. Surround him with light and guard him with angels—Your fiercest sentinels. Help him feel the strength and power to overcome evil. Please surround him with the light of love. Let him be protected until his wounds are healed. Help me be a shield for him and not a weapon." In the days and weeks after the retreat, I would often pray for angels to protect our home and shield my husband. I could almost see warrior angels, complete with armor and sword, guarding our home and protecting him from darkness. I know my prayers were answered. I began a consistent meditation practice and felt closer to my Heavenly Parents and my Savior. I received more inspiration for myself and my family. I was filled with greater love and forgiveness. My husband began doing the addiction meditation and had a hypnotherapy session with Felice to rewrite some subconscious scripts. In the nine months since, he has regained his temple recommend and experienced the peace only available from becoming reborn and renewed by the power of the Atonement. His desires are full of light. Our marriage is stronger now than ever. Three months ago, our new baby was born into a home filled with love and light. I did not fall again into the darkness of postpartum depression as I had with my first child. I can't help but feel a consistent practice of Kundalini Yoga and Meditation has inspired and enabled me to remain close to the Source of All Light and Love.

A few months ago, before meditating, I asked Heavenly Father to tell me what He would want me to know specifically in that moment and for my life—what it was that I had been overlooking. Some things came to mind: forgiveness, loving "sinners," and being reminded that Christ ate with sinners. But then the bull's-eye answer came: "I fix broken things." I often lose hope when something is "broken" in my mind—a person, a marriage, a heart—forgetting that Christ can heal all things. I was grateful for that gentle reminder to have faith in Him and His ability to heal, for I have seen and experienced it in my own life.

Kundalini Yoga and Our Adoption Miracles | Mandi Felici

I was introduced to Kundalini Yoga and Meditation one year ago, and it has changed my life. After a few weeks of doing Kirtan Kriya, I began to feel more calm and balanced. I was more patient with my family. I felt the Spirit strongly every day. I felt inspired and enlightened. My thoughts changed. My desires and goals changed. I redid my vision board several times, and as I listened to God's voice, my path became clearer. I received great insight into His plan for me. Each morning as I meditated and then prayed, my heart and mind were opened to amazing things. Let me share with you how these amazing revelations led to the miraculous adoption of our little girl.

We adopted our son, Leo, as a newborn four years ago. He has brought us so much joy. We had hoped and prayed for a second baby to join our family for the last three years. On New Year's Eve, I was updating my vision board for 2014. A friend asked why I had dates on everything, except for the photo "We welcome a healthy new baby into our family." I told her that it was really on God's time and that I couldn't put a date on it. She said, "Everything is in God's time!" She was right, of course. I rewrote it, adding "in January 2014."

Two weeks later, we got a phone call from our adoption agency. There was a birth mom named J. who was looking at our profile. The agency e-mailed us some information about her and asked if we were interested. I read over the file and learned that J. was in prison, serving time for some drug charges. She had done drugs (heroin and meth) during the first two months of the pregnancy, so we were concerned about possible complications for the baby. But we signed the form and submitted it, stating that were we interested in J. seeing our file.

Over the next two days, we submitted forms for three other birth mothers who seemed like better matches because there were no drugs or alcohol reported. We were starting to get excited and feeling like we would be getting a baby very soon. We started preparing the baby room and getting ready.

A few days later, I got another e-mail from the agency about J. It was about the final cost breakdown and approval sheet. I let the e-mail sit in my inbox. I didn't sign it because I still had some concerns, and besides we were being looked at by those other birth moms. But for two straight days, I had this nagging feeling . . . "Sign the form" . . . "Sign the form."

Friday afternoon the agency called, asking if we had signed the form for J. I asked the caller a few more questions and then hung up the phone. I was still very nervous about it. With the form in my hand, I said a silent prayer. "God, is this the baby for us? Is she supposed to be in our family? Will she have major health concerns because of the drugs? Will she be okay?" My answer was a single line from a song: "I walk by faith." I could hear the tune so clearly in my head. I hummed it out loud and then began to sob as I signed the form. "I sign by faith."

I felt scared and unsure but also calm. I knew that everything would work out like it was supposed to.

Three days later, we got the call—J. had picked us! A baby girl would be joining our family just a week or two later! We were so excited.

The next day we learned a tiny bit more about J. The circumstances surrounding her conception had not been ideal and she didn't know much about the father. She did some drugs during the first two months of the pregnancy and was currently in prison, serving an eight-month sentence. She would be moved to a hospital for the birth. Our poor little baby. She and her birth mom had been through so much already. I felt incredibly grateful that God had given me some extra tools to help her—energy work, essential oils, prayer, and meditation. I knew that we could help her. I knew that she was going to be okay.

A few days later, I had the most wonderful experience while meditating. I was asking God what the baby's name should be. We had liked the names Lucy and Lena for a very long time, and they are both names from our grandmothers. I asked God what her name should be. The name Mary came to me. I tried to dismiss it because it's such a common name and we prefer more-unique names. But that is what I thought of: Mary.

The following day, as I was praying and meditating about it again, I asked if Lena was the right name. I was told to look it up. The first website that came up said that Lena is a form of Magdalena, as in Mary Magdalena. "Oh—I love her!" I thought. Then I read this paragraph: Mary Magdalene (or Magdalena), a character in the New Testament, was named thus because she was from Magdala. She was cleaned of evil spirits by Jesus and then remained with him during his entire ministry, witnessing the crucifixion and the resurrection.[1]

Wow! What a perfect name for our little girl, who was coming into this world with so much to overcome. I believed she would need to be cleansed of some evil spirits. She would need Christ's healings in so many ways. But she would remain with Him—always.

I was so moved by this. I cried silent tears as I praised God for this beautiful answer to my prayer. I then asked Him about a middle name for Lena.

God told me that it should be Love. I thought, *Really? Love? Is it too cheesy?* Would she grow up hating it? And I heard clearly, "It's not cheesy. It's an affirmation. Love will be the affirmation for her life. She will overcome all things with Love."

Again, I was moved by this tender voice speaking to my heart. Lena Love. What a beautiful name for our beautiful little girl. I could feel her spirit with me, and I could feel the strength of her spirit. She has a special mission on this earth. And I have a special mission to help her accomplish it. I felt so honored and so blessed to become her mother.

I shared this experience with Felice, and she responded with this:

This morning I was meditating and I felt your baby come to me, and I just started weeping.

---

1 "Meaning of Names," *BabyCenter*, last modified February 17, 2013, http://community.babycenter.com/post/a40051630/meaning_of_names.

She was saying, "Thank you." I don't know why I was privileged with a visit, but it was awesome. She is so happy to come to your family. I think she had a little fear it would never work out. I also got the feeling that you should do some work on her before she is born to clear some DNA stuff from the line she had to come through. My feeling is that it is not a ton of work, but she wants it done before birth.

Felice was busy, so she referred me to Wendy, who is an energy healer who also does Kundalini Yoga. I immediately called Wendy, and we did two sessions of energy work for our little Lena. She cleared a lot of blocks, false beliefs, and bad conception energy. She could also see that during the drug use, there were evil entities that entered J.'s body, which scared the baby, and this fear was crystallized in her brain. Wendy meditated for two days and was finally able to clear this from the baby and replace it with healing, peaceful energy. She also cleared the need for addiction, feelings of worthlessness, and a host of other things. We could both feel Lena's Aura brighten as Wendy did all of this. It was a powerful and spiritual experience.

Lena wanted me to know that she chose to come to earth this way so that she could learn and grow. She also chose her birth mom because she wants to help J. Lena has a deep love for J. Lena also wanted me to know that she knows she is coming to our family, and she is excited. She wanted me to know that she will always have energetic ties to her birth family and that part of her mission on earth is to heal that family tree. I knew that the energy work we were doing right then was the beginning of that process. Wow. What a privilege to be part of that. I began doing a healing meditation each day—sending lots of love and healing to J. and to Lena. I asked God to place a protective shield around them. I asked healing angels to perform miracles on them, to nurture and protect them. And I know that He has.

We flew to Utah and met with J.'s mom and sister. They were so nice, and they told us a lot about J. They told us that she has a really big heart and that she loves everyone. She is truly a compassionate soul. If she sees a homeless person, she wants to help him or her and weeps for days if she is unable to help. She is very social, a people person, and loves everyone. She is extremely intelligent, with an IQ of 160. She loves to travel and to try new things.

The caseworker told us that J. went through dozens and dozens of family profiles. She picked ours first—we were her number-one choice. She loved that we value education, that we travel a lot, and that we love the cultural diversity in our area. She told the caseworker: "This is Leo's little sister."

They told us that J. would be transported from the prison to the hospital for just a very short time. She would be shackled to the bed, and a guard would be at the door. That broke my heart. She couldn't have her mom or a friend there to help her during the delivery. She would be feeling so alone and scared. That made my heart break. It was so cruel.

That night I woke up at 3:00 a.m. and was thinking about J. and the baby. And then the most wonderful thing occurred to me. There is a picture on my vision board of some children, with the phrase "Liberate the Captives." This comes from my favorite scripture, Jacob 2:19: "And after ye have obtained a hope in Christ ye shall obtain riches, if ye seek them; and ye will seek them for the intent to do good—to clothe the naked, and to feed the hungry, and to liberate the captive, and administer relief to the sick and the afflicted."

This scripture became my mantra about a year ago, as I was building my business. God told me that it was okay to build a successful business if my intent was to do good. Truly, my vision is to clothe the naked; feed the hungry; administer to the sick and afflicted (with essential oils); and to liberate the captive (which had meant, for me, advocating for adoption—truly the liberation of innocent little babies from captivity).

I have this scripture on my wall, and I think about it constantly. In fact, part of it is on my vision board ("Liberate the Captives") because I want to start a foundation that advocates for adoption. It is part of my mission on this earth. I want to help as many babies as I can. So, that night, as I thought about baby Lena, I realized that she was in prison right at that very moment. We were liberating her from captivity, literally. I was stunned and overcome with emotion and gratitude for God's tender mercies.

I told all this to Felice, and she told me that Mukunday is one of the names of God and means "Liberator" and that I might want to look up a mantra called Har Har Mukunday. I realized that I had a mantra with the word *Mukunday* in it that I had been chanting in my head for weeks. I couldn't get that line out of my head. I had heard Felice say that mantras have embedded within them the ability to bring you everything you need, even when you don't know what you need. Again, I was astounded at the wondrousness of God. He was caring for Lena and caring for us during every part of this journey. I also realized that intentionality is powerful. That vision boards are powerful. Whatever we envision, we can create. And the Word is powerful. God answers our prayers and guides us along our path if we stay close to Him and cocreate our lives with Him.

A year ago, I could not have imagined the inspiration and miracles that are now a part of my everyday life. I really am more enlightened and so much more in tune. I know it's because of my daily meditation practice and that I am making time to really connect with God each morning. I am so grateful for this ancient technology of Kundalini Yoga and Meditation. I truly believe that all truth can be circumscribed into one great whole. Kundalini complements and strengthens my testimony of the restored gospel, my faith in Christ, and my relationship with Him. It has changed my life. It has changed me. Wahe Guru!

Kundalini Yoga Led Me Back To Christ | Shannon

I had been doing Kundalini Yoga sporadically for about six years when my marriage came to an end. At that point, I started going more often to help me through my divorce. But I never had a personal daily meditation practice until two years ago when I took Felice's class. I did the 40-day Kirtan Kriya meditation challenge. Right away I found that I slept better, I was more cheerful during the day, more patient with my kids, and really enjoying life. Other people could notice a difference too. I even had a co-worker tell me that I was glowing.

When I added the Meditation For Healing Addictions, I suddenly decided to stop dating. That is also when I decided to do a teacher training, which was a life changing experience. I had so many spiritual experiences, and it made me want to strengthen my relationship with Heavenly Father. I had been inactive throughout my twenties and I had gone back to church, but I was just going through the motions. I was showing up, but I wasn't really invested.

When I started my teacher training, my dad freaked out and thought I was going down a path that was going to lead me away from the Church. The following weekend in teacher training, I learned about a mantra that can heal opposite gender parent relationships (Bandh Jammeeai), so I started playing it. After a while, my dad and I had a total 180, and he became more interested in what I was doing.

During teacher training I got a download to start a business to help people using Kundalini Yoga and Meditation, essential oils, and energy work. That was unexpected, but I did it, and it makes me very happy to help others now.

After teacher training, I had more intuition, and I wanted to develop more spiritual gifts and be closer to Christ. I also decided that I wanted to go back to the temple (after sixteen years without a recommend). That took eight months of preparation, but in preparing for it I got to experience the gift of the Atonement and just feel how much my Savior loves me. There were moments when I literally felt Him wrap his arms around me.

My mom came to town with a family friend and a few other friends joined me, and I went back to the temple. It was a very beautiful peaceful experience. After sixteen years I finally have a temple recommend in my wallet. I attribute the changes in my life to Kundalini Yoga, and I am grateful for how it led me back to Christ.

The Kundalini rises
not just because of exercises
but because of a
total lifestyle
of consciousness.

— Felice Austin

AWAKE AS IN ANCIENT DAYS, PAGE 23

Yogic
Lifestyle

Yogic Lifestyle

Raising the Kundalini is not just about physical exercises; it involves a total lifestyle of consciousness. Because Kundalini Yoga is not a religion, it is not a requirement to do everything that the yogic lifestyle prescribes. It is acceptable to pick and choose what works for you; however, there are physical, mental, and spiritual benefits to everything, and I have found them all worth investigating. Many aspects of the yogic lifestyle should be familiar and complementary to a person living a faith-filled life and living the Lord's law of health, or the Word of Wisdom, as Latter-day Saints call it. The Word of Wisdom was given through revelation to the prophet Joseph Smith "in consequence of evils and designs which do and will exist in the hearts of conspiring men in the last days" (Doctrine and Covenants 89:4).

A primary aspect of the yogic lifestyle is rising early to meditate. The Lord's law also recommends early rising. Doctrine and Covenants 88:124 says, "Retire to thy bed early, that ye may not be weary; arise early, that your bodies and your minds may be invigorated." The yogic technology of *Ishnaan* is very invigorating and is shared in the box on the following page.

Adherents to this yogic path are not required to live a monastic lifestyle. Kundalini Yoga is a technology suited for householders—people who have families and children and jobs and houses. Marriage is not only encouraged but considered the highest yoga. Every marriage is considered not only a union between two people but also between the couple and God.

In this yogic discipline, it is not necessary to give up wealth or possessions. In fact, material prosperity is important for developing society and having the resources to fulfill your destiny. Giving one-tenth to God (what most Christians call tithing) is encouraged not only in money but in all activities.

There are also yogi do's and don'ts, known as yamas and niyamas. In an acorn shell, the Five Yogic Observances are purity, contentment, determination, study, and devotion/ recognition of the One. The Five Yogic Abstinences, or things the yogi or yogini commits

ISHNAAN: The Science of Hydrotherapy, or the Yogi Cold Shower

The ancient yogis knew the benefits of a cold shower in the ambrosial hours, before meditating. And they had to work hard to get it, carrying buckets of water to the top of a ladder. We are fortunate to have running water and removable shower heads. But there is more to this practice than just cold water; it is an ancient and sacred science. What else did you expect?

This science is called *ishnaan*—when the body, by its own virtue, creates the temperature that can beat off the coldness of the water. Ishnaan is not just wetting your body. There is a grace to it.

I recommend beginning by massaging the body with organic, cold-pressed almond oil or sesame oil. Use a dry brush to bring the blood to the surface of the skin until the skin is hot.

Then, put your extremities under the cold water. Start with the feet. Then the hands and arms. Use one foot to massage the other while under the cold water. Let the water hit different parts of your body; you will experience different energetic effects. Then stand away from the stream for a while, and use both hands to massage your body until your body gets hot.

Then get under the cold stream of water again, and massage your body again. Continue this process for about ten to fifteen minutes or until you feel warm. Chanting a mantra makes it much easier! When you come out, your entire caliber will be different. You will have a radiant glow, and all of your organs will be rebuilt.

The body's automatic response to the cold water will be to bring blood flow to the central organs, which will flush the organs and the capillaries. Flushing the organs changes the secretions of the glands, leading to youth in not only the physical appearance of the body but also the way the body runs and regulates.[1]

Precautions

There are a few important cautions. Be sure to start with your feet and hands. The thighs, genitals, and head should never be first. Avoid cold showers during pregnancy and menstruation. Cold showers should also be avoided if you have a fever, rheumatism, or heart disease. If you have high blood pressure or sciatic nerve problems, start slowly.[2]

---

1 Yogi Bhajan, *KRI International Teacher Training Manual, Level 1*, 4th ed. (Santa Cruz, NM: Kundalini Research Institute, 2007), 248.
2 Ibid.

to adhere to, are non-violence, being truthful, not stealing, controlling the senses, and not being greedy.[1] The yogi lives a life filled with *seva*, or selfless service.

The Kundalini Yoga lifestyle is lacto-vegetarian, which means that meat and eggs are not eaten. With regard to consuming meat, the Lord counsels: "Yea, flesh also of beasts and of the fowls of the air, I, the Lord, have ordained for the use of man with thanksgiving; nevertheless they are to be used sparingly; and it is pleasing unto me that they should not be used, only in times of winter, or of cold, or famine" (Doctrine and Covenants 89:12–13).

When considering meat consumption from a health point of view, meat is one of the most acid-producing foods. Blood that is more acidic is ideal for cancer growth.

---

1 Yogi Bhajan, *The Aquarian Teacher: KRI International Kundalini Yoga Teacher Training Level 1 Yoga Manual* (Santa Cruz, NM: Kundalini Research Institute, 2007), 44.

Meat leaves toxins in our bodies because of the components of animal protein and the process required to break down these proteins. Meat it is among the greatest sources of cholesterol, and consuming meat can lead to hardening of the arteries and heart disease. Also important to consider is that most animals raised for consumption today are given chemicals and hormones to benefit in the production process, but these chemical and hormones can be harmful to consume.[2]

Other foods that yogis are recommended to avoid are white sugar, salt, nicotine, white bread, caffeine, and alcohol.

The Kundalini Yoga lifestyle also includes being drug free. Kundalini Yoga and drugs do not mix—even so-called natural drugs like marijuana, which Yogi Bhajan says is actually one of the worst drugs because it smokes the gray matter in your brain.[3] Yogi Bhajan says the following: "Drugs are not being taken for any other reason than that people cannot face their reality, yet drugs take them to non-reality. At that moment give them survival, that's all. Every stimulant, every drug, every love, every relationship is based on affirmation of non-reality."[4]

The Lord's law of health likewise eschews drugs and other harmful substances. According to Elder M. Russell Ballard: "The battle over man's God-given agency continues today. Satan . . . uses addiction to steal away agency. . . . Researchers tell us there is a mechanism in our brain called the pleasure center. When activated by certain drugs or behaviors, it overpowers the part of our brain that governs our willpower, judgment, logic, and morality. This leads the addict to abandon what he or she knows is right."[5]

The blessings and promises that come from living the Lord's law of health are astounding: "And all saints who remember to keep and do these sayings, walking in obedience to the commandments, shall receive health in their navel and marrow to their bones; And shall find wisdom and great treasures of knowledge, even hidden treasures; And shall run and not be weary, and shall walk and not faint. And I, the Lord, give unto them a promise, that the destroying angel shall pass by them, as the children of Israel, and not slay them" (Doctrine and Covenants 89:18–21).

---

2 Bhajan, *The Aquarian Teacher*, 250.
3 Bhajan, *The Aquarian Teacher*, 250.
4 Ibid.
5 M. Russell Ballard, "O That Cunning Plan of the Evil One," *Ensign,* November 2010, http://www.lds.org/general-conference/2010/10/o-that-cunning-plan-of-the-evil-one.

My Bald Eagle | Wendy Cleveland

When I was ten, I saw a bald eagle. It completely took my breath away. I didn't expect to see anything in the sky, and when I looked up, there the eagle was, soaring so majestically right above my head. Being only ten years old didn't stop me from appreciating the immense beauty of the moment. It was something that I have never forgotten and think about often. And oftentimes, I find myself gazing up at the sky, waiting for my next encounter with one of these supernal creatures.

After I started to meditate, I witnessed my life changing. Not slowly, like I was used to witnessing progress in my life. Meditating has affected me in countless ways. I could write a novel about it, but for now I would like to share how meditation helped me find my joy again.

I had been living a beautiful, blessed life with a beautiful family and incredible friends. There was so much that God had blessed me with. But in the state I was in, I hadn't felt joy in many years. I was living in a kind of numb state where I could only feel the negative emotions in my life. Feeling things like love and joy was as rare as seeing a bald eagle soaring in the sky.

When I began meditating, I started with Kirtan Kriya. This meditation helps clear generational issues and promotes change. I set an intention to clear any generational chains I was carrying from ancestors and to clear any negative issues in my own body. I started seeing a difference right away. Since then, the big metaphorical rock I had been carrying on my shoulders has disappeared.

Through meditating, I have learned how to listen to my spirit and commune with the Holy Ghost in everything I do. I have learned that God oftentimes sends me dreams to communicate with me. In one dream, God showed me all the times in my life that I had felt joy. In every instance, I had been surrounded by my family. I learned from that dream that I hadn't felt joy (real joy, which starts from within and radiates out of you like a bright light) for a long time, and I learned what it was like to feel joy again.

From that day on, it was my goal to feel joy at least once a day. Some days I did, some I didn't. But when I did it was joy from my family. I had to let go of any distractions that were keeping me from enjoying my beautiful family. But eventually I found a little joy in every day, until I got to the point where I was basking in joy almost continually, praising God for my family and for my joy. It was like looking up into the sky and seeing the elusive bald eagle everyday. I know that having joy in our posterity is the mode of heaven and earth. God wants us to feel that joy. Meditation helped me get my joy back. And I am forever grateful.

Healing for Families | Katy Willis

Healing has not only been an individual and couple experience but also a family experience. In the past few years, we have become aware that my husband and my children are chain breakers. There have been dysfunctional and toxic family issues that we have looked at squarely, and we are the generation to make changes. Although I am not a chain breaker myself, I am key in creating an incubator environment for my children, where healthy patterns are offered and modeled.

Kundalini Yoga and Meditation has affected my family through my being calm and balanced. I have noticed that especially my little ones mirror my state of being—whether calm or unbalanced. Kundalini Yoga was a comfortable addition to the healing technologies we have been using to make change for future generations. As I introduced Kundalini Yoga mantras to my three children (ages six, five, and three), all were excited to learn. They love it when I teach them a new one! Sometimes it takes singing the mantra for a few days, but my children have caught on to each one and remember them all. Their favorites are "I am Happy, I am Good," "I am Beautiful, I am Bountiful, I am Blissful," "Sa Ta Na Ma," and "Ek Ong Kar."

We have a children's Kundalini mantra CD I turn on while I make breakfast. One by one my children come to the kitchen singing along. We homeschool, and we added Kundalini Yoga to our school day after prayer. I catch them singing and humming throughout their day on their own too. We also sing mantras before bed as I apply essential oils to their feet.

I have loved watching my children make connections. For example, I taught my children Kirtan Kriya and how to use their index fingers to point and sing "I Am Happy". My daughter has been so terrified of the dark that she wants someone to walk with her if she has to go into a dark room alone. She sings the mantra when she is afraid and has noticed it calms her.

My three-year-old has asked to sing "I Am Happy, I am Good" after discussing issues such as hitting a sibling. I think singing this mantra helps him remember he is a good boy and his goodness is separate from his choices.

I love that Kundalini Yoga is another tool in my children's toolbox and that they are learning to tap into this technology to tune into their needs. It has helped them to be protected, strong, and happy as they make this journey.

Pulling Weeds | Name Withheld

This morning while doing my meditation, I had the hardest time sitting still. I almost couldn't wait for it do be done so I could move. This was the first time I have been so unsettled. Toward the end, I could picture these deep-seated negative thoughts and habits beginning to be pulled out of my body. They are deep down and they don't want to come out. I am picturing weeds in a garden.

When I was young and my parents would tell us we needed to clear an area of our yard from weeds, we would usually go water that area first. We did this for two reasons: (1) It made the ground softer so it would be easier to pull out the weeds after the water soaked for an hour or so. (2) We could put off actually working for an hour or two. After the area soaked, we would start pulling out the stubborn weeds and clearing the area.

So I am picturing that all of the time I have spent meditating so far I have been soaking the ground. Now it is time to pull out the weeds, and they might not want to come out. But after they are cleared, I am hoping to feel the difference in my life.

He wakeneth
morning by morning,
he wakeneth
mine ear to hear
as the learned.

— Isaiah 50:4

Sadhana

Sadhana

The regular daily practice of yoga, meditation, and related exercise is called *sadhana* (pronounced SOD-nuh). The word means "self-discipline," and sadhana is a self-discipline that allows you to express the Infinite within yourself. We practice every day because that is what self-discipline is:

> We consciously choose to rise up, to exercise the body and meditate. Each day is different. Each day we are different. Every 72 hours all the cells of the body totally change. Sickness comes and goes. Motivation waxes and wanes. But through all the flux of life, through all the variations of the mind and heart, we consciously choose to maintain a constant and regular practice.[1]

Sadhana is also a sacrifice—the practice of making sacred a set time to give praises to God, who is the Great Giver.

Sadhana is best practiced in the morning, before the sun rises. Sadhana is a time each day to notice the patterns that lead away from higher consciousness and then to transcend those patterns. Many yogis practice sadhana for at least two and a half hours per day before the rising of the sun. This time represents giving one-tenth of the day to God, similar to the law of tithing. However, anyone can receive all the benefits of sadhana by beginning with a short daily practice. I usually have students begin with a seven-minute meditation and a three-minute yoga kriya each day (which means they only need to rise ten minutes earlier than normal). Then, on their own timetable, they can increase the amount of time as they wish. Even with just seven minutes a day, the results of consistent practice create what Yogi Bhajan calls spiritual fitness:

---

1 Yogi Bhajan, *KRI International Teacher Training Manual, Level 1*, 4th ed. (Santa Cruz, NM: Kundalini Research Institute, 2007), 144.

There is a dynamic triangle within each of us between practice, experience, and our experience of the experience. There is a constant cycle between these three. If you have many beliefs and no *sadhana,* how are you really changing? If you believe very good things about people and serve no one, what good is that? *Sadhana* becomes a key. In terms of the body and posture there is one law for *sadhana:* "Get up, set up and keep up." If you don't set up for the day, if you don't posture yourself, ready to engage the day, how are you going to keep up?

And how are you going to have a set up if things are already happening before you even get up? So first you have to get up before things are happening. Then you can set yourself in a posture, attitude, and commitment, ready to engage. Then you have the potential to keep up. If you keep up, you will start having a momentum above Time. And the effective human is timeless above Time. As long as you feel you are just at the whim of Time, you are not at the level of extraordinary human that is your normal potential. And it all starts with *sadhana* and posture. That's what a spiritual posture is. It gives you spiritual fitness.[2]

THE AMRIT VELA

Amrit Vela means "ambrosial hours" or "nectar hour."[3] It is the three hours before dawn, usually from three to six o'clock or from four to seven o'clock. Rising to meditate during the Amrit Vela is an ancient practice known to many cultures. The Hindus and Buddhists knew the sacredness of the Amrit Vela and so did the Persian Poet Rumi, who wrote the following:

The breeze at dawn has secrets to tell you.
Don't go back to sleep.
You must ask for what you really want.
Don't go back to sleep.
People are going back and forth across
the doorsill
Where the two worlds touch.
The door is round and open.
Don't go back to sleep.[4]

As mentioned, it is best to get up before time gets up and before your story begins. Though you can do your sadhana at other times of the day, there are many benefits to morning sadhana. For one thing, there are fewer disturbances. The masses are asleep, and the

---

2 Ibid., 148.
3 Ibid., 215.
4 Dharam Singh, "Group Sadhana," accessed March 24, 2014, www.amritvela.org.

global vibration is quiet and sacred. Where night and day overlap, there is a crack between worlds. At this time the veil of *maya* is thinnest. During these hours, the mind is less prone to worldly anxieties and thoughts. For all of these reasons, the Amrit Vela provides an ideal atmosphere for remembering and communicating with God.

Simply being vertical and leaning in the direction[5] at this time has profound effects on the subconscious. There are also enormous health benefits. The power of *prana* is more concentrated and can cleanse and revitalize your body more easily.[6] Yogi Bhajan said that doing Sadhana a "person becomes defeatless. Sadhana is self-victory and it is a victory over time and space. . . . When you get up it is a victory on time and when you do it, it is a victory on space. . . . Sadhana is only for you. Sadhana is self-victory."[7] Additionally,

SYMBOLISM OF THE SHEEPSKIN

Through the ages, yogis have sat on animal skins for meditation. In the story of Gideon in the Hebrew Bible, a sheepskin was selected as a sacred sign between Gideon and God in Gideon's request for a second witness of the Lord's words:

Behold, I will put a fleece of wool in the floor; and if the dew be on the fleece only, and it be dry upon all the earth beside, then shall I know that thou wilt save Israel by mine hand, as thou hast said (Judges 6:37).

It is traditional (though not required) for many Kundalini Yoga practitioners to sit on a sheepskin while meditating and practicing yoga. The sheepskin is great for yoga because it is soft and comfortable for the ankles. Yogi Bhajan recommended sheepskin for meditation because it is a natural fiber, it grounds the practitioner, and it blesses and liberates the soul of the dead animal. Indeed, many people experience deeper states of connection to God when using a sheepskin rather than a sticky yoga mat[1] or cushion.

I find it difficult to ignore the symbolism of the sheepskin and the sacrificial lamb.. Starting in the days of Adam, men were required to offer a blood sacrifice to God—an unblemished, first-born male animal, which of course, was symbolic of the sacrifice of the coming Christ. Then Jesus fulfilled this law and ended the need for blood sacrifice:

And ye shall offer up unto me no more the shedding of blood; yea, your sacrifices and your burnt offerings shall be done away. . . . And ye shall offer for a sacrifice unto me a broken heart and a contrite spirit. And whoso cometh unto me with a broken heart and a contrite spirit, him will I baptize with fire and with the Holy Ghost (3 Nephi 9:19–20).

One student, Kylie, described her relationship with sheepskin as follows: "I got my sheepskin and used it first on a new moon. I had a big realization that His sacrifice is the foundation that makes my sacrifice possible. He is our foundation for progression and enlightenment. It makes it all the more meaningful to sit on a literal foundation reminding me of the ultimate sacrifice upon which all my life and progression rest. So great!"[2]

---

1 It is said that synthetic yoga mats can shrink the Aura by one third.
2 Personal communication via Facebook group. Accessed March 8, 2014.

---

5 By "lean in the direction" it is meant that even if you can't do a pose or a posture perfectly, just do your best.
6 amritvela.org
7 Yogi Bhajan lecture July 7, 1981

"Sadhana is a test of self-grit. If your sadhana is more important than your neurosis, you are fine. If your neurosis is more important than your sadhana, you are not."[8]

Though I haven't collected enough data on the subject, it is my hypothesis that when the lives of all great world leaders and game changers are examined, most will be found to be early risers. President and prophet Gordon B. Hinckley arose every morning at four o'clock, as did the prophet Joseph Fielding Smith, who was fond of telling his children, "People die in bed, and so does ambition."[9]

I realize that rising early may be the most difficult part of sadhana for some people, but it doesn't have to be difficult. The simple way to begin is to set your alarm for one minute earlier each week. After a year of doing so, you would be rising nearly an hour earlier. If you would like to go straight for the glory, you could start by waking up fifteen minutes earlier (woah!) and doing a small daily practice. Most of my students have never meditated before and start with a daily seven-minute meditation. As this practice becomes easy and pleasurable, they begin to add more time.

SADHANA GUIDELINES

Here are some guidelines for starting your sadhana practice:

- Sahana truly begins the night before, so it is best to eat early, eat light, and pray before you go to sleep so that your highest self will wake you up feeling refreshed and happy.

- Rise during the Amrit Vela or a little earlier than you are now.

- Eliminate.

- Set your energy for the day by taking an invigorating cold shower (see the instructions on page 161).

- Dress in natural fiber clothing, cover your head, and remove any footwear.

- Prepare the environment around you. Make sure it is as uplifting as possible. Your body is a temple of God, and your preparations should reflect your intention to cleanse, heal, and uplift yourself and others. Choose a firm but soft surface to practice on.

- Sit on a natural fiber rug, sheepskin, or yoga mat. For those with physical limitations or injuries, sitting in a chair with your feet flat on the floor is okay.

- Tune in with the Adi Mantra (see page 190). This step is not optional. Always tune in to begin your sadhana.

---

8 Yogi Bhajan lecture January 22, 1991.
9 Smith and Steward, Life of Joseph Feilding Smith, 3 (found on lds.org)

- Warm up with Cat-Cow Pose (see page 194) or other exercises or a good Pranayam.

- Complete the yoga kriya of your choice.

- Complete one or more meditations of your choice.

- Relax. You may want to have a shawl or blanket handy to wrap around yourself.

- Pray.

- Tune out with the "Long Time Sun" song and a long Sat Nam (see page 292).

You may move the order of some of these items around and add in scripture reading and personal prayer wherever you choose, but always begin by tuning in and end by tuning out. If you do not have time to complete a full yoga kriya in the early morning hours, it is okay to do it at another time. I also recommend doing yoga kriyas in groups as often as you can. I encourage you to complete a full Kundalini Yoga class once a week in a group setting, which will provide community and the support of a teacher who can answer any questions and assist you in selecting a meditation.

QUESTIONS TO CONSIDER

Many people ask me what they should do for their sadhana. I usually encourage people to start with a simple yoga kriya like Basic Spinal Energy Series or Awaken Your Ten Bodies, and a core meditation like Kirtan Kriya or Sat Kriya. But over time, you might want to change your sadhana. It is best to trust your intuition when building your sadhana practice, but here are some questions that might be worth considering and praying about.

- What Yoga Kriya would help me with my intention of ____?

- Should my sadhana include more than one meditation? Which meditation would help me most all around? And which would help most for the specific intention of ____?

- How long should I do the meditations (minutes as well as days in a row)?

- Should I include a pranayam as part of my sadhana?

- What pranayam should be my go-to pranayam throughout the day?

- What mantra should be my go-to throughout the day?

- Do any of my Ten Bodies need balancing/strengthening. What is the priority?

- What scripture mantras do I need in my life right now?

- What is it You want me to know/do today?

- What questions should I be asking?
- What should I be praying for?
- Is there a specific name of God I should be using as I pray for ___ intention?
- Are there spiritual gifts I am ignoring? What can I do to develop them?

Healing My Childhood | Hannah Worthington

When Felice started doing the meditation webinar, I felt a strong urge to join the class, but I put it off, being too busy with small children, having a husband with a low-paying job, and scraping through with finances. I put the webinar out of my mind for a year or so, until a good friend pestered me to join the class as it was repeating. She kept telling me to e-mail Felice. And so I did (eventually), and I will be grateful forever for that friend and for Felice. Meditation, and knowing how to do it effectively, has changed how I think, and it's still changing me and making me a better me.

When I started my first forty days, my intention was to find myself easily having more patience. I realized that for years, I was instinctively reacting to my children in the same way my mother had reacted to me as a child. Despite my rational belief in gentle, positive parenting, I was still failing. I was lashing out and being angry over things that I felt I ought to have been able to cope with rationally and patiently. By the end of the forty days, I no longer felt the urge to lash out. Not ever. The instinct had been totally driven out of me, to the extent that I am amazed when I look back on the day and how challenging things have been and how calm and patient I have remained. I know it is my practice of Kundalini Yoga and Meditation, working through the Atonement of Christ, that this is possible.

My favorite part of the forty days was the time at home-education camp. I sat in the back of my car with the boot open and chanted Kirtan Kriya to the setting sun in the middle of the Peak District. The experience was beautiful. I remember during one meditation session, as I was chanting I felt the Spirit so strongly. I felt it testify that Jesus had atoned and given His life for us. I knew I was loved and a cherished sister.

I always feel far more positive, energized, and ready to face whatever is in store for me after Felice's classes. It always feels like there is something there just for me, just what I needed to hear or the exercise my body needed to experience.

After my forty days, I added in a meditation for releasing childhood anger. I can feel it working in me. My face tingles, and I feel my body shedding the incorrect beliefs and the cellular memories it has been holding onto. During a difficult time at the beginning, after much prayer and a lot of tears, I felt the presence of my Heavenly Parents, dressed in white, on either side of me, holding me and letting me know that They loved me. I knew in that moment that I would be okay, that this was something that would pass, and that I could come out stronger when it was finished.

Keep Up and You'll Be Kept Up

Susan thought that after forty days of meditation, all of her problems would go away. But they didn't, so she quit meditating. They definitely did not go away after that.

Ashley completed forty days of Kirtan Kriya, and it changed her life significantly. She stopped meditating because she figured she had already received all the benefits. Her life quickly changed back to the way it was before.

I think that forty is a nice round symbolic number, and it's fun to do a forty-day meditation. But the fortieth day is not meant to be the end, or a one-time event, and expectations should be released to God. Here is what the teachings say:

> It is written that, in 40 days, a practitioner using Kundalini Yoga as an experience creates uplift and liberation. It may take 20 years using other techniques. But that was assuming the person who engages in this should first be mentally stable, have strong habits, have a clear mind, and a pure body. Most people do not fit these qualifications and it takes a little longer to use the same practices to clear the subconscious and organize the mind toward the soul and the Infinite, instead of toward our finiteness and neurosis.[10]

The above quote explains why results vary and why religious people who live a clean life and are stable are able to accelerate faster. However, even though the technology is fast, it is not always helpful to look for proof of your progress or to compare your progress with others. Proofs will come along the way and you'll take note of them, but don't get hung up on proof. Some people may see colors or feel sensations in their bodies, and while these experiences can be fun, Yogi Bhajan called them "glitter at the bottom of the ladder." They don't necessarily indicate a mighty change or awakening, which, through the Kundalini Yoga technology, can often happen very subtly and without fireworks.

---

10 Yogi Bhajan, *KRI International Teacher Training Manual, Level 1*, 4th ed. (Santa Cruz, NM: Kundalini Research Institute, 2007), 286.

There may be days that nothing at all seems to be changing, but things are happening outside of your awareness. I challenge people to complete a forty-day meditation because forty days in a row is the right amount of time to make a change from one state of being to another, but your own personal meditations can be done for ninety days, one hundred twenty days, a thousand days, or your entire life. Real transformation continues to unfold in layers as each beat of the heart rewrites your destiny.

There may be a honeymoon period with meditation, there may be interference, and there may also be times when it seems your "progress" has fallen off. Maybe tragedy strikes, challenges arise, or unhealed parts of yourself come up. It is important to remember that these things are sacred too. After all, happiness and sorrow are the opposing forces that swirl the heart chakra. In difficult times, the only thing to do is to *keep up*. I have been through dark times. I testify that if you keep up, you *will* be kept up and there will be glorious days ahead.

I love the following quote from M. Catherine Thomas:

With eyes to see, we find that we are participants in a highly interactive universe, a dynamic laboratory, in which the Governing Powers lead us and even provoke us to 'be conformed to the image of [God's] Son' (Romans 8:29). To this end, the Lord, knowing what we do not yet understand about our own soul, what has not yet been healed or resolved in us, allows circumstances and events to provoke the tutorials which will set us free in love.[11]

I've found that if you want to assess your progress, the best practice is to circle a date on the calendar nine months from now. We travel through life in nine-month cycles, and it seems the right amount of time for rebirth. On the date you've circled, look back and assess your progress. You might find that the landscape looks quite different.

> One part of the sadhana should stay constant long enough for you to master, or at least experience, the changes evoked by a single technique. Each kriya and mantra has its individual effects, although they all elevate you toward a cosmic consciousness. Learn to value the pricelessness of one kriya, and all others will be understood in a clearer light.
>
> —Yogi Bhajan, *The Aquarian Teacher: KRI International Kundalini Yoga Teacher Training Level I Yoga Manual* (Santa Cruz, NM: Kundalini Research Institute, 2007),150

---

11 M. Catherine Thomas, *Light in the Wilderness: Explorations in the Spiritual Life* (Salt Lake City, UT: Digital Legend Press, 2010), 164.

Forever Changed | Bonnie Hansen

When I first decided to do the Intro to Kundalini Yoga Meditation Webinar, I had no idea how it would change my life, my perspective, and my soul. I just wanted more peace, more clarity, a closer relationship with God, and a greater ability to handle the everyday stresses of life.

Just this morning as I pondered what I would say if someone asked me to stop my meditation practice, I realized that to give this up would be like asking me to stop saying my prayers. It would be like asking me to build an impenetrable wall between me and my Savior. It would be asking me to return to the depressed, discouraged, frightened, wounded little girl I had been most of my life. It would be asking me to give up my newfound ability to stay calmer with my kids, my ability to now truly see and appreciate their awesomeness and their worth to Heavenly Father. It would be taking away a valuable tool to help my husband heal from his own childhood wounds. It would be like asking me to sever the connections between me and Heavenly Father, my Savior, and my higher self that I have built and formed one daily meditation session at a time for over a year now. I hope I am never asked to give that up, because I never could give up the sweet, blissful connection to God and myself—my true self—I feel each morning.

Meditation hasn't always been easy or blissful. Some days, especially in the beginning, I learned things I didn't want to know, things that ripped my heart out, things that filled me with grief. But I was never alone. Always, God was there with me, guiding me, comforting me, holding me. Ancestors were there too, and so were angelic friends I have no mortal memory of. I felt loved and cared for and knew that I was on the right path. After each new revelation and subsequent healing, I was lighter, happier, and more in tune with who I really am. It was time for the darkness to leave, and I was ready for it. The beauty of it was that it came gently, only as fast as I could handle, only as fast as I had the faith to believe that, with God's help, I could overcome it.

Every new webinar Felice offered I signed up for. Each class always had one more song or mantra, one more meditation, one more tidbit of information that I needed just at that time to help me continue and progress on my healing journey. I learned again how completely God is involved in the details of our lives, how He brings people into our lives just at the time that we need it. I learned in my heart, *and not just my mind*, that I am strong, that I am valued by the One who matters most, that I have a divine purpose to help heal all my brothers and sisters.

I stand up straighter and taller now. I look younger. I am healthier and fitter. I am happier. I love people more. I am gaining a greater ability to forgive myself and others, no matter how grave or serious the offense. All of it is covered by the Savior's Atonement, and I have learned that on a deep, personal level during my daily sadhana. I have learned that He has never left me, that I can give Him all my pain and He can heal me, no matter how deep the pain or the wound. I knew these things on an intellectual level before, but now I know them deep in my heart because I have felt them. Kundalini Yoga and Meditation has awakened my true self from a deep sleep. I now feel truly alive. I know Kundalini Yoga and Meditation can change the world because it has forever changed me.

Weird But Amazingly Effective | Breynn

I have no idea why I decided to start meditating. I came across Felice's website through *The Gift of Giving Life* blog, which I found through another friend's blog. A round about way to get there, I know. I really was feeling out of touch with my life and needed some way to release the pressure that was building. I decided to give meditation a try even though it sounded weird to me. I am glad I did.

I have been meditating for about seventy days at the time of this writing. The first thing I noticed that changed was some of my habits, particularly my nail-biting habit. I haven't bit my nails since about the second week, when I started doing the meditation for releasing addictions. It feels great. I have tried to stop so many times. I am thirty-four, and I have bit my nails since forever. My mom tried to get me to stop when I was little. As an adult I have tried everything I can think of to quit—yucky nail polish, self-determination, pretty nail polish, anything else that promised to work. But nothing did. So when I started meditation and soon after was able to stop biting my nails, I was amazed.

Some other things I have noticed that have changed in my life are things that I have wanted to change or implement for a long time but have never had the ability to really make them work. I have been studying my scriptures every morning. I have always been good at reading everyday, but I had gotten into the habit of reading two verses or so before bed. Not so much studying, but more or less not wanting to give up what I knew could be good for me. Now I have been studying every morning. It has been nice. I am enjoying it more too. I hope to just get better and better the more I read.

I have also started reading the Book of Mormon with my kids every morning. We have talked about doing this for a while, but I have just never had the energy to really pull it off. We have been reading for about three weeks or so now. It's just a little bit—some days a few verses, some days more. But the kids are enjoying it and asking good questions. We have also been doing scripture lessons at night before we read books. The kids are actually learning a lot about the teachings of the scriptures and LDS church history. They are very tuned into the lessons we are learning. It is nice to see them understanding the church and the gospel.

I have noticed that my dishes are getting done so much more easily now. I used to have a pile of dishes left for me after the kids were put to sleep. It was really depressing to be tired after getting them to sleep and realize that I had a mountain of dishes to do. I have been getting dishes done right after dinner now. It hasn't been hard or a huge change or anything that I have felt. I just have gotten them done. We haven't been turning on the TV at nights as much anymore. Not that I have stressed about it or anything, it just hasn't been turned on. Positive changes.

One big thing for me was watching late-night TV. I had a love/hate relationship with late-night TV. At night, I felt pulled to just sit and veg in front of the TV. I needed my "me time." During the day when I was very conscious, I realized that I really hated the effects that came from watching TV at night. I hated how tired I was. I also hated the shows I was watching. They left me with bad feelings and with bad images in my mind. Other shows were just not morally good. During the day I could tell this practice was not good, but at night I just couldn't stop. But I have finally stopped. I haven't watched late-night TV for a while now. Occasionally I will watch something small, but it is always uplifting and usually short. I don't feel the same pull anymore to the TV. I have been going to bed instead. Sometimes I will read for a bit first, but it feels great to go to bed now. I feel so much better.

After writing this all out, I can see there have been many things that have changed in my life. The only thing that I have really made myself do daily is meditate. I really do make sure that I do that. The rest has just fallen into place more or less. It is all stuff that I have been wanting to change or implement for a long time. None of these things were new goals for me, but they have all started working in my life after I began my daily meditation.

Interestingly, none of these things were my top priorities for why I started to meditate. I have three things that are incredibly important to me that I need divine help with. Three things that I know I cannot do on my own. None of these three things have been changed (that I can see right now). Maybe things are changing and I just can't see it yet. It would be easy to look at those three things and not see any change and decide that meditation just isn't helping. But I can't ignore all of the other things that have been changed so far. The three things I am still waiting on are big—like really big. Maybe they will just take time, or maybe some prep work needs to be done first before they can change. I don't know really. But I have seen too many results from meditating to quit now. I am really enjoying it. To be honest, I still find meditation a little weird, but I also find it amazingly effective.

Interference

The light shineth in darkness, and the darkness comprehendeth it not.
—John 1:5

Ever since Adam and Eve were cast out of the Garden of Eden and were separated from God, humans have lived in a world of opposites. Sometimes when people begin to meditate, they experience an opposition response, or what some people call *interference*. Interference is basically the darkness in and around you that is having a hissy fit about all the light you are adding. Your subconscious is also programmed to resist change, regardless of its value, and the devil and his angels don't want people to clean out their minds, commune with God, or practice or teach any science that can lead to becoming more like God.

Interference can manifest in unique ways. I won't give you any examples, because I don't want them to become suggestions. The important thing to remember is that if anything strange starts to happen, don't stop. Keep meditating, and cast out the scorner and his minions.

From the beginning, Satan threatened to do everything he could to possess our bodies, and he's following through. The reality is that dark spirits can access our bodies any time we sin or invite them in through dark emotions, like hate, anger, and unrighteous judgment. These emotions, even though they may be buried in the subconscious, create an emotional back door through which these entities can enter. Often these dark spirits work very subtly to avoid detection (sometimes for years), and at other times, though less frequently, they use a lot of dramatic flare and scare tactics to prevent forward motion. Even when we are doing what is right, Satan may try to attack, as Elder Jeffrey R. Holland reminds us. He explains that opposition turns up almost anyplace something good has happened or is about to happen. He reminds us of two examples of the adversary trying to stop righteousness from progressing:

> Joseph said he had scarcely begun his prayer when he felt a power of astonishing influence come over him. Thick darkness, as he described it, gathered around him and seemed bent on his utter destruction. But he exerted all his powers to call upon

God to deliver him out of the power of this enemy, and as he did so a pillar of light brighter than the noonday sun descended gradually until it rested upon him. At the very moment of the light's appearance, he found himself delivered from the destructive power that had held him bound. What then followed is the greatest epiphany since the events surrounding the crucifixion, resurrection, and ascension of Christ in the meridian of time. The Father and the Son appeared to Joseph Smith, and the dispensation of the fulness of times had begun. (See JS—H 1:15–20.)[12]

Thankfully this darkness didn't send Joseph running or stop his quest for truth. Joseph's example shows us what to do when Satan shows up: Hold stronger to the light. Satan also attempted to interfere with righteous progress after Moses had a face-to-face conversation with God and the Glory of God was upon Moses. Though it seems ridiculous that Satan tried to tempt Moses after such a spiritual high, Satan's pattern is to constantly oppose the light. If he can't stop you from beginning, he may show up at the end of a spiritual high, as he did to Moses, saying, "Worship me" (Moses 1:12).

Moses of course didn't buy it, and he dismissed the devil (Moses 1:16). But Satan only became more nasty, and for a brief moment when Moses began to fear, he "saw the bitterness of hell" (Moses 1:20), which is instructive about the affects of fear. When Moses finally called upon God, he was able to pull himself together. Then, in the name of the Savior—those were the the magic words—Moses commanded Satan to depart (Moses 1:21).[13] Satan left, and Moses had another amazing vision wherein he beheld God, and God gave him the power to command the waters (Moses 1:25), which as you may know came in handy later on in Moses's life.

May these examples give you hope and also help you stay strong. Elder Holland encourages, "After you have gotten the message, . . . go forward. Don't fear, don't vacillate, don't quibble, don't whine."[14]

Kundalini Yoga and Meditation might be new or strange to you, but many of the Lord's mysteries might be considered strange to outsiders. We can follow the example of Jesus Christ, who always did the will of His father, regardless of how unusual the instructions. For example, Jesus never questioned His divine intuition to heal by spitting in a blind man's eyes (Mark 8:23) or by sticking His fingers in a deaf man's ears (Mark 7:33).

Trust in God. Trust the feelings of the Spirit as you read this book. Forty or one thousand days from now, keep trusting those feelings. Kundalini Yoga and Meditation has been the answer to the prayers of many worthy and active members of The Church of Jesus Christ of Latter-day Saints. As Elder Holland says, "Stay the course and see the beauty of life unfold for you."[15]

---

12 Jeffrey R. Holland, "Cast Not Away Therefore Your Confidence" (devotional, Brigham Young University, Provo, UT, March 2, 1999), accessed March 21, 2014, http://speeches.byu.edu/?act=viewitem&id=795.
13 The scriptures and the temple ordinances are full of examples of how to cast out devils. Other resources are listed in the resource section at the end of this book.
14 Holland "Cast Not Away Therefore Your Confidence."
15 Ibid.

I Asked Them To Leave | Chelsea Proctor

I don't mean to focus on the dark side, but I think it is worth sharing. A week ago I was going strong with my meditation. The problem was I started feeling miserable and guilty but couldn't remember what it was that I had done wrong because there wasn't anything to merit those feelings. When I'd meditate, I'd started feeling like there was someone else there and I didn't feel safe. One night I went to bed without meditating but couldn't sleep, so I got up and did my meditation. I felt a bit better and went back to bed and decided to pray. I prayed about those feelings I was getting, and I felt that it was probably due to bad spirits making me feel the way I did. I then asked that if this was true that they leave. Almost immediately after asking that in the name of Jesus Christ, my mind cleared and my body relaxed dramatically so that I could finally go to sleep, which I did promptly after praying.

I am grateful for what I have learned so far with meditating while implementing the other very important things I need to do to grow closer to God. I've seen in my own life that Kundalini Yoga and Meditation and the gospel work together, and miracles can and will happen if put together. I love it!

Lifting The Fog | Robyn Allgood

Negative thought patterns are like cancer in the brain. After the death of my son, I didn't realize how many negative thoughts I had allowed to grow until I initiated the Forty-Day Meditation Challenge at the urging of my friend, Felice. And while I don't think that I held on to negative thoughts about my son's death, there were other kinds of negative thoughts that I had fed myself that needed healing.

Other than missing meditation while very sick and for a time after having my baby, I have been meditating for almost a year. I am letting go of the negative thoughts bit by bit and allowing the Atonement to heal my mind. I believe that is what meditation (among other spiritual endeavors like prayer, scripture study, and singing a hymn) does. It allows the Atonement in to heal. So the fog is lifting, little by little, and I thank heaven for it.

One thing I have noticed is that whenever I am nearing a milestone, I run into some form of opposition to complete the 40, 80, or 120 days. Once I realize that I am almost to the milestone, I realize why I have been doubting myself or feeling unmotivated. Satan does not want me to experience the change and transformation that come by sustained, diligent meditation. For me, this becomes the catalyst to see it through. It is after climbing the wall that I see the blessings.

USING THE TEACHINGS IN THIS BOOK

CONTENTS

SOME IMPORTANT THINGS TO KNOW BEFORE YOU BEGIN

※ Always begin every meditation session or yoga session by tuning in with the Adi Mantra: Ong Namo Guru Dev Namo. To tune in, chant this mantra three or more times. Tuning in connects you to your highest consciousness and to the golden chain of teachers (see page 190).

※ When practicing the yoga kriyas, it is essential that you follow the instructions, do the exercises in the indicated order, and do each exercise as instructed to the best of your ability.

※ You do not have to do the exercises for the full times listed. Many of the times listed are for advanced students; even just a minute of each exercise will be sufficient to receive the desired benefits from the kriya. If you wish to do less time, usually it is best to decrease times by the same percentage.

※ It is very important that you never do more than the recommended time limits, even if you feel strong or like the exercise.

※ One of the purposes of each posture is to serve as a self-diagnostic tool for the yogi. Learn to listen to your body as you move through the exercises.

※ It is recommended to warm up the physical body before doing a Kundalini Yoga kriya or meditation. A good pranayam may also be used as a warm up.

※ In the absence of other instruction:

- All breathing is through the nose and is long, slow, and deep. Jalandhara Bandh (Neck Lock) should be applied at all times. (See page 198 for an explanation of the Bandhs.)

- Close the eyes, and focus on the Third Eye Point.

- Apply Mul Bandh (Root Lock) at the end of each exercise and before you relax out of the posture. (See page 198.)

- Relax with a straight spine for a minute or two between exercises to assimilate the effects.

※ Although not required I recommend covering your head, preferably with natural white fabric. The head covering helps to concentrate the energy. Covering the head is also how humans have historically come into the presence of God. Any head covering will do, but some people choose to wear a turban. The turban is a symbolic self-crowning, reminding us that we are all kings and queens. A turban will also give you a nice cranial adjustment.

※ At the end of your practice, tune out with the "Long Time Sun" song and a long "Sat" and short "Naam" (see page 292).

Music Recommendations

Sometimes a meditation or yoga kriya will recommend that a certain mantra or song be played or chanted. You can find most of this music online on most sites where music is sold, but the mother source is http://www.spiritvoyage.com. For ease of searching, I have included some artist and album recommendations where appropriate.

Essential Oils

Essential oils can be a wonderful complement to your personal Kundalini Yoga and Meditation practice. Essential oils are natural aromatic compounds that are extracted from plants. They have been used for thousands of years as natural medicines, and many are referred to in the Bible. Some were even given to baby Jesus by the "wise men from the east." As you can read on page 6, these gifts had both practical and symbolic meanings.

Though used for millenia, essential oils fell out of use for a time and were "rediscovered" in the 1920s and 1930s. Medical science is starting to take notice, and the research is proving just how powerful essential oils are. Many people are embracing them as effective alternatives to pharmaceutical drugs and chemical cleaning products. In addition to being antibacterial, antiviral, and antifungal, essential oils hold hundreds of natural compounds that work with the body to relieve pain, improve digestion, decrease inflammation, calm anxiety and stress, and enhance connection with God and the divine within. Essential oils are very high vibration substances and can even act as a shield against dark and negative energies.

You should always follow the instructions on the bottle of oil. Most good-quality oils can be applied safely to adult skin. Some oils, like oregano and cinnamon, should always be diluted with a carrier oil when used topically. Please ensure you understand your oils before using them (see the Resources section at the end of this book for resources on essential oils).

The recommendations on the following pages regarding essential oils are merely suggestions and are not part of the teachings of Yogi Bhajan. They are my own recommendations. Remember that you are the expert on your own body. You may use any oils you choose or none at all. You can apply the oils where you feel you need them—over your heart, across your forehead, on the soles of your feet, and so forth. You can also have a very powerful experience by using the oils aromatically. Apply one to two drops of oil on your hands; rub your hands together, cup them around your nose and mouth, and then breathe in the oil. The aromatic molecules of the oil will enter the limbic system of the brain and trigger changes in your mood and emotional state, helping you release negative programming and be more open to receiving something new. You can also apply a small amount of oil to your hands and then practice Alternate Nostril Breathing (see page 276).

TUNING IN

Before beginning any meditation or kriya, we tune in. If you think of a radio, you have to tune in to the right station in order to hear your programming. This is true of meditation. The Adi Mantra is a sacred mantra that tunes us into the receive the highest spiritual frequency for meditation; it connects us energetically to the golden chain of teachers, and will protect and guide you in your practice.

The Adi Mantra is: ONG NAMO GURU DEV NAMO (see page 89 for translation).

Come sitting in easy pose with your hands in prayer mudra and chant the mantra three times.

I also recommend chanting the mangala charn mantra (AAD GURAY NAMEH) three times (see page 89) for protection after tuning in and before you practice yoga and meditation. However, this step is optional.

Videos demonstrating how to tune in can be found on at youtube.com/treeoflifekundalini

POSTURES

Kundalini Yoga is a science of angles and triangles. Angles produce leverage. For example, a very skinny rod may move a large rock if placed at an angle and used as a lever. Every angle created with the body has a corresponding energetic effect. For instance, lifting the legs thirty degrees affects the Navel Point. Lifting the arms sixty degrees affects the heart and lungs.[1]

While it is important to be precise about angles and posture, there is no universal perfect. Though we have done our best to represent the ideal postures in this book, each person is unique; if an individual can only lean in the correct direction, he or she will receive all the benefits of a kriya. With practice, many postures will feel more natural. Sometimes what is easy one week is not the next week as we confront stiffness in our minds and egos.

Each asana, or posture, in a kriya is

- an exercise that isolates muscle groups;

- a meditation that connects mind and body;

- a connection to energy flow, opening energy channels; and

- a self-diagnostic tool for the yogi, providing signals of discomfort, pleasure, and pain.

This section outlines some frequently used postures as well as postures that may be used as warm-ups or on their own.

---

1 Yogi Bhajan, *KRI International Teacher Training Manual, Level 1*, 4th ed. (Santa Cruz, NM: Kundalini Research Institute, 2007), 102.

Easy Pose is the most basic of the sitting postures. To get into this position, bend the knees and cross the legs underneath each other. Straighten the spine. If this pose is difficult for you, you may try elevating your hips by sitting on a firm meditation pillow.

Lotus Pose Very few exercises and meditations require Lotus Pose, but it is recognized as one of the best asanas for deep meditation. To get into this position, bend the left leg so the left heel comes to the groin. Lift the left foot onto the upper right thigh. Bend the right leg so that the right foot goes over the left thigh as close to the abdomen as possible. (The legs may also be reversed.) Straighten the spine. In this position you will feel locked in place.

Half Lotus Pose For those who can't do full Lotus Pose, Half Lotus Pose is an alternative. In this pose, only one leg is pulled up onto the thigh. The other leg remains on the ground underneath the opposite thigh.

Rock Pose To achieve Rock Pose, start by kneeling on both heels, with the tops of the feet flat on the ground. The heels are under the sitting bones. It is said the whosoever masters this pose can "digest rocks." Rock Pose and Easy Pose may be used interchangeably if one is more comfortable for you.

Sitting in a chair with a straight spine or with feet flat on the floor is also an option for those who are unable to sit in any of the other sitting positions.

The benefits of this exercise are numerous. It balances the emotions as well as the hormones. It releases fear and anger and helps to open the heart. It massages internal organs and is even said to take wrinkles out of the skin. When practiced for 3 minutes, it is a complete kriya.

Cat-Cow Pose For this pose, come to all fours, with the hands underneath the shoulders and the knees under the hips, hip-width apart. Point the fingertips forward. Inhale and let the belly drop as you open the heart and lift the neck up. Lift the head and chin, and stretch the tailbone back, creating an arch in the spine that resembles a sagging cow. Exhale and curl the back, pulling the navel toward the spine and tucking the chin and tailbone under. This move will create a rounded spine and is the "cat" part of the movement. The navel is the center point of the movement.

The benefits of this pose are similar to Cat-Cow Pose.

Spinal Flexes Sit in Easy Pose. Hold the shins or the knees. Inhale and arch the spine, opening the heart, pulling the shoulder blades together, and using arm strength to increase the stretch.

Exhale and let the spine roll back, opening wide the space between the shoulder blades and dropping the chin to the chest. Generally, the head stays level and the neck does not arch with the movement of the spine.

This exercise works on the kidneys and liver, releases fear and anger, and helps the body relax and unwind.

Pelvic Circles/Sufi Grind Pose Begin in Easy Pose with the hands on the knees, and move the upper body in a circle as if you were stirring the bowl of the pelvis with the spoon of the spine. As you inhale, moving forward around and around, the heart opens and the shoulder blades come toward each other. As you exhale back and around, the back opens and the shoulder blades expand. After 1–2 minutes, reverse the direction.

Generally, 3 minutes is a good time length for this exercise. By the end of 3 minutes all the glandular secretions released will have spread throughout the body, and you will feel great.

Ego Eradicator Sit in Easy Pose. Raise the arms to a sixty-degree angle. Curl the fingertips onto the pads at the base of the fingers, and plug the thumbs into the sky. Close the eyes. Concentrate at the Third Eye Point, and do Breath of Fire (see page 278).

To end, inhale and touch the thumb tips together overhead, hold the breath, extend the fingertips toward the sky and apply Mul Bandh (Root Lock). Then exhale, relax, and sweep the arms down.

One of the benefits of this pose is that it raises the sexual energy to the Heart Center.

Frog Pose Squat down so the buttocks are on the heels. The heels should be touching and off the ground. Put the fingertips on the ground between the knees. Keep the head up. Inhale, straighten the legs up, bring the head down, and keep the fingers on the ground. Exhale, squat back down, and bring the head up and the face forward. The inhale and exhale should be strong.

This exercise engages the life nerve, sometimes called the sex nerve, which runs down the inside of the leg. The life nerve is where your creative energy lies. This exercise can remove creative blocks, increase potency, and transform sexual energy.

Life-Nerve Stretch Begin by sitting, with the legs stretched out in front or spread wide. If possible, grab the toes in finger lock (the index and middle fingers pull the toe, and the thumb presses the nail of the toe). Otherwise, rest the fingers on the shins. Exhale and bend forward from the navel, lengthening. Inhale and use the legs to push up. The head follows last. This exercise can also be done from side to side with the body alternately folding over each leg on the exhale.

Corpse Pose Usually at the end of every Kundalini Yoga set, there is a layout in this pose. This is one of the most important poses because it allows the body to integrate all the energy it has awakened and all the changes that have occurred. This is the time to completely relax and let go of the breathing, the focus, and the body. Never cross the ankles. Arms are by the sides with the palms face up.

BANDHS (BODY LOCKS)

The purpose of Kundalini Yoga is to allow and direct the flow of life-giving energy through the body and the Aura, allowing us to access our divine qualities and powers. To help move and direct energy, we use *bandhs*, which are body locks (or seals). The bandhs allow the energy to be accumulated, deepened, or sealed into the body as part of the process of transformation.[1]

Mul Bandh (Root Lock)

The Root Lock is like a hydraulic lock at the base of the spine, directing excess sexual energy into creativity and bodily repair. This lock will also correct a lack of sexual vitality. The key function is to blend the *prana* and *apana* (eliminating force) at the Navel Point. Mul Bandh redirects the apana from its normal course downward. When the prana and apana meet and blend, the two opposing forces cause an inner heat. This heat creates the power to open the entrance to the shushmana so that the energy can rise and the process of transformation can begin. This bandh is frequently used at the end of an exercise to seal its effects.

To apply this lock: Apply the following three actions in a smooth motion: Contract the anal muscles upward and inward. Then contract the sex organs with an upward drawing motion, as if you were stopping the the flow of urination. Finally, contract the lower-abdomen muscles as you pull the Navel Point inward and upward toward the spine. This lock can be applied with the breath held in or out.

Uddiyanna Bandh (Diaphragm Lock)

The name of Uddiyanna Bandh comes from the Sanskrit word meaning "to fly up." The diaphragm is a physical, muscular barrier but also an energetic barrier. The functions that occur below the diaphragm are unconscious and reactive; the functions above the diaphragm are conscious and more flexible. This lock crosses the midbody barrier, integrating the unconscious and conscious qualities, and facilitates the pranic flow from the lower to the upper triangle through the central channel (*shushmana*). This lock also gently massages the heart and the intestines. Never apply this lock when the stomach is full.

To apply this lock: Fully exhale the breath. Pull the entire abdominal region, especially the area above the Navel Point, upward and back toward the spine, lifting the diaphragm as far into the thoracic cavity as possible. The navel itself does not contract, though it is pulled

---

1 All of the content in this section is from Yogi Bhajan, *The Aquarian Teacher: KRI International Kundalini Yoga Teacher Training Level I Yoga Manual* (Santa Cruz, NM: Kundalini Research Institute, 2007), 107–108.

upward from above. Lift the chest. Apply for **10–60 seconds**, depending on how long you can hold with a mood of calmness. Exhale gently without lifting the chin or releasing Jalandhar Bandh (Neck Lock).

Jalandhar Bandh (Neck Lock)

This is a very subtle lock and is an essential part of sitting with a straight spine and should be applied to all meditations unless otherwise specified. This subtle lock directs the flow of of pranic energy into the central channel past the neck and into the cranial area (rather than somewhere else, which could cause dizziness). It calms the heart, allows the energy to flow, and allows for an increase in connectedness between the glands.

To apply this lock: Sit comfortably, with the spine straight. Lift the chest and the sternum. Gently stretch the back of the neck by pulling the chin toward the back of the neck. Keep the head level; it should not tilt in any direction. Relax the neck, throat, face, and brow.

Maha Bandh (Great Lock)

Maha Bandh involves simultaneously applying the three locks (Mul Bandh, Uddiyanna Bandh, and Jalandhar Bandh). The perfection of this lock rejuvenates and harmonizes the glands, nerves, and chakras. Applying this lock is also said to cure many ailments, including sexual dysfunction, blood pressure issues, menstrual cramps, poor circulation, irregularity, wet dreams, and excessive preoccupation with fantasy. Maha Bandh is also said to increase longevity.

MUDRAS (SEALS)

A mudra is a position of the hands that locks (seals) and guides energy flow and reflexes in the brain. The hands are an energy map of our consciousness and health. Each area of the hand connects to a certain part of the body or brain, representing different emotions and behaviors.

The most commonly practiced way to seal a mudra is to touch the tip of the thumb (the fleshy part, not the nail) to each of the fingertips. Exert enough pressure to feel the flow of energy but not enough to whiten the fingertips.

Prayer Pose In Prayer Pose, the palms of the hands are flat and pressed together to neutralize the male and female sides of the body. Always use Prayer Pose to center yourself with the Adi Mantra before starting a kriya.

Gyan Mudra: Seal of Knowledge To form Gyan Mudra, place the tip of the index finger on the tip of the thumb. The energy of the index finger is associated with Jupiter, representing expansion. This seal is one of the most commonly used mudras. It gives receptivity and calmness. This seal stimulates knowledge, wisdom, and the power to compute.

Shuni Mudra: Seal of Patience To form Shuni Mudra, place the tip of the middle finger on the tip of the thumb. The middle finger is associated with the energy of Saturn, which represents the taskmaster, the law of karma, and the responsibility and courage to hold to duty. This mudra is said to give patience, discernment, and commitment.

Surya or Ravi Mudra: Seal of the Sun, Seal of Life
Surya or Ravi Mudra is formed by placing the tip of the ring finger on the tip of the thumb. The ring finger represents the power of the Sun and Uranus. The Sun represents energy, health, and sexuality. Uranus symbolizes nervous system strength, intuition, and change. Practicing this mudra gives revitalizing energy, nervous system strength, good health, and the power to win.

Bhuddi Mudra: Seal of Mental Clarity To form Buddhi Mudra, place the tip of the pinkie finger on the tip of the thumb. The pinkie finger is associated with Mercury, which symbolizes quickness and the mental power of communication. Practicing this mudra opens the capacity to communicate clearly and intuitively. This mudra also stimulates psychic development.

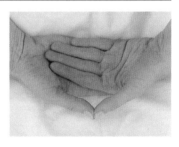

Bhudda Mudra To form Bhudda Mudra, rest the hands face up in the lap, with the thumb tips touching. For men, the right palm is on top. For women, the left palm is on top.

Christ Mudra In Christ Mudra, the index and middle fingers are extended, and the thumb locks down the ring and pinkie finger.

Venus Lock is used frequently in exercises. This mudra connects the positive and negative sides of the Venus Mound—the fleshy area at the base of the thumb—to the thumb on each hand.

For men, place the palms facing each other. Interlace the fingers, with the left pinkie finger on the bottom. Put the left thumb tip just above the base of the thumb on the webbing between the thumb and index finger of the right hand. Press the tip of the right thumb against the fleshy mound at the base of the left thumb. For women, reverse the finger sequence, with the right pinkie finger on the bottom.

The thumbs represent the ego. The Venus Mound is associated with the planet Venus and the energy of sensuality and sexuality. This mudra channels the sexual energy and promotes glandular balance. This mudra also brings the ability to concentrate easily if you rest the hands in your lap while in a meditative posture.

YOGA KRIYAS

Some people become confused about the difference between a yoga kriya and a meditation. The word *kriya* means "complete"—or an action that leads to completeness. A yoga kriya is a set of exercises taught in a particular order that have a specific energetic outcome. Some yoga kriyas work on all the systems in the body, giving you a great overall tune-up. Others have more specific outcomes and may not work all the body systems. This is why it is helpful to do warm-ups.

Some people will call a yoga set a kriya, for short. Some meditations have the word kriya in the name, but these meditations are not necessarily yoga sets.

To maintain clarity, I have tried to use the words *yoga kriya* when talking about a yoga set (versus a meditation). However, I will now contradict what I just said and tell you that the lines are sometimes blurry—a few kriyas qualify as both a yoga kriya and a meditation (e.g., Sat Kriya), and many yoga kriyas have meditations embedded within them. Also, each asana (posture) is in itself a meditation.

It is best to do a yoga kriya before you meditate, because the yoga and its energetic effects prepare the body and mind for even deeper meditation.

Awakening to Your Ten Bodies

TIME: **20–48 MINUTES**

1 Stretch Pose: Lie on the back, with the arms at the sides. Raise the head and the legs six inches. Also raise the hands six inches, with the palms over the hips and slightly facing each other to build energy across the Navel Point. Point the toes, keep the eyes focused on the tips of the toes, and practice Breath of Fire for **1–3 minutes**.

2 Nose to Knees: Bring the knees to the chest, with the arms wrapped around the knees. Tuck the nose between the knees, and practice Breath of Fire for **1–3 minutes**.

3 Ego Eradicator: Sit in Easy Pose. Raise the arms to a sixty-degree angle. Curl the fingertips onto the pads at the base of the fingers. Plug the thumbs into the sky. With the eyes closed, concentrate above the head, and practice Breath of Fire for **1–3 minutes**. To end, inhale, and touch the thumb tips together overhead. Exhale and apply Mul Bandh. Inhale and relax.

4 Life-Nerve Stretch 1: Sit with the legs stretched wide apart, and raise the arms overhead. Inhale. Then exhale while stretching down and grabbing the toes of the left foot. Inhale while coming straight up. Then exhale while stretching down and grabbing the toes of the right foot. Continue for **1–3 minutes**.

5 Life-Nerve Stretch 2: Sit with the legs stretched wide apart. Hold onto the toes of both feet. Exhale while stretching down, bringing the forehead to the floor. Then inhale while coming straight up. Continue for **1–3 minutes**.

6 Spinal Flex (Camel Ride) 1: Sit in Easy Pose. Grab the front of the shins with both hands. Inhale. Flex the spine forward, and rock forward on the buttocks. Exhale. Flex the spine backward, and roll back on the buttocks. Keep the head level and the arms fairly straight and relaxed. Continue for **1–3 minutes**.

7 Spinal Flex (Camel Ride) 2: Sit on the heels. Place the hands flat on the thighs. Inhale while flexing the spine forward. Exhale while flexing backward. Focus at the Third Eye Point. Continue for **1–3 minutes**.

8 Spinal Twist: Sit on the heels, and grasp the shoulders with the fingers in front and the thumbs in back. Inhale and twist to the left; exhale and twist to the right. Keep the elbows high and parallel to the floor. (Do not reverse.) Continue for **1–3 minutes**.

9 Grasp the shoulders with the fingers in front and the thumbs in back. Inhale and raise the elbows so that the backs of the wrists touch behind the neck. Exhale and lower the elbows to shoulder height. Continue for **1–3 minutes**.

10 Arm Pumps: Interlace the fingers in Venus Lock (see page 203). Inhale and stretch the arms up over the head. Then exhale and bring the hands back to the lap. Continue for **1–3 minutes**.

11 Alternate Shoulder Shrugs: Sit in Easy Pose, with the hands resting on the knees. Inhale and raise the left shoulder. Exhale and raise the right shoulder as you lower the left shoulder. Then inhale and raise the left shoulder as you lower the right shoulder. Continue for **1 minute**. Then, reverse the breath so that you inhale while raising the right shoulder and lowering the left shoulder, and you exhale while raising the left shoulder and lowering the right shoulder. Continue for **1 minute**.

12 Shoulder Shrugs: Inhale and raise both shoulders. Exhale and lower the shoulders. Continue for **1 minute**.

13 Neck Turns: Sit in Easy Pose, with the hands on the knees. Inhale and twist the head to the left. Exhale and twist the neck to the right. Continue for **1 minute**. Then reverse the breath so that you inhale while twisting to the right and then exhale while twisting to the left. Continue for **1 minute**. Inhale deeply, concentrate at the Third Eye Point, and slowly exhale.

14 Frog Pose: Squat down so the buttocks are on the heels. The heels should touch and be off the ground. Put the fingertips on the ground between the knees. Keep the head up. Strongly inhale while straightening the legs, keeping the fingers on the ground. Strongly exhale and come back to squatting position, face forward. Continue this cycle **54 times**.

15 Relaxation: Deeply relax on the back.

The following meditation is recommended to follow this kriya.

Laya Yoga Meditation

Sit in Easy Pose, with the hands on the knees in Gyan Mudra (page 201) Chant "Ek Ong Kaar-(uh) Saa-Taa-Naa-Maa-(uh) Siri Wha-Uh Hay Guroo." On "Ek," pull the navel. On each "Uh," firmly lift the diaphragm. The "Uh" sound should be more of a powerful movement of the diaphragm than a purposeful projected sound. Relax the navel and the abdomen on "Hay Guroo." With the breath, visualize the sound spiralling up from the base of the spine to the top of the head in 3.5 circles. Continue for **11–31 minutes**.

MUSIC: During the relaxation after any kriya, I like to play the gong or a gong recording. Harijiwan Singh Khalsa has a great gong suite on his album *Resound*.

ESSENTIAL OIL RECOMMENDATIONS: Basil, Cypress, Frankincense, Grapefruit, Patchouli

Basic Spinal Energy Series

TIME: 26–36 MINUTES

Spinal flexes have a multistage reaction pattern that alters the strengths and proportions of alpha, theta, and delta waves.

1 Spinal Flex 1: Sit in Easy Pose, and grab the ankles with both hands. Deeply inhale and flex the spine forward, lifting the chest up. Exhale, flexing the spine backward. Keep the head level during this movement so it does not flop. Repeat **108 times**, and then inhale and **rest 1 minute**.

2 Spinal Flex 2: Sit on the heels, placing the hands flat on the thighs. Inhale and flex the spine forward. Exhale, flexing the spine backward. Mentally chant "Sat" on the inhale and "Nam" on the exhale. Repeat **108 times**, and **rest 2 minutes**.

3 Spinal Twist: Sit in Easy Pose, and firmly grasp the shoulders, placing the fingers in front and the thumbs in back. Inhale and twist to the left, and then exhale and twist to the right. Make the breaths long, deep, and rhythmic. Complete this pattern **26 times**, and then inhale and face forward. **Rest 1 minute**.

4 Bear Grip: In Easy Pose, lock the fingers in Bear Grip at the Heart Center. Move the elbow in an up-and-down, see-saw motion, breathing deeply with each lift. Complete this pattern **26 times**, and then inhale, exhale, and pull the Mul Bandh (Root Lock). **Relax for 30 seconds**.

5 Spinal Flex 3: Sit in Easy Pose, grasping the knees firmly. Keep the elbows straight, and begin to flex the upper spine. Inhale forward, and then exhale backward. Repeat **108 times**, and then **rest 1 minute**.

6 Shoulder Shrugs: Sit in Easy Pose. Lift both shoulders while inhaling, and then lower the shoulders while exhaling. Repeat this for less than **2 minutes**. At the end, keep the shoulders pressed up, inhale, and hold for 15 seconds. Relax the shoulders.

7 Neck Rolls: Sit in Easy Pose, with the spine straight. Slowly roll the neck clockwise **5 times** and then to the left **5 times**. Inhale and pull the neck straight.

8 Bear Grip: Lock the fingers in Bear Grip at the level of the throat. Inhale and apply Mul Bandh (Root Lock). Exhale and apply Mul Bandh. Then raise the hands above the top of the head. Inhale and apply Mul Bandh. Exhale and apply Mul Bandh. Complete this cycle **2 more times**.

9 Sat Kriya: Sit on the heels, raise the arms overhead, and bring the palms together. Interlace the fingers except for the index fingers, which point straight up. Men cross the right thumb over the left thumb; women cross the left thumb over the right thumb. Chant "Sat" while pulling the Navel Point in; chant "Naam" while relax the Navel Point. Continue this chant and motion with a powerful, steady rhythm for at least **3 minutes**. Then inhale. Apply Mul Bandh (Root Lock), squeezing the energy from the base of the spine to the top of the skull. Exhale, holding the breath out and applying all the locks. Inhale and relax.

7 Relax: On your back, completely relax for **15 minutes**.

Age is measured by the flexibility of the spine: to stay young, stay flexible. This series works systematically from the base of the spine to the top. All 26 vertebrae receive stimulation and all the chakras receive a burst of energy. This makes it a good series to do before meditation. Many people report greater mental clarity after regular practice of this kriya. A contributing factor is the increased circulation of the spinal fluid, which is crucially linked to having a good memory.

Beginners can reduce the 108 repetitions to 24 repetitions and extend the rest periods from 1 minute to 2 minutes.

ESSENTIAL OIL RECOMMENDATIONS: Cypress, Peppermint, Wild Orange, Lime

Exercises to Create a Disease-Free Body

TIME: **53 MINUTES**

This movement stimulates the nervous system, which ultimately is the base power. If the base power is well stimulated, human effectiveness increases.

1 Lie down flat on the back, with the legs straight and the heels touching. Place the hands under the neck, touching the skin. Move the hips vigorously left and right, up and down like a jumping bean. After **2.5 minutes**, begin Breath of Fire and continue the movement for **1 minute**.

2 Remain on the back, with the legs straight and the heels touching. Cross the hands over the Heart Center (the most neutral energy posture possible). Inhale through the nose, and raise the legs to ninety degrees. Exhale through the mouth while lowering the legs. Continue these leg lifts for **5 minutes**.

3 Keeping the hands in the same position, lift the legs to ninety degrees. Hold this position. Listen to Kulwant Singh's "Chatr Chakr Vartee" while inhaling through the nose and exhaling through the mouth. Continue for **2 minutes**. Hold the position, and sing along with the recording for an additional **3 minutes**. Sing from the rib cage. Sing from the heart.

4 Keeping the hands and legs in the same position, criss-cross the legs. Sing along with this movement for **7 minutes**.

5 Keeping the hands in the same position, lower the legs so they are resting on the ground. Alternately raise each leg to ninety degrees; while raising one leg, lower the other all the way to the ground. Keep the knees straight. Sing along with this movement for **4 minutes**.

This movement stimulates the lymph glands to get the poison out. It is a prayer. Move your hands to create a vacuum pressure to move the Kundalini Shakti up. Do it with sacredness.

6 Sit in Easy Pose. Raise the arms in the air, with the palms facing forward. Begin opening and closing the arms, criss-crossing them over the head. Keep the elbows straight. Sing along with this movement for **7 minutes**.

Then, continue the movement, but instead of singing, inhale through the nose and exhale through the mouth for **2 minutes**.

7 Sit in Easy Pose, with the hands on the shoulders. Twist left and right, moving from the hips. Vigorously move the rib cage. Inhale through the nose and exhale through the mouth for **2.5 minutes**. Then sing along with the motion for **1.5 minutes**.

This exercise can help relieve gas. If your knees don't obey you, you can use your hands to press your knees to your chest.

8 Lie on the back, bend the legs, and bring the knees to the chest. Extend the legs straight out, allowing the heels to touch the ground. When the feet touch the ground, bring the knees back to the chest. Continue the movement for **3 minutes**.

During this exercise, Yogi Bhajan played 5 minutes of Kulwant Singh's "Chatr Chakr Vartee" and then 3.5 minutes of Singh Kaur's "Beloved God" from the *Peace Lagoon* recording.

9 Relax every part of the body. Meditatively move through the body, relaxing each part. Remain relaxed and motionless, allowing the body to recuperate. Fly away from the body. Meditate on the heavens, beauty, and excellence. Don't move for any reason for **8.5 minutes**.

10 Remain on the back, and rotate the wrists and ankles for **2 minutes**.

11 Remain on the back, and raise the arms straight up to ninety degrees, with the fingers wide open. Relax the feet, resting them on the floor for 30 seconds. Move the arms in circles with no bend in the elbows for **1 minute**.

12 Relax.

"When your circulation is strong, disease doesn't like to visit you. This set moves your blood, lymph and prana. It activates the nervous system from the navel center, distributing energy so you can relax and live fear-free and full of health"

—Gurucharan Singh Khalsa, as qtd. in "Kriya—Exercises to Create a Disease-Free Body," accessed March 24, 2014, http://www.shaktakaur.com/kriyas/exercises_to_create_a_disease_free_body.htm).

MUSIC: Most of the music mentioned in this kriya is available on spiritvoyage.com. I also really like to play the song "Heal Me" by Nirinjin Kaur from the album *Adhara*.

ESSENTIAL OIL RECOMMENDATIONS: Patchouli, Eucalyptus, Grapefruit

Kriya for Elevation

TIME: **42 MINUTES**

This easy set of exercises is excellent as a tune-up. It systematically exercises the spine and aids in the circulation of prana to balance the chakras.

This exercise opens the lungs, brings the hemispheres of the brain to a state of calmness, and consolidates the magnetic field.

1 Ego Eradicator: Sit in Easy Pose. Raise the arms to a sixty-degree angle. Curl the fingertips onto the pads at the base of the fingers. Plug the thumbs into the sky. Close the eyes, concentrate above the head, and complete Breath of Fire for **1–3 minutes**. To end, inhale and touch the thumb tips together overhead. Exhale and apply Mul Bandh (Root Lock); inhale and relax.

This exercise stimulates and stretches the lower and mid spine.

2 Spinal Flex: Sit in Easy Pose, and grasp the shins with both hands. Inhale, flexing the spine forward and lifting the chest. Exhale, flexing the spine back and keeping the shoulders relaxed and the head straight. Continue with deep, rhythmic breaths for **1–3 minutes**. Then inhale, exhale, and relax.

This exercise stimulates and stretches the lower and mid spine.

3 Spinal Twist: Sit in Easy Pose. Grab the shoulders, with the thumbs in back and the fingers in front. Keep the elbows high, with the arms parallel to the ground. Inhale while twisting the head and torso to the left. Exhale while twisting to the right. Continue for **1–4 minutes**. To end, face straight forward, exhale, and relax.

This exercise stimulates the lower and upper spine.

4 Front Life-Nerve Stretch: Stretch both legs straight out in front. Grab the toes in Finger Lock (the index and middle fingers pull the toe, and the thumb presses the nail of the big toe). Exhale, lengthening the core of the spine by bending forward from the navel. The head follows last. Inhale and use the legs to push up. The head comes up last. Continue with deep, powerful breathing for **1–3 minutes**. Inhale and hold the breath briefly. Stay up and exhale completely, holding the breath out briefly. Inhale and relax.

This exercise helps with elimination, stretches the sciatic nerve, and brings circulation to the upper torso.

5 Modified Maha Mudra: Sit with the right heel tucked into the perineum and the left leg extended forward. Grasp the big toe of the left foot with both hands, applying pressure against the toenail. Pull the Jalandhar Bandh (Neck Lock). Exhale while bringing the elbows to the ground and lengthening the spine, bending forward from the navel to continue lengthening the spine. Bring the head to the knee. Keep the spine straight. Hold the position for **1–2 minutes** while practicing Breath of Fire. Inhale. Exhale and stretch the head and torso forward and down. Hold out the breath briefly. Inhale, **switch legs, and repeat** the exercise. Relax.

This exercise develops flexibility in the lower spine and sacrum and charges the magnetic field.

6 Life-Nerve Stretch: Spread the legs wide, grasping the toes in Finger Lock (see exercise 4). Inhale and stretch the spine straight, pulling back on the toes. Exhale, bend at the waist, and bring the head down to the left knee. Inhale while bringing the upper body back to the center position, and then exhale, bringing the head to the right knee. Continue with powerful breathing for **1–2 minutes**. Then inhale, rising to the center position, and exhale, bending forward from the waist and touching the forehead to the floor. Continue this up-and-down motion for **1 minute**. Then inhale, bringing the upper body back to the center position and stretching the spine straight. Exhale, bringing the forehead to the floor. Hold out the breath briefly as you stretch forward and down. Inhale and relax.

This exercise balances sexual energy and draws the prana to balance apana so that the Kundalini energy can circulate to the higher centers in the following exercises.

7 Cobra Pose: Lie on the stomach, with the palms flat on the floor under the shoulders. Bring the heels together, with the soles of the feet facing up. Inhale into Cobra Pose, arching the spine, vertebra by vertebra, from the neck to the base of the spine until the arms are straight. Begin Breathe of Fire, and continue for **1–3 minutes**. Then inhale, arching the spine to the maximum. Exhale and hold out the breath briefly; apply Mul Bandh (Root Lock). Inhale. Exhaling slowly, lower the arms and relax the spine, vertebra by vertebra, from the base of the spine to the top. Relax, lying on the stomach, with the chin in the floor and the arms by the sides.

This exercise balances the upper chakras and opens the hormonal gate to the higher brain centers.

8 Shoulder Shrugs: Sit in Easy Pose. Place the hands on the knees. Inhale and lift the shoulders up toward the ears. Exhale and drop the shoulders. Continue rhythmically shrugging the shoulders with the powerful breathing for **1–2 minutes**. Inhale. Exhale and relax.

9 Neck Rolls: Sit in Easy Pose. Begin rolling the neck clockwise in a circular motion, bringing the right ear toward the right shoulder, then the back of the head toward the back of the neck, the left ear toward the left shoulder, and the chin toward the chest. Keep the shoulders relaxed and motionless. Allow the to gently stretch as the head circles around. Continue for **1–2 minutes**, and then roll the neck in the opposite direction for **1–2 minutes**. Bring the head to a central position and relax.

Continued on following page. . .

Sat Kriya circulates the Kundalini energy through the cycle of the chakras, aids in digestion, and strengthens the nervous system.

10 Sat Kriya: Sit on the heels, with the arms overhead and the palms together. Interlace the fingers except for the index fingers, which point straight up. Men cross the right thumb over the left thumb; women cross the left thumb over the right thumb. Chant "Sat Naam" emphatically in a constant rhythm, about 8 times per 10 seconds. Chant the sound "Sat" from the navel point and solar plexus, and pull the navel all the way in and up. On "Naam," relax the navel. Continue for **3–7 minutes**, and then inhale and tightly squeeze the muscles from the buttocks all the way up the back, past the shoulders. Mentally allow the energy to flow through the top of the skull. Exhale. Inhale deeply. Exhale completely and apply Mul Bandh (Neck Lock), with the breath held out. Inhale and relax.

Deep relaxation allows you to enjoy and consciously integrate the mind/body changes that have been brought about while practicing this kriya. This step allows you to sense the extension of self through the magnetic field and the Aura and allows the physical body to deeply relax.

11 Relax: Relax in Easy Pose or on the back, with the arms at the sides and palms up.

ESSENTIAL OIL RECOMMENDATIONS: Sandalwood, Rose, Roman Chamomile

Kriya for the Fourth Chakra (Green Energy Series)

TIME: **52 MINUTES**

This set balances the Heart Center, which is the center of Christ consciousness. The Heart Center is also the true source of prosperity. This kriya balances the energies of giving and receiving and allows the person to attract opportunities. This kriya will also clear blocks around the heart.

1 Sit in Rock Pose. Inhale and flex the upper body forward. Mentally chant "Sat," focusing on the first chakra. Exhale and flex backward, mentally chanting "Naam" and focusing on the third chakra. Continue for **2 minutes**. To finish, inhale, apply Mul Bandh (Root Lock), and hold 10 seconds. Repeat ending 3 times.

2 Sit with the legs stretched out. With the hands beside the hips, push down, lifting the body momentarily off the floor before letting it drop again. Keep the spine straight. Continue this movement rapidly for **2 minutes**.

3 Squat in Crow Pose, with the spine straight. Clasp the hands, with the index fingers pointing straight out. Extend the arms at the level of Heart Center. With the eyes open, look into Infinity. Maintain with Breath of Fire for **2 minutes**. To finish, inhale and hold as long as possible while continuing to project from the Heart Center.

4 Run in place, bringing the knees above the hips and punching with alternating arms. Continue for **3 minutes**.

5 Sit in Kundalini Lotus Pose. Hold for **2 minutes** while practicing Breath of Fire. To finish, inhale and hold while drawing energy up the spine. Exhale and relax.

6 Sit on the left heel, and place the right foot on the left thigh. Cup the hands just below the Navel Point. Pull the diaphragm up, and chant "Ong So Hung" in a heart-centered, powerful way for **3 minutes**.

7 Sit in Easy Pose, with the eyes closed and the arms extended, palms up. Visualize energy arching over the head, flowing in through the left palm and out through the right palm. Continue with Breath of Fire for **2 minutes**. To finish, inhale and hold as long as possible, continuing to feel the flow of energy. Exhale and relax.

8 Sit in Easy Pose, and place the hands in Venus Lock behind the neck. Inhale and bring the forehead to the floor, mentally chanting "Sat." Exhale and raise the upper body while mentally chanting "Naam." Continue for **2 minutes**.

9 Sit in Easy Pose, with the arms extended. While inhaling, raise the right arm to sixty degrees; exhale and lower the arm to horizontal. Inhale and raise the left arm to sixty degrees; exhale and lower the arm to horizontal. Move rapidly for **2 minutes**. To finish, bring the arms together at Brow Level. Inhale and hold the breath while projecting from the Third Eye into Infinity. Exhale and relax.

10 Sit in Easy Pose, with the hands in Venus Lock about four inches above the seventh chakra. With the eyes closed, look out of this chakra. Hold with Breath of Fire for **2 minutes**.

10a Extend the index fingers, and breathe long and deep for **2 minutes**.

10b Open the hands so that only the tips of the fingers and thumbs touch. Switch back to Breath of Fire for **2 minutes**. To finish, inhale and hold, projecting up and out. Exhale and relax.

11 Sit in Easy Pose, with the palms forward and raised to shoulder level. Visualize green energy, and chant "Haree Haree Haree Har" from the heart, feeling the navel pulse as you chant. Continue for **11 minutes**. To finish, inhale, exhale, and relax.

12 Meditate in Gyan Mudra. Feel loved. Know that opportunities are being attracted to you. Radiate love for all.

MUSIC: There is as yet no music for the Haree Har mantra exactly as it is in this kriya. So you must use the sound of your own voice. You can find a good version of "Ong So Hung" on Guru Singh's album *The Guru Singh Experience*.

ESSENTIAL OIL RECOMMENDATIONS: Rose, Geranium, Melissa, Ylang Ylang, Basil

Kriya for Relaxation and Releasing Fear

TIME: 65 MINUTES

This exercise benefits the kidneys and the liver.

1 From a standing position, bend forward from the waist, keeping the back parallel to the ground. Reach behind to hold onto the calves or wherever you can reach to maintain balance. Begin to flex the spine as you would in the Cat-Cow Pose. Inhale and flex the spine downward, with the neck arched up. Exhale and flex the spine upward, bringing the chin to the chest. Keep the legs straight. Continue the movement, maintaining rhythmic coordination with the breath, for **7 minutes**.

This exercise rejuvenates the spleen and the liver. As the liver releases toxins, you may feel nauseated.

2 Remain standing, and place the hands on the hips. Rotate the torso from the waist in large circles. Continue this motion rapidly and with power for **9 minutes**.

This movement exercises the kidneys. The neck must move to allow blood to flow to the brain.

3 Sitting in Easy Pose, make fists and place them in front of you as if grasping a steering wheel, with the elbows bent and the arms parallel to the floor. Twist the torso powerfully from side to side, twisting as far as possible in each direction. Allow the neck to follow this movement; consciously keep the elbows up. Continue for **4 minutes**.

This exercise prevents arthritis in the fingers. If you already have arthritis, this exercise will help reduce the arthritis.

4 Sitting in Easy Pose, extend the arms up at a sixty-degree angle. The palms face up, with the fingers straight and the thumbs extended. Close the hands rapidly, continuing to keep the fingers straight, bringing the tips of the fingers to the base of the palms. Then quickly open the hands again. Continue rapidly opening and closing the hands for **2 minutes**.

This exercise removes tension from the neck and purifies the blood. Your fears will leave you as you powerfully project outward on the exhale.

5 In Easy Pose, extend the arms out to the sides, parallel to the ground. Make fists with the hands, touching the thumbs to the base of the pinkie fingers. Inhale through the mouth, and bend the elbows, bringing the fists to the front of the body at the shoulders. Exhale through the mouth, returning the arms to the extended position. Moving rapidly and powerfully, coordinate the motion and breathing for **6 minutes**.

This exercise adjusts the muscles under the breasts. If this area is tight, you will feel tense. This exercise will relieve the tightness and tension.

6 Sitting in Easy Pose, assume the same hand position as in exercise 5, with the palms of the fists facing down. Stretch the arms straight out in front of the body. Rotate the fists in circles—the left fist counterclockwise, the right fist clockwise. The fists should be tight and held at the level of the heart, with the elbows straight. Move the shoulder blades and the muscles underneath the shoulders. Continue with power for **2 minutes**.

7 Sit in Crow Pose (a crouching position, with the knees drawn into the chest and the soles of the feet flat on the floor; if necessary, the heels may rest on a rolled mat or firm folded blanket as a prop). Keep the spine straight. Make fists, with the thumbs out. Place the thumbs at the neck to help with balance. Keeping the hands stationary, inhale and stand up. Exhale and lower back down to Crow Pose. Continue for **3 minutes**.

This exercise, Sitali Pranayam, is effective against anger and bad moods. If your mouth becomes bitter, that means you have bad breath (prana), but it is being cleaned out as you complete this pranayam. "Dukh Bhanjan" was sung in promise of the place where many were healed by a sip and dip in the nectar tank at the Golden Temple.

8 Sit in Easy Pose, and place the hands on the knees. Keep the spine straight. Curl the tongue, and protrude it slightly past the lips. Inhale deeply and smoothly through the tongue and mouth. Exhale through the nose. Make the breaths long and heavy. After **4–5 minutes**, play "Dukh Bhanjan" if available and meditate on the healing vibrations of the Golden Temple and the Sound Current of the shabd. Continue for **2 minutes**, breathing in rhythm with the music.

9 Continue listening to the music. Sit in Easy Pose and raise the arms, curving them upward. Close the eyes, and move rhythmically to the music. Stop thinking and move with the beat. If you can bring your body into exact rhythm with the music, you can go into a state of ecstasy. Continue for **10 minutes**.

This exercise has been known to heal people from kidney and gall bladder stones.

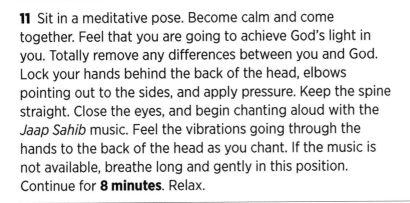

10 Sit on the heels in Rock Pose. Place the hands on the thighs. Listen to *Jaap Sahib* mantra. Bow the forehead to the floor to the Namastang rhythm, bowing 4 counts and resting 1 count with the music. Without the music, complete the movement in 10 beats, as follows: bow down on 1, sit up on 2, bow down on 3, sit up on 4, bow down on 5, sit up on 6, bow down on 7, sit up on 8, and stay up for beats 9 and 10. Continue for **8 minutes**.

11 Sit in a meditative pose. Become calm and come together. Feel that you are going to achieve God's light in you. Totally remove any differences between you and God. Lock your hands behind the back of the head, elbows pointing out to the sides, and apply pressure. Keep the spine straight. Close the eyes, and begin chanting aloud with the *Jaap Sahib* music. Feel the vibrations going through the hands to the back of the head as you chant. If the music is not available, breathe long and gently in this position. Continue for **8 minutes**. Relax.

MUSIC: In addition to the music mentioned in the kriya, I like to play any mantras that remove fear, such as "Chattr Chakkr Vartee." Nirinjan Kaur has a great version on her album *From Within*. I might also play the mantra "Aap Sahee Hoa" from her *Adhara* album.

ESSENTIAL OIL RECOMMENDATIONS: Rosemary, Cassia, Lavender, Myrrh

Kriya for Relieving Inner Anger

TIME: **29 MINUTES**

> "You think snoring is a funny thing. It's not. It will relax you right there."

1 Lie down flat on the back in a relaxed posture with arms at the sides, palms open and legs slightly apart. Pretend to snore for **1½ minutes**.

> This exercise balances anger. it puts pressure on the Navel Point in order to balance the entire system.

2 Still lying on the back, straighten the legs, point the toes and raise them both up to 6 inches. Hold for **2 minutes**.

3 Remaining in the posture, stick out the tongue and do Breath of Fire through the mouth for **1.5 minutes**.

4 Still on the back, lift the legs up to 90 degrees. Keep the arms on the ground by your sides. Begin to beat the ground with all the anger you can achieve. Beat hard and fast for **2.5 minutes**, keeping the arms stiff and straight. Get the anger out!

> "This is Bhajan (stone) Pranayam. It can make even a stone head think right."

5 Still on the back, bring the knees into the chest, and stick the tongue out. Inhale through the open mouth and exhale through the nose. Continue for **3 minutes**.

6 Sit in Celibate Pose, buttocks on the floor between the heels. Cross the arms over the chest and press them hard against the rib cage. Bend forward and touch the forehead to the floor as if you are bowing. For **2.5 minutes** move at a pace of approximately **30 bows per minute**, then for another **30 seconds** move as fast as you can.

"When the inverted anger becomes part of the body, the simple effect is that you have absolutely no relationship with your Self. . . . Inferiority complex or superiority complex are a cover up of inner anger. Manipulation and lying is part of inner anger. Not being self sustaining or having a foundation to work it out is an inner anger. Misbehavior, wrong calculation, self destruction, destroying the business, destroying the relationship is all inner anger. . . . On the other hand, anger comes from the place of the Agaan Granthi. It is the area of the heart, it is the blood, it is the circulation, it is the diaphragm, it is the heart pumping. . . . The whole life depends on it. So it is the center of the heart, it is the furnace. Either it can cook for you or it can burn down your house and there is nothing in between. That is the tragedy of it."

—YOGI BHAJAN (September 21, 1988)

7 Sitting with the legs straight out in front, begin to beat all parts of your body with open palms. Move fast for **2 minutes**.

8 Stand up. Bend forward, keeping the back parallel to the ground, and let the arms and hands hang loose. Remain in this posture and sing for **3 minutes**. (In class Yogi Bhajan played a recording of Guru Guru Wahe Guru, Guru Ram Das Guru.) This is called "forced circulation." If you get dizzy in this posture, sit down immediately.

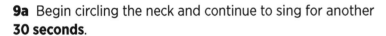

9 Continue singing and come into Cobra Pose. Lying on the stomach, place hands under the shoulders with palms flat. Elongate the spine, lift the chest and heart up, drop the shoulders, and stretch the head back. Straighten the arms. Continue for **1 Minute**.

9a Begin circling the neck and continue to sing for another **30 seconds**.

10 Still in Cobra Pose begin kicking the ground with alternate feet for **30 seconds**.

11 Sat Kriya in Easy Pose: Sit in Easy Pose and close the eyes. Stretch the arms overhead, keeping the elbows straight. Interlace the fingers with the Jupiter (index) fingers extended and pointing straight up. Squeeze the Navel Point in and up as you chant "Sat." Release as you chant "Naam." Continue **3 minutes**. To end: inhale and squeeze the muscles tightly from the buttocks all the way up the back. Mentally allow the energy to flow through the top of the skull. Exhale and relax.

12 Relaxation: Lie down and nap on your back for **5 minutes**. Yogi Bhajan played the gong.

MUSIC: Snatam Kaur has several beautiful versions of "Guru Guru Wahe Guru Guru Ram Das Guru."

ESSENTIAL OIL RECOMMENDATIONS: Thyme, Black Pepper, Cilantro

Kriya to Throw off Stress

TIME: **36 MINUTES**

This exercise adjusts the ovaries (or testes), stimulates the life-force energy, and releases stress.

1 Sit in Easy Pose, with the spine straight. Bring the hands up by the shoulders, with the palms forward and the fingers pointing upward. Touch the thumb and the index finger, and then touch the thumb and the ring finger. Continue rapidly touching the thumb with each of the two fingers. Keep the eyes open, and concentrate on the tip of the nose. The ideal speed for this action is 9 touches per second, but 3 touches per second is acceptable. After **5.5 minutes**, begin inhaling and exhaling powerfully through the mouth. Breathe through the mouth for **2 minutes**, and then complete Breath of Fire through the nose for **30 seconds**. Inhale deeply and relax.

This exercise stimulates and stretches the lower and mid spine.

2 Cross the hands over the Heart Center, with the left hand on top of the right hand. Close the eyes and breathe extremely deeply and slowly for **4 minutes**; feel the healing strength of the hands on the heart.

2a Put both hands on the forehead, feeling the healing effect of the hands. Concentrate on "I am, I am" as you listen to Nirinjan Kaur's "Bountiful, Blissful, and Beautiful" for **7 minutes**.

3 Put both hands on the Navel Point, and press with all your force. Breathe slowly and meditate deeply on Nirinjan Kaur's "Ong Namo, Guru Dev Namo" for **8 minutes**. Inhale deeply, open the eyes, and shake the hands.

This step changes the neurons in the brain.

4 Twist the wrists back and forth, keeping the fingers and thumbs spread open; continue for **2 minutes**.

Your total health will benefit by opening up your rib cage in this movement. It's a partnership between you and your shoulders, not just an up and down movement.

5 Place the hands on the shoulders, and sing along with Guru Shabad Singh's recording of "Pavan Pavan." Make the shoulders dance to the music. Dance to free the rib cage. Dance with style for **5 minutes**.

This self-massage will balance the calcium and magnesium in your body and reduce the effects of old age.

6 Use open palms to beat the inner thighs. Use the rhythm of "Punjabi Drums" to pace the movement; continue for **3.5 minutes**.

"All the strength of the Universe is within you. It cannot be found outside. Those who do not develop strength from inside cannot get it from outside either."

—YOGI BHAJAN

MUSIC: Jai Jagdeesh has a great version of "Pavan Pavan" on her album *Of Heaven and Earth*.

ESSENTIAL OIL RECOMMENDATIONS: Basil, Lavender, Ylang Ylang

Renew Your Nervous System and Build Stamina

TIME: **26 MINUTES**

This exercise can give you totally new nerves and stamina. It will break up blockages in the lungs. This exercise can also relax the body, remove muscle fatigue, and make you steady.

1 Sit in Easy Pose, with the spine straight. Bend the left elbow, and rest it close to the rib cage. Face the left palm upward, with the fingers pointing straight ahead. Make an O shape with the mouth, and breathe through the mouth in the following manner: Inhale in three strokes as you touch the floor on the right side with the palm of the right hand (touch or hit the floor once per stroke) and bring the right hand back toward the left palm. As the right palm touches the left palm, exhale in one stroke through the mouth. Time the motion of the right hand so that you touch the floor and return within the three strokes of the inhale. Exhale in one stroke as the right palm touches the left palm. Continue in this manner, breathing powerfully from the diaphragm, for **4 minutes**.

2 Close the eyes, and continue exercise 1, but move faster. Continue for **3.5 minutes**.

3 While inhaling and exhaling through the O-shaped mouth, move the arms in outward circles in front of the chest. The motion is similar to scooping water out of the lap, dashing it on the face, and circling the arms back to the lap. Move vigorously to open the chest and to exercise the muscles of the shoulder blades. Continue for **3.5 minutes**.

This exercise sends new serum to the brain and can help relieve depression.

4 Rest the right hand on the left hand at the center of the chest at about shoulder height. Face the palms down. Keep the hands touching as you rapidly move them four to six inches up and down. Breathe through the O-shaped mouth in time with the movement. Continue for **1.5 minutes**.

After opening the diaphragm in the preceding exercises, this dance process is necessary. This exercise is good for circulation.

5 Stand up and dance, shaking the entire body to the rhythmic beat of Bhangra music. Lift the arms in the air, and loosen the shoulders, spine, and hips. Break up the body blocks with rhythmic movement. Move vigorously and make yourself sweat. Continue for **11 minutes**.

6 Spread the legs shoulder-width apart, keeping the knees straight. Lean over so that the torso is parallel with the ground. Rest the hands on the knees to support the torso. Let the lower back stretch out, and allow it to open up. Continue for **1 minute**. Move directly to the next exercise.

7 Relax the arms, and allow the body to hang forward. Bounce slowly and gently, allowing the weight of the body to stretch the spine and the muscles in the back of the legs. Continue for **30 seconds**. Inhale and gently rise up straight.

8 To finish, move in a relaxed manner from one position to the other in the following way: Inhale as you relax forward. Exhale as you rise up straight. Continue inhaling as you relax forward and exhaling as you straighten. Repeat **5 times** total.

If a person's shoulders get tight, that person feels old and lifeless. You cannot be sick if you neither allow crystals to form in your feet nor allow your shoulders to get tight.

MUSIC: For dancing I recommend an album called *Kundalini Remix*, or remixes by DJ Krishan.

ESSENTIAL OIL RECOMMENDATIONS: Basil, Lemon, Peppermint, Wild Orange

Nabhi Kriya

TIME: **57 MINUTES**

Nabhi is the nerve plexus around the Navel Point. This exercise set gets the navel area in shape very quickly, but the effects reach far beyond a strong core. This kriya activates the power of the third chakra, which is the center of a person's identity, self-esteem, and willpower. This kriya can improve many kinds of mental illnesses because most mental illness results from a problem with the lower chakras.

The times indicated are for advanced students. Beginners should start with 3–5 minutes on the longer exercises.

This exercise benefits the lower digestive area.

1 Lie on the back. Inhale and lift the right leg to ninety degrees. Exhale and lower the leg. Repeat with the left leg. Continue the deep, powerful breathing and leg lifts for **10 minutes**. Move directly to the next exercise.

This exercise improves the upper digestive system and the solar plexus.

2 Inhale and lift both legs to ninety degrees. Extend the arms straight up, palms facing each other, for balance and energy. Exhale as you lower the legs. Continue for **5 minutes**.

This exercise eliminates gas and relaxes the heart.

3 Bring the knees to the chest, clasping them with the arms. Allow the head to relax back. Rest in this position for **5 minutes**.

This exercise charges the magnetic field and opens the Navel Center.

4 Begin in the same position as exercise 3. Inhale while opening the arms straight to the sides on the ground and extending the legs straight out to sixty degrees. Exhale and return to the starting position. Continue for **15 minutes**. Move directly to the next exercise.

This exercise sets the hips and the lower spine.

5 Bring the left knee to the chest, hold it there with both hands, rapidly raise the right leg to ninety degrees, and then lower the right leg. Inhale as the leg raises, and exhale as the leg lowers. Continue for **1 minute**. Switch legs and repeat for **1 minute**. **Repeat** the cycle one more time. Move directly to the next exercise.

This exercise benefits the spinal fluid and the Aura.

6 Stand up straight, with the arms overhead, hugging the ears. Press the fingers back so that the palms face the sky. Exhale as you bend forward and touch the ground (not shown), keeping the arms straight and hugging the ears. While exhaling, apply Mul Bandh (Root Lock). Then inhale deeply as you rise very slowly. Complete the front bends slowly for **2 minutes**, then complete the front bends rapidly for **1 minute**.

7 Completely relax or meditate for **10–15 minutes**.

MUSIC: I like to play music with a good rhythmic beat during the leg lifts. I prefer to use a mantra that also removes fear during this kriya. Such as "Rakhe Rakhan Har" by Singh Kaur album *Rakhe Rakhan Har* or Kulwant Singh's "Chttr Chkkr Vartee."

ESSENTIAL OIL RECOMMENDATIONS: Bergamot, Oregano, Ginger, Black Pepper, Peppermint

Wake-Up Sequence

The following is a recommended wake-up sequence after a deep relaxation session in corpse pose.

1 In corpse pose, become conscious of the breath. Inhale. Exhale. Wiggle the fingers and toes.

2 Make small circles with the wrists and ankles.

3 Stretch the arms over the head.

4 Bring the right knee to the chest, and then allow one knee to cross the body, keeping the shoulder blades on the ground. Inhale and twist. Exhale and release the leg. Repeat with the other leg.

5 Rub together the soles of the feet; rub together the palms of the hands.

6 Bring the knees to the chest, and rock from side to side. Then rock along the length of the spine (ensure that you are on a soft surface) until you come sitting back upright.

7 If you have finished your practice, you can Tune Out. Instructions for tuning out are on page 292.

MEDITATIONS

The purpose of meditation is to cleanse the subconscious mind and align the mind with the Infinite. Silence awakens us to what is in the subconscious mind and allows it to begin to dump. Then, to change the deepest subconscious, a seed is needed. The seed is the Word, or sound/mantra. It is the fulcrum through which we can leverage our thoughts to the plane of the Infinite. The seed contains all of the DNA of the Infinite. It is a template from which we can remodel the mind. When this merger through rhythm and *Naad* takes you into *anahat*, or the "unstruck sound" of the heart, it changes the structure of the subconscious itself—it changes the desire field. When finite and Infinite merge, all powers will prevail through you. All creation will serve you. I encourage you to experience God in you through your own consistent daily practice.

Adi Shakti, Namo, Namo Meditation

Pose: Sit in Easy Pose, with a slight Jalandhar Bandh (Neck Lock). Keep the spine straight.

Mudra: Make fists of both hands, thumbs on the outside. Bend the elbows by the sides of the torso, and bring each fist toward the corresponding shoulder, palms facing forward and index fingers pointing straight up. Hold the position.

Eye Position: Keep the eyes closed, and focus on the Third Eye Point.

Mantra: Chant aloud to the Adi Shakti mantra:

> *Adi Shakti, Adi Shakti, Adi Shakti, Namo, Namo*
> *Sarab Shakti, Sarab Shakti, Sarab Shakti, Namo, Namo*
> *Pritham Bhagwati, Pritham Bhagwati, Pritham Bhagwati, Namo, Namo*
> *Kundalini Mata Shakti, Mata Shakti, Namo, Namo*

Chant from the Navel Point. Sing with it; merge with it.

Time: Continue for 11–31 minutes.

Commentary: This mantra tunes you into the creative primal (first/original) power in the universe. This creative power is often thought of as feminine. The meditation can be used to tune into the divine feminine power as well as to develop creative and intuitive gifts. It is said that whoever can master this mantra can make God dance. Whenever you are in trouble, chant this mantra; everything will become clear.

It is also said that when Indian women recited this mantra, India was a land of milk and honey. When the women forgot the mantra, the country became a living hell. A woman who learns and uses this mantra will be a living goddess, and God will be manifest in her.

Yogi Bhajan said, "If there is a time in your life where you have a miserable situation, exhaustive environments come to confront you, which comes in everybody's life, this is the Maha Shakti Mantra. Do this meditation, and let the past die and let prosperity live. Let you die, and let your power live! This mantra can manifest Maha Shakti in you."

MUSIC: 31-minute call-and-repeat version by Gurudass Kaur from the album *Adi Shakti*, or 11-minute version by Sada Sat Kaur from the album *Angels Waltz*

ESSENTIAL OIL RECOMMENDATIONS: Myrrh, Clary Sage, Melissa, Ginger, Cassia, Bergamot

Meditation for Healing Addictions

Pose: Sit in Easy Pose, with a light Jalandhar Bandh (Neck Lock). Keep the spine straight, and ensure the first six lower vertebrae are locked forward.

Mudra: Make fists of both hands, and extend the thumbs straight. Place the thumbs on the temples, and find the spot where the thumbs fit. (This location is the lower anterior position of the frontal bone above the temporal-sphenoidal suture.) Lock the back molars together, and keep the lips closed. Keeping the teeth pressed throughout, alternately squeeze the molars tightly and then release the pressure. A muscle will move in rhythm under the thumbs. Feel it massage the thumbs, and apply a firm pressure with the hands.

Eye Position: Keep the eyes closed, and focus on the Brow Point.

Mantra: *Saa Taa Naa Maa*

Silently vibrate the mantra at the brow.

Time: Continue for 5–7 minutes. With practice, the time can be increased to 20 minutes and ultimately to 31 minutes.

Commentary: This meditation can be used to alleviate all kinds of mental and physical afflictions. The pressure exerted by the thumbs triggers a rhythmic reflex current that flows into the central brain. This current activates the brain area directly underneath the stem of the pineal gland. An imbalance in this area makes mental and physical addictions seemingly unbreakable. In modern culture, this imbalance is pandemic. If we are not addicted to smoking, eating, drinking, or drugs, we are addicted subconsciously to acceptance, advancement, rejection, emotional love, or something else. This meditation is excellent for everyone but particularly effective for those rehabilitating from drug dependence, mental illness, and phobic conditions.

ESSENTIAL OIL RECOMMENDATIONS: Bergamot, Frankincense, Vetiver, White Fir

Antar Naad Mudra

Pose: Sit in Easy Pose, with a slight Jalandhar Bandh (Neck Lock). Keep the spine straight.

Mudra: Extend the arms straight, and rest them over the knees. Make Buddhi Mudra (page 202) with both hands by touching the tips of the thumbs to the tips of the pinkie fingers; the other fingers are relaxed and straight. Become completely still physically and mentally, like the calm ocean. If listening to the mantra in music, listen to the chant for a minute. Feel its rhythm in every cell of the body. Then join in the mantra.

Mantra: *Saa Ray Saa Saa, Saa Ray Saa Saa*
Saa Ray Saa Saa, Saa Rang
Har Ray Har Har, Har Ray Har Har
Har Ray Har Har, Har Rang

Time: Continue for 11–31 minutes.

Commentary: Antar Naad Mudra (also called Kabadshe Meditation) opens the chakras for the full effect of all other mantras. It is a sensitizing meditation for the impact of the inner Sound Current. It is the base of all mantras. The original practice of mantras required mastering this mantra before practicing any other mantras.

The esoteric structure of the mantra is coded in the qualities represented by each of the sounds, as well as in the rhythm that weaves the sounds together into a coherent and powerful effect. Sa is the Infinite, the totality, God. It is the element of ether. Sa initiates and contains all other effects; it is subtle and beyond. Har is the creativity of the earth. Har is the dense element, the power of manifestation, the tangible, and the personal. The sounds of "Sa" and "Har" are woven together and then projected through the sound of Ang, or complete totality, like the original sounds "Aum" and "Ong."

Anyone who practices this meditation is granted prosperity, creativity, and protection against attacks. This meditation gives new power to your words and brings luck even if you are a scoundrel.

Antar Naad Mudra as a Full-Moon Meditation

Mudra: Press the hands against each other in Prayer Pose at the Navel Point. As the mantra starts ("Saa Ray Saa Saa"), bring the palms up the center front of the torso, about four to six inches in front of the body. While passing the Heart Center to the level of the Brow Point, open the hand mudra to make an open lotus by the time it reaches the brow. (To form an open lotus, press the base of the palms together, connect the tips of the pinkie fingers and the tips of the thumbs, and spread open the rest of the fingers.)

When the mantra reaches "Har Ray Har Har," turn the fingers to point down, with the back of the hands touching (the reverse of Prayer Pose). Slowly bring this mudra down the chakras in rhythm with the music until the fingertips reach the Navel Point on the sounds "Har Rang." Then turn the hands around and begin again.

Commentary: The cycle of the music and the mudra is key to opening the flow of Kundalini. The new awareness will give you the authority to make the right choices and conquer the ugliness of life. You will be peaceful and secure.

MUSIC: 31-minute track on Guru Shabd Singh Khalsa's album *The Legacy Collection Volume 1* or 11-minute version by Nirinjan Kaur on the album *Prem Siri*

ESSENTIAL OIL RECOMMENDATIONS: Lavender, Cypress, Basil, Clove

Bringing Mental Balance

Pose: Sit in Easy Pose. Keep the spine straight.

Mudra: Interlace the fingers at the base, with the palms facing up, fingers pointing up at a gentle sixty-degree angle, and thumbs straight. Hold the inverted Venus Lock at the solar plexus.

Eye Position: Keep the eyes one-tenth open.

Mantra: Chant the Guru Gaitri Mantra:

> *Gobinday, Mukanday, Udaaray, Apaaray,*
> *Hareeang, Kareeang, Nirnaamay, Akaama.*

The above are eight aspects of God, loosely translated as the following:

> Sustainer, Liberator, Enlightener, Infinite,
> Destroyer, Creator, Nameless, Desireless.

Chant as fast as possible so that the words are indistinguishable. The chant should turn into a sound current.

Time: Start with 11 minutes, and over time build up to 31 minutes.

Commentary: When you're at your wits' end, when you don't know what to do, when nothing else works, this meditation does! This meditation is one of five Yogi Bhajan gave specifically "to prepare for the gray period of the planet and to bring mental balance".

MUSIC: No music. Chant as fast as you can.

ESSENTIAL OIL RECOMMENDATIONS: Basil, Frankincense, Myrrh

Meditation for a Calm Heart

Pose: Sit in Easy Pose, with a straight spine and a light Jalandhar Bandh (Neck Lock).

Mudra: Place the left hand at the Heart Center. Place the palm flat against the chest, with the fingers parallel to the ground and pointing to the right. Make Gyan Mudra with the right hand, and then raise the right hand to the side, with the elbow bent as if you were taking an oath.

Eye Position: Either close the eyes or look straight ahead with the eyes one-tenth open.

Breath Pattern and Visualization: Imagine the flow of the breath, and consciously regulate each part of it as you use the following pattern: Inhale slowly and deeply through the nose. Hold the breath in, and raise the chest. Hold as long as possible, and then exhale gradually, smoothly, and completely. When the breath is completely expelled, lock out the breath for as long as possible.

Time: Continue for 3–31 minutes.

In a class, try this meditation for 3 minutes. If you have more time, try the meditation for three periods of 3 minutes each, with 1 minute of rest between, for a total of 11 minutes. For an advanced practice of concentration and rejuvenation, build up to 31 minutes.

End: Inhale and exhale strongly three times. Relax.

Commentary: This meditation is perfect for beginners because it opens awareness of the breath and conditions the lungs. When you hold the breath in or out for "as long as possible," you should not gasp or be under strain when you let the breath flow again.

To master breath holding is to master the inflow and outflow of life itself. The proper home of the subtle force, prana, is in the lungs and heart. In this meditation, the left hand is placed at the natural home of prana, creating a deep stillness at that point. The right hand, which throws you into action and analysis, is placed in a receptive, relaxed mudra, in a position of peace. The entire posture creates a still point for the prana at the Heart Center, inducing the feeling of calmness.

Emotionally, this meditation adds clear perception to your relationship with yourself and your relationships with others. If you are upset at work or in a personal relationship, sit in this meditation for 3–15 minutes before deciding how to act. Then act with your full heart. Physically, this meditation strengthens the heart and lungs.

ESSENTIAL OIL RECOMMENDATIONS: Lavender, Lemon, Patchouli, Sandalwood

Fists of Anger (Meditation for Releasing Anger)

Pose: Sit in Easy Pose or Rock Pose, with a light Jalandhar Bandh (Neck Lock).

Mudra: Touch each thumb to the mound at the base of the pinkie finger. Close the rest of the fingers over the thumbs to form fists. Raise the arms, and begin a backstroke type movement over the head through the Arcline. Alternate swinging each arm up, over, and back around again, as if you were doing the backstroke in a swimming pool. The movement is heavy and strong. Cross your Arcline about 2–3 times per second. Get angry.

Eye Position: Close the eyes.

Breath: Through an O-shaped mouth, strongly inhale and then exhale in sync with the arm movements. The breath is heavy and fast. Keep the lips in an O shape throughout the meditation.

Time: Continue for 3 minutes maximum, then finish with the ending. One should never do this meditation for more than 3 minutes.

End: Interlock the fingers, and stretch the arms up over the head, palms facing up. Inhale deeply through the O-shaped mouth. Hold the breath for 10 seconds. Exhale strongly (cannon breath) out through the O-shaped mouth. Repeat ending breath 3 times.

Commentary: The mudra, movement, and breathing are continuous and strong. Throughout the meditation, intentionally think about everything that makes you angry, negative, or commotional. Yogi Bhajan said, "Get angry and eat up your own inner anger."

ESSENTIAL OIL RECOMMENDATIONS: Thyme, Black Pepper, or Cilantro

Ganputi Kriya

Pose: Sit in Easy Pose, with a light Jalandhar Bandh (Neck Lock).

Mudra: Place the wrists over the knees, hands in Gyan Mudra, with the arms and elbows straight.

Eye Position: Keep the eyes one-tenth open, and focus on the Third Eye Point.

Mantra: *Saa Taa Naa Maa*
Raa Maa Daa Saa
Saa Say So Hung

PART 1: Chant the mantra in a single breath, pressing each fingertip in sequence with the syllable of the mantra. Use a monotone voice in the Tibetan form, or use the same melody as used for Kirtan Kriya.

MUSIC: The gong may be played throughout part 1 of this meditation.

TIME: Continue for 11–62 minutes.

PART 2: Inhale deeply and hold the breath. With the breath held, move the upper body, twisting and stretching each muscle. Move the head, torso, arms, back, belly, and hands (shake like a wet dog). Exhale powerfully. Repeat 3–5 times.

PART 3: Sit straight. Look at the tip of the nose. Become totally calm and absolutely still. Continue this pose for 2–3 minutes.

Time: 13–65 minutes.

Commentary: This meditation is also known as a meditation to make the impossible possible because it can break through any block. Ganputi Kriya meditation clears the blocks from your past, present, and future. It allows you to let go of the attachments to the mind and the impacts of past actions so that you can create and live a fulfilled life with integrity in the present moment and live a perfect future.

Healing with the Siri Giatri Mantra

Pose: Sit in Easy Pose, with a light Jalandhar Bandh (Neck Lock).

Mudra: Tuck the elbows comfortably against the ribs. Extend the forearms out from the center of the body at a fifteen-degree angle. The palms are flat, facing up, with the wrists pulled back, the fingers together, and the thumbs spread. Consciously keep the palms flat during the meditation.

Mantra: Raa Maa Daa Saa Saa Say So Hung

Pull in the navel powerfully on "So" and "Hung." Note that Hung is not long and drawn out. Clip it off forcefully as you pull in the navel. Chant one complete cycle of the mantra, and then inhale deeply and repeat the cycle. To chant this mantra properly, remember to move the mouth fully with each sound. Feel the resonance in the mouth and the sinus areas. Let the mind concentrate on the qualities that are evoked by the combination of sounds.

Time: Chant powerfully for 11–31 minutes.

End: Inhale deeply and hold the breath while offering a healing prayer. Visualize the person you wish to heal (potentially yourself) as being completely healthy, radiant, and strong. Imagine the person entirely engulfed in healing, white light and completely healed. Then exhale and inhale deeply again, hold the breath, and offer the prayer again. Then lift the arms high and vigorously shake out the hands and fingers.

Commentary: Certain mantras are to be cherished like the most rare and beautiful gem. One such jewel is the Siri Gaitri Mantra. It captures the radiant healing energy of the cosmos just as a gem captures the light of the sun. Like a gem, the Siri Gaitri Mantra can be used in many settings for different purposes and occasions. When Yogi Bhajan shared this technology, he gave a series of meditations that use the inner dynamics of this mantra. If you master any of these practices, you will be rewarded with healing and awareness.

The Siri Gaitri Mantra is also called a Siri Mantra and a Sushmuna Mantra. The mantra has eight sounds that stimulate the Kundalini to flow in the central channel of the spine and in the chakras. As this process occurs, there is usually a huge metabolic adjustment to the new level of energy in the body. The brain is also involved: the sounds balance the five zones of the left and right hemispheres of the brain to activate the Neutral Mind.

The mantra uses a sound current. The sounds create a juxtaposition of energies.

- Ra means the energy of the sun: strong, bright, and hot. Ra energizes and purifies.

- Ma is the energy of the moon. Ma is a quality of receptivity, coolness, and nurturing.

- Da is the energy of the earth. Da is secure, personal, and the ground of action.

- Sa is the impersonal Infinity. Saa is the cosmos in all of its open dimensions and totality. The repetition of Saa in the mantra is a turning point. The first part of the mantra is ascending and expands into the Infinite. The second part of the mantra pivots those qualities of the highest and most subtle ether and brings them back down. This process interweaves the ether with the earth. Sa is the impersonal Infinity.

- Then comes Say, which is the totality of experience and is personal. It is the feeling of a sacred "Thou." Say is the embodiment of Sa.

- So is the personal sense of merger and identity.

- Hung is the Infinite, vibrating and real. The two qualities together (So and Hung) mean "I am Thou."

While chanting this mantra, complete a cycle of energy and go through a circuit of the chakras. You will grow toward the Infinite and then convert the linkage of finite and Infinite at Sa. Then you will revert to an embodiment and blend of purity.

If a group is completing this meditation, it can be done in a circle. Members may lie down in the center of the circle if they wish to.

MUSIC: "Ra Ma Da Sa" by Snatam Kaur on the album *Grace*

ESSENTIAL OIL RECOMMENDATIONS: Helichrysum, Geranium, Eucalyptus, Rose

Developing The Power to Heal

Pose: Sit in Easy Pose.

Mudra: Place the left hand on the Navel Point. Place the right arm by the right side of the torso, elbow bent and the palm facing forward. Hold the right hand up as if taking an oath. Chant out loud or meditate silently. The movement of the kriya is timed with the chanting.

Mantra: Raa Maa Daa Saa Saa Say So Hung

At "Raa," begin to slowly move the right arm forward from the starting position; continue slowly moving the arm so that at "Hung," the arm is straight out in front of the body, with the palm facing down (as if giving a blessing). Then move the right arm back to the starting position (by the side of the torso). Begin the movement again at "Raa."

Time: Start with 11 minutes, and work up to 31 minutes. Gradually, you may increase the time to a maximum of 2 hours.

Commentary: Yogi Bhajan said that this is a meditation to practice your whole life. This meditation is a simple exercise that can give you the power to heal.

MUSIC: "Ra Ma Da Sa" by Snatam Kaur on the album *Grace*

ESSENTIAL OIL RECOMMENDATIONS: Helichrysum, Geranium, Eucalyptus, Rose

I am Happy Meditation for Children

Pose: Sit in Easy Pose

Mudra: In the rhythm of the mantra, the children shake their index fingers up and down (like their parents might sometimes do when scolding the children).

Eye Position: Either close the eyes or look straight ahead with the eyes one-tenth open.

Mantra: I Am Happy, I Am Good
I Am Happy, I Am Good

Sat Naam Sat Naam Sat Naam Ji
Wahe Guru Wahe Guru
Wahe Guru Ji

Commentary: Yogi Bhajan gave this meditation specifically for children to use in times when their parents are fighting or going through a crisis—to give children the experience of remaining stable and unaffected. Of course, the meditation can be done anytime.

Children, especially those under the age of six, have a much shorter attention span than adults. All meditations with movement and variation work well. Children like simple celestial communication.

MUSIC: "I am Happy" by Snatam Kaur of the album: *Feeling Good Today!*

ESSENTIAL OIL RECOMMENDATIONS: Ylang Ylang, Geranium, Rose, or Lavender

You can visit youtube.com/treeoflifekundalini to learn how to do a celestial communication to this mantra.

Kirtan Kriya

This kriya is one of three meditations that Yogi Bhajan said would carry civilization through the Aquarian Age, even if all other teachings were lost. Practicing Kirtan Kriya correctly involves four principal components: mantra, mudra, voice, and visualization.

Eye Position: Focus on the Brow Point.

Mantra: This kriya uses the five primal sounds—or the Panj Shabd: Saa Taa Naa Maa—in the original bij form of Sat Naam:

> Saa: Infinity, cosmos, beginning
> Taa: Life, existence
> Naa: Death, change, transformation
> Maa: Rebirth
> Chant from the Navel Point. Sing with it; merge with it.

The Panj Shabd is the cycle of creation. From the Infinite comes life and individual existence. From life comes death or change. From death comes the rebirth of consciousness. From rebirth comes the joy of the Infinite, through which compassion leads back to life.

Mudra: Keep the elbows straight, with the hands in Gyan Mudra. Each finger touches, in turn, the tip of the thumb with a firm but gentle pressure, following the pattern below:

> Saa: The index finger touches the thumb.
> Taa: The middle finger touches the thumb.
> Naa: The ring finger touches the thumb.
> Maa: The pinkie finger touches the thumb.

Each repetition of the entire mantra takes 3–4 seconds. After finishing one repetition, begin again with the index finger.

Visualization: As you meditate on the primal sounds, imagine a flow of energy that moves into the top of the head and then moves down and out through the Third Eye in an L form. By doing so, you will feel a constant flow of cosmic energy into your Solar Center, or Tenth Gate (the Crown Chakra). As the energy enters the top of the head, place "Saa," "Taa," "Naa," or "Maa" there. As you chant "Saa," for example, the "S" sound starts at the top of your head and the "aa" sound moves down and out through the Brow Point, projected to Infinity. This energy flow follows the energy pathway called the Golden Cord—the connection between the pineal gland and the pituitary gland. Some people may occasionally experience headaches from practicing Kirtan Kriya if they do not use the L form. The most common reason is improper circulation of prana in the Solar Centers.

Voice: The mantra is chanted in the three languages of consciousness:

Aloud (the voice of the human): Awareness of the things of the world

Whisper (the voice of the lover): The longing to belong

Silent (the voice of the divine): Meditation on Infinity or mental vibration

To Practice: Chant aloud for 5 minutes. Then whisper for 5 minutes. Then go deeply into silence, mentally vibrating the sound for 10 minutes. Then whisper for 5 minutes. Then chant aloud for 5 minutes.

End: Close the meditation with a deep inhale. Hold the breath as long as comfortable—up to 1 minute—relaxing completely to achieve 1 minute of absolute stillness and silence. Then, stretch the hands up as far as possible and spread the fingers wide. Stretch the spine, and take several deep breaths. Relax.

Time: Including the end of the meditation, 31 minutes. (Timing can be increased or decreased so long as the ratio is the same and always ends with one minute of silence.) Maximum time for this meditation is 2.5 hours.

Commentary: Practicing this meditation brings a total mental balance to the individual psyche. As you vibrate on each fingertip, you alternate your electrical polarities. This brings a balance in the electro-magnetic projection of the Aura. Practicing this meditation is both a science and an art. It is an art in the way it molds consciousness and the refinement of the sensation and insight it produces. It is a science in the tested certainty of the results it produces. Because it is so effective and exact, it can lead to problems if not done properly. Through this constant practice, the mind awakens to the infinite capacity of the soul for sacrifice, service, and creation.

MUSIC: This meditation is best done with only the sound of your own voice. To keep track of the precise timing, I recommend making a recording of yourself to practice with, or using an interval timer app.

ESSENTIAL OIL RECOMMENDATIONS: Cilantro, White Fir, Frankincense, Wintergreen, Lavender, Rosemary

Patience and Temperament

Pose: Sit with the spine straight.

Mudra: Interlock the middle finger of the right hand with the middle finger of the left hand, and bring this lock two to three inches in front in front of the Heart Center. Face the right palm down, and face the left palm toward the chest. Ensure that only the middle fingers are touching, and pull these fingers with maximum capacity for 3 minutes while breathing slowly and deeply. (When done correctly, this technique is usually a little painful in the middle fingers.)

Eye Position: Close the eyes nine-tenths, and look straight ahead at the Third Eye Point.

Breath: Inhale and exhale slowly and deeply.

Time: 3 minutes.

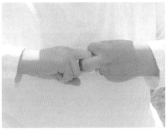

Commentary: When you are finished, you will feel much more calm and patient. The benefits of this technique can been seen after only 1 minute, which is why this technique is sometimes referred to as the Emergency 1-Minute Meditation for Patience.

ESSENTIAL OIL RECOMMENDATIONS: Tree Oil Blend, Patchoili, Myrrh, Birch

The instructions for this kriya/meditation are from the personal notes of David S. Khalsa and thus were not reviewed by KRI.

Meditation for Prosperity

Pose: Sit in Easy Pose, with a light Jalandhar Bandh (Neck Lock).

Mudra: Place the elbows by the sides, with the forearms angled up and outward, the fingers at the level of the throat, and the palms facing down.

Alternately hit the insides of the hands together, and then open the hands so the palms face up. When the palms face up, the pinkie fingers and the bottom of the palms touch. Then hit the insides of the hands together again, and open the hands so the palms face down. When the palms face down, the sides of the index fingers touch and the thumbs cross below the hands, with the right thumb under the left thumb. Yogi Bhajan said that the thumbs crossing this way is the key to the meditation.

Eye Position: Keep the eyes nine-tenths closed, and focus on the tip of the nose.

Mantra: *Har Har*

Chant continuously from the Navel Point, using the tip of the tongue.

Time: Yogi Bhajan said, "This meditation can be done for up to 11 minutes. It is so powerful in bringing prosperity that more than 11 minutes would be greedy."

Commentary: Yogi Bhajan said, "This meditation stimulates the mind, the Moon Center, and Jupiter. When Jupiter and the Moon come together, there is no way in the world you will not create wealth."

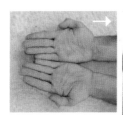

MUSIC: Though not required, "Tantric Har" by Simran Kaur is perfect for this meditation.

ESSENTIAL OIL RECOMMENDATIONS: Wild Orange, Ylang Ylang, Peppermint

Releasing Childhood Anger

Pose: Sit in Easy Pose, with the arms stretched out straight to the sides. Do not bend the elbows. Use the thumbs to lock down the pinkie and ring fingers in Christ Mudra, and extend the index and middle fingers. The palms face forward, and the fingers point out to the sides.

Breath: Inhale deeply by sucking air through closed teeth, and exhale through the nose.

Time: Continue for 11 minutes.

End: To finish, inhale deeply and hold the breath for 10 seconds while stretching the spine up and stretching the arms out to the sides. Exhale. Repeat two more times.

Commentary: This meditation provides subtle powers; it will change you inside and out. The meditation can be completed in the morning or in the evening; if you complete it in the evening, the next morning you will find that your whole caliber and energy have changed.

ESSENTIAL OIL RECOMMENDATIONS: Thyme, Ylang Ylang, Wild Orange

Meditation to Rebuild and Strengthen the Arcline

Pose: Sit in Easy Pose. Keep the spine straight.

Mudra: Extend the elbows toward the sides. Place the hands a few inches in front of the Heart Center. The hands should be parallel, with the left hand on top, palm down, and the right hand four inches below, palm up.

Eye Position: Keep the eyes opened and focused on the tip of the nose.

Breath: Inhale through the nose in eight rapid, equal strokes. Then, exhale through the nose in eight rapid, equal strokes. To understand this procedure, imagine inhaling an amount of air equal to about one-eighth of the volume of the lungs, consecutively adding one more eighth during each short inhalation. Then, consecutively exhale one-eighth of the air in the lungs in each of eight strokes. Start with small volumes in order to reach eight strokes in and eight strokes out without completely filling or emptying the lungs prematurely. Do not pause between inhale and exhale. Each complete breath cycle takes about 10 seconds.

Mantra: *Saa Taa Naa Maa*

When breathing, use the mantra instead of counting the parts. Say the mantra twice for the inhale and twice for the exhale.

Time: Continue for 11 minutes (no more or less).

End: Inhale deeply, and hold the breath for 35 seconds while maintaining the hand posture. Then exhale and relax.

Commentary: According to Yogi Bhajan, this technique is also referred to as the Eight-Stroke Breath Meditation and has been taught as a therapy to strengthen and rebuild the Arcline.

ESSENTIAL OIL RECOMMENDATIONS: Basil, Melaleuca, Clove, Frankincense, Juniper Berry, Myrrh, Birch

The instructions for this kriya/meditation are from the personal notes of David Shannahoff Khalsa and thus were not reviewed by KRI.

Sat Kriya

Pose: Sit on the heels.

Mudra: Raise the arms overhead, with the palms together. Interlace the fingers except for the index fingers, which point straight up. Men cross the right thumb over the left thumb; women cross the left thumb over the right thumb.

Mantra: *Sat Naam*

Chant "Sat" while pulling in the Navel Point; chant "Naam" while relaxing the Navel Point.

Time: Continue for at least 3 minutes.

End: Inhale, apply the Mul Bandh (Root Lock), and tightly squeeze the muscles from the buttocks all the way up the back, past the shoulders. Mentally allow the energy to flow through the top of the skull. Exhale, hold the breath out, and apply all the locks. Inhale and relax.

Relax for 6 minutes after completing 3 minutes of Sat Kriya.

You may build the time of the kriya to 31 minutes, but remember to complete a long, deep relaxation immediately afterward. A good way to build up to 31 minutes is to complete the kriya for 3 minutes and then rest for 2 minutes. Repeat this cycle until you have completed 15 minutes of Sat Kriya and 10 minutes of rest. Finish the required relaxation by resting an additional 15–20 minutes. Do not try to jump to 31 minutes even if you feel strong or virile or you are a yoga teacher. Respect the inherent power of the technique. Let the kriya prepare the ground of your body properly to plant the seed of higher experience. Sat Kriya is not just an exercise; it is a kriya that works on all levels of your being—both known and unknown. By pushing the physical body too much, you could block the more subtle experiences of higher energies; you could have a huge rush of energy. Or you could have an experience of higher consciousness but not be able to integrate the experience into your psyche. So prepare yourself with constancy, patience, and moderation, which will ensure the ideal end result.

Notice that you emphasize pulling in the Navel Point. Don't try to apply Mul Bandh. Mul Bandh occurs automatically if the navel is pulled in. Consequently, the hips and lumbar spine do not rotate or flex. The spine stays straight, and the arms make only a slight up-and-down stretch with each vocalization of "Sat Naam" as your chest lifts.

Commentary: Sat Kriya is fundamental to Kundalini Yoga and should be practiced every day for at least 3 minutes. Its effects are numerous.

This kriya directly stimulates and channels the Kundalini energy, so it must always be practiced with this mantra.

Sat Kriya strengthens the entire sexual system and stimulates its natural flow of energy, thereby relaxing phobias about sexuality. This kriya allows you to control insistent sexual impulses by rechanneling sexual energy to creative and healing activities in the body.

People who are severely maladjusted or who have mental problems also benefit from this kriya since maladjustments and mental disturbances are always connected with an imbalance in the energies of the lower three chakras.

Further, general physical health is improved since all the internal organs receive a gentle rhythmic massage from this exercise. The heart gets stronger from the rhythmic up-and-down pattern of blood pressure generated from the pumping motion of the Navel Point.

If you have time for nothing else, make this kriya part of your daily efforts to keep your body a clean and vital temple of God.

ESSENTIAL OIL RECOMMENDATIONS: Frankincense, Sandalwood, Myrrh

Technique for Managing Fears

Pose: Sit with the spine straight.

Mudra: Group the four fingertips and the thumb tip of the left hand, and press very lightly into the Navel Point, like a plug. Place the four fingers of the right hand on the forehead just above the root of the nose, with the four fingers pointing left over the Third Eye Point, as if taking your temperature.

Eye Position: Close the eyes.

Mantra and Visualization: Play the mantra Chattra Chakkra Vartee in the background for 3 minutes maximum while imagining and assessing all your fears and consciously relating to the mental experience of each fear.

Commentary: This technique helps to manage severe states of fear and eliminate negative images and emotions that have come from fearful experiences. The technique will replace the negative emotions with positive emotions, thus creating a different mental association with the stimulus. *This unique effect can only be achieved with the Chattra Chakkra Vartee mantra.*

MUSIC: "Chattr Chakkr Vartee" by Nirijan Kaur on the album *From Within*

ESSENTIAL OIL RECOMMENDATIONS: Juniper Berry, Birch, Cypress, Lavender, Myrrh

The instructions for this kriya/meditation are from the personal notes of David Shannahoff Khalsa and thus were not reviewed by KRI.

When You Don't Know What To Do

Mudra: Sit in Easy Pose or in a chair, with the spine straight. Relax the arms at the sides of the body. Bend the elbows, raise the hands, and bring them together at the center of the chest. Cross the hands, with both palms facing toward the chest. Rest one palm in the other (the position of the left and right hands is interchangeable). Cross the thumbs, and point the fingers up at a comfortable angle.

Eye Position: Look at the tip of the nose.

Breath: First, inhale through the nose, and then exhale through the nose. Second, inhale through the mouth, and then exhale through the mouth. Third, inhale through the nose, and then exhale through the mouth, Fourth, inhale through the mouth, and then exhale through the nose. Continue this sequence.

All breaths should be deep, complete, and powerful. When breathing through the mouth, purse the lips almost as if to whistle.

Time: Start by practicing this kriya for 11 minutes. You may gradually increase the time to 31 minutes.

Commentary: Try this meditation when you don't know what to do. It is very simple but very powerful if done correctly. This kriya coordinates both areas of the brain, provides powerful insight, and coordinates the mystery of spiritual phenomena with the mastery of the three bodies (physical, mental, and spiritual). Sometimes called the Gyan Mudra Kriya, this meditation solves many complications.

ESSENTIAL OIL RECOMMENDATIONS: Clary Sage, Lemon, Peppermint, Rosemary

Venus Kriyas

The first step in developing a healthy, sacred relationship is to develop your relationship with the Infinite in yourself—your true, divine self. The second step is to establish trust and commitment. Third is to communicate and then to communicate some more. Fourth is to establish a joint spiritual practice. Yoga and meditation are wonderful technologies for connecting to the Infinite together.[1]

Venus Kriyas are a unique kind of meditation taught by Yogi Bhajan. They are meant to be completed with a partner, usually of the opposite sex. Venus Kriyas are categorized as a more advanced Kundalini Yoga practice because they intensify the experience of the exercise through the polarities of the male and female interaction.

Anciently, Venus Kriyas were used as a kind of marriage therapy and a way to enhance an already healthy relationship. Venus Kriyas help heal and bring greater dimension and connection to any committed relationship, helping partners address issues of trust and communication as well as heighten and develop the spiritual dimension of the relationship. Venus Kriyas are never used to seduce or sensually excite a partner. These kriyas are used to elevate the sexual and sensory energy to a connection based on awareness and the capacity to see the sacred in the other.

This section presents one Venus Kriya as well one other meditation that is not a Venus Kriya but can be used by couples for similar purposes.

How to Practice Venus Kriyas

Always tune in with the Adi Mantra—"Ong Namo Guru Dev Namo"—before practicing Venus Kriyas. When practicing as a couple, always tune in facing each other.

It is recommended that the couple begin with a Yoga Kriya or another complete meditation before beginning.

Venus Kriyas are not used to sensually or sexually seduce one's partner. The purpose of Venus Kriyas is to elevate the relationship and the polarities to a purity and the highest vibration. If done with the wrong intention, Venus Kriyas lose their effectiveness and, in fact, can be more damaging than helpful.

Always limit the exercise to 3 minutes (unless specifically taught otherwise by Yogi Bhajan)

---

1 Jivan Joti Kaur, "Sacred Union (with 3 Venus Kriyas for Couples)," accessed March 17, 2014, http://www.3ho.org/3ho-lifestyle/authentic-relationships/sacred-union-3-venus-kriyas-couples.

Kirtan Kriya for Clearing the Clouds

Kirtan Kriya is one of the foundational meditations (described on page 262) and can be done individually or as a couple. It is not a Venus Kriya, but when practiced as a couple, Kirtan Kriya can have many of the same benefits. When done with a partner, it is called Kirtan Kriya for Clearing the Clouds because it is known to change the weather in a relationship. Couples should tune in facing each other but then sit back to back, spine to spine, for this meditation. This meditation is a good kriya to complete before beginning a Venus Kriya.

Pose: Sit in Easy Pose, back to back with your partner. Hands are in Gyan Mudra at the knees. Focus the eyes on the Third Eye Point.

Mantra: Saa Taa Naa Maa

Time: For the full meditation, 31 minutes. To shorten the meditation, see the instructions on page 263.

Mitna Kriya (Pushing Palms)

Pose: Sit in Easy Pose facing your partner, with knees touching. Look into your partner's eyes, and place your palms on your partner's palms. Begin pushing the palms alternately while rhythmically chanting the Guru Giatri Mantra (the woman chants the mantra first, and then the man chants the mantra):

Gobinday, Mukunday, Udaaray, Apaaray, Hareeung, Kareeung, Nirnaamay, Akaamay

MUSIC: Sada Sat Kaur's album *Shashara*

PRANAYAM

Pranayam is the use of breathing techniques to control the movement of prana.

The first thing an aspiring yogi or yogini should be aware of is their own simple, natural breathing. In correct Simple, Natural Breathing, the Navel Point moves out on the inhale and in and up on the exhale. We use the inhale to make ourselves wider, and we use the exhale to make ourselves longer. Many people learn to breathe backward. I encourage you to observe your natural breathing by sitting with the spine straight and the eyes closed. A natural breath uses the nose. Learning to breathe properly is probably the most important thing a student of Kundalini Yoga learns.

In this section I have included several pranayams that are commonly used in Kundalini Yoga or that may be useful for your everyday life.

Alternate Nostril Breathing

Alternative Nostril Breathing is a simple yet powerful technique that can take you through all the stages of your yoga practice.

Alternative Nostril Breathing includes the following steps:

In this *pranayam*, the breath is always relaxed, deep, and full.

The left hand is in Gyan Mudra.

Use the thumb of the right hand to close the right nostril, and use the index or ring finger of the right hand to close the left nostril. (This breathing technique is sometimes called U Breathing because of the mudra.)

Close the right nostril, and gently and fully inhale through the left nostril.

Close the left nostril, and exhale through the right nostril.

Inhale through the right nostril.

Close the right nostril, and exhale through the left nostril.

Repeat this pattern, alternating nostrils after each inhalation.

The following are benefits of Alternate Nostril Breathing:

- Creates whole-brain functioning by balancing the right and left hemispheres

- Integrates and grounds

- Gently purifies the ida and pingala nadis

- Creates a deep sense of well-being and harmony physically, mentally, and emotionally

- Helps alleviate headaches, including migraines, and other stress-related symptoms

- Inhaling left and exhaling right increases calmness and integrates unwanted negative emotions and stress (excellent by itself before bed)

- Inhaling right and exhaling left gives clarity and a positive mood, helping you focus on what is important

Breath of Fire

Breath of Fire is one of the foundational breathing techniques used in Kundalini Yoga. Breath of Fire accompanies many postures and has numerous beneficial effects. It is important to master this breathing technique so that it is done accurately and becomes automatic.

Breath of Fire is rapid, rhythmic, and continuous. The inhale and the exhale are of equal lengths, with no pause between them (approximately two to three cycles per second).

Breath of Fire is always practiced through the nostrils, with the mouth closed, unless stated otherwise. Breath of Fire is powered from the Navel Point and the solar plexus. To exhale, the air is expelled powerfully through the nose by pressing the Navel Point and the solar plexus back toward the spine. This action feels automatic if you contract the diaphragm rapidly.

To inhale, the upper abdominal muscles relax, the diaphragm extends down, and the breath seems to come in as part of relaxing rather than through effort.

The chest stays relaxed and slightly lifted throughout the breathing cycle.

When done correctly, there should be no rigidity in the hands, feet, face, or abdomen.

Begin practicing Breath of Fire for **1–3 minutes**. Some people find it easy to practice Breath of Fire for **10 minutes** right away. Others find that the breath creates an initial dizziness or giddiness; if these sensations occur, take a break. Some tingling, travelling sensations, and lightheadedness are completely normal as your body adjusts to the new breath and new stimulation of the nerves. Concentrating at the Brow Point may help relieve these sensations. Sometimes these symptoms are the result of toxins and other chemicals released through the breathing technique. The symptoms may be relieved by drinking a lot of water and changing to a light diet.

Breath of Fire is not hyperventilation, nor is it Bellows Breath.

Do not practice Breath of Fire while pregnant and during the heavy days of menstruation.

An easy way to practice Breath of Fire is to sit in Easy Pose, place one hand on the Navel Point, and place one hand on the diaphragm. Begin panting like a dog with the tongue out. Feel how the Navel Point naturally moves in with the exhale. Then close the mouth, and continue the movement of the breath through the nose.

The following are three common mistakes when practicing Breath of Fire:

Many people learn to breathe backward—they inhale by pulling the belly in, thus making the space for the breath less rather than more. This practice is called paradoxical breathing. It can be easily changed by placing one hand on the chest and one hand on the belly while practicing Breath of Fire slowly with total awareness.

Some people mistakenly do Bellows Breath, which involves breathing with an exaggerated pumping of the belly. Breath of Fire is not the deep bellows cleansing breath that pumps the stomach with complete exhales and inhales. Breath of Fire comes from higher up, near the solar plexus.

Some individuals do not focus on achieving a balanced ratio of the inhales and exhales. To address this issue, listen to the sound of the breath and create a steady rhythm.

The following are benefits of Breath of Fire:

- Releases toxins and deposits from the lungs, mucous linings, blood vessels, and other cells

- Expands lung capacity and increases vital strength

- Strengthens the nervous system's ability to resist stress

- Repairs the balance between the sympathetic and parasympathetic nervous systems

- Strengthens the Navel Chakra

- Increases physical endurance and prepares you to act effectively

- Adjusts the subtle psychoelectromagnetic field of the Aura so that the blood becomes energized

- Reduces addictive impulses for drugs, smoking, and bad foods

- Increases oxygen delivery to the brain, facilitating a focused, intelligent, and neutral state of mind

- Boosts the immune system and may help prevent many diseases

- Promotes synchronization of the biorhythms of the body's systems

Long Deep Breathing

Long, Deep Breathing uses the full capacity of the lungs by using three chambers of the lungs: the abdominal or lower chamber, the chest or middle chamber, and the clavicular or upper chamber. Long, Deep Breathing starts by filling the abdomen, then expanding the chest, and finally lifting the upper ribs and clavicle. The exhale is the reverse: first the upper chamber deflates, then the middle, and then finally the abdomen pulls in and up as the Navel Point pulls back  toward the spine. A good way to practice Long, Deep Breathing is by lying on the back, with one hand on the stomach and one hand on the chest. Try isolating each part and feeling the differences as the breath moves through the cavities.

Long, Deep Breathing has many benefits:

- Relaxes and calms, due to its influence on the parasympathetic nervous system

- Increases the flow of prana

- Reduces and prevents the buildup of toxins in the lungs

- Stimulates endorphins, which help fight depression

- Brings the brain to a new level of alertness

- Pumps spinal fluid to the brain, giving greater energy

- Stimulates the pituitary gland and intuition

- Readjusts the magnetic field

- Cleanses the blood

- Increases vitality

- Clears nerve channels

- Speeds up emotional and physical healing

- Aids in breaking subconscious habits, such as insecurities and fears

- Aids in fighting addictions

- Reduces or eliminates pain

Sitali Pranayam

To do Sitali Pranayam, sit in Easy Pose, with a light Jalandhar Bandh (Neck Lock). Roll the tongue into a U, with the tip of the tongue just outside of the lips. Inhale deeply through the rolled tongue, and exhale through the nose. Continue for **3 minutes**.

Alternatively, practice this technique 26 times in the morning and 26 times in the evening. Repeating this technique 108 times is a deep meditation and a powerful healer for the body and the digestive system.

This pranayam gives power, strength, and vitality. It can have a cooling, cleansing effect. Initially, the tongue tastes bitter, but it eventually becomes sweet.

Victory Breath

Victory breath is a tool you can use anywhere. It takes just 40 seconds, and no one will ever know you are doing it.

Inhale for 2–3 seconds, and hold the breath. While holding the breath, mentally chant "Vic-tor-y." Exhale. The entire sequence should take less than 10 seconds. Repeat several times. Practicing Victory Breath for **40 seconds** will change your state.

PREGNANCY

Pregnancy is a sacred time when the temple-body of a woman expands to fit another soul. Many Kundalini Yoga kriyas may not be appropriate for pregnant women. I encourage pregnant women to find a Kundalini-inspired yoga class or video specifically for pregnancy (SEE THE RESOURCES SECTION).

However, many pregnant women still enjoy and benefit from going to Kundalini Yoga classes and keeping up their meditation practice. Here are a few precautions to consider when participating in a regular Kundalini Yoga class while pregnant.

Pregnant women should not practice Breath of Fire or hold the breath for any length of time. If pregnant, one should also avoid pulling the navel or Mul Bandh (Root Lock) and should never practice inversions such as Shoulder Stand or Plough. After the sixteenth week of pregnancy it is advisable not to lie flat on the back for more than a few seconds.

Pregnant women are encouraged to consult with a health care provider, meditate (babies love it), practice Long Deep Breathing, talk or sing to your baby (especially mantras), take long walks, do comforting exercises like Cat-Cow Pose and Pelvic Circles, dance with your baby, and above all befriend and listen to your body. I also recommend several other exercises on the following pages. Bringing a child into the world through conscious pregnancy is a gift to that child and to the world. May you be blessed on your journey.

Butterfly Pose

With a straight spine, bring the soles of the feet together. If you wish to sit in this posture for an extended period, you may lean against a wall to keep your spine straight. This posture opens up the hips and pelvis and has numerous benefits for pregnant women.

Pregnancy Squats

Squats are one of the best things you can do when pregnant. For centuries, women have given birth in a squatting position, as squatting opens the pelvis and allows the baby to drop down with gravity's help. When pregnant, some precautions are needed when squatting. Many people will need support under their heels (such as a rolled-up yoga mat or cushion). Inhale, raise the arms, bring the hands together above the head, and then bring the hands down into Prayer Pose at the Heart Center as you come into a squat. To rise, place the hands flat on the ground, raise the buttocks, and then slowly roll up one vertebra at a time.

Keep-Up Exercises

A Keep-Up Exercise is any arm exercise or meditation maintained for 3 minutes. In this example, Nancy is gently moving her arms up and down eight inches, like flapping wings. The idea of a Keep-Up Exercise is to train the mind to experience power through an intense feeling. Though 3 minutes of arm exercises might be difficult at first, with practice and by using the breath, such an exercise can be easily done. This mind-body training is preparation for birthing time; if you can complete a 3-minute Keep-Up Exercise with power and grace, you can get through a 1-minute birthing wave in the same manner.

Jap Walking Meditation

As you walk, you can chant Sa-Ta-Na-Ma as you touch each finger (similar to Kirtan Kriya page 262). Long walks with your partner can strengthen your bond. Long walks also tone the uterus and prepare the body to birth.)

YOGA FOR KIDS

People often ask me if their children can participate in Kundalini Yoga and Meditation. The answer is that yes, and it is never too early. Ultrasound imagery shows that babies make all 84 yoga postures inside of the womb, and as soon as they acclimate to gravity outside the womb, you will see them attempting these exercises again. It is my personal belief that we go to yoga to remember how to "become as a little child." So if you have the opportunity to expose your child to Kundalini Yoga and Meditation, do it as soon as possible, so they don't forget what they already knew.

The I Am Happy Meditation (page 261) is a favorite meditation of all ages, but children and teens can do much more. Children can meditate for longer than you think, especially when motivated and when it is their idea. When teaching yoga to children, I usually shorten the times of each exercise in yoga kriya. When teaching very young children, I just have them to do simple warm ups (modeled by Amarjot Kaur on the the next page) to get them to move their bodies, and then we meditate.

The best way to entice your children to meditate is to be an example. I have taught yoga and meditation to hundreds of parents and when when one or both parents begin a regular practice, the children, like moths, are drawn to the light. Don't be surprised if your kids know all the words of the mantras or start meditating on their own or with you.

Warm Ups For Kids

CAT

COW

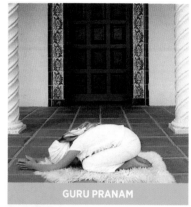
GURU PRANAM

BABY POSE

COBRA POSE

KUNDALINI TRIANGLE POSE

FORWARD BEND A

FORWARD BEND B

Kids Can Meditate!

TUNING IN

ADI SHAKTI MEDITATION

KIRTAN KRIYA

3-MINUTE TECHNIQUE FOR MANAGING FEARS

MEDITATION FOR COMMUNICATION

Have

Fun!

I was trying to define the mantra language to my carpool kids when they got in the car while I was listening to a mantra song. My thirteen-year-old defined mantras beautifully: "An ancient language that praises God." Not sure if that was something I had taught him or if he came up with it on his own.

—SHERIDAN RIPLEY, MOM OF 3

"The angel that is right there on the ceiling said

"Mom, my teacher said she was losing her mind so I told her to meditate and she would find the part she needed."

— AUDREY, 6 YRS OLD

that if I do this yoga I will be happy."—AMARJOT KAUR, 8 YEARS OLD

"Oh, that meditation was so good, Mom. I think I better keep my head covered all day to hold it in there."

—HYDEE, 4 YRS OLD

After we were done meditating last night, my eight-year-old said, "It feels like we're in a fish bowl that's never been cleaned in 5,000 years, and it's just been cleaned 10 seconds ago."

— CHERISE SANT, MOM OF 4

Tuning Out

When you have finished your practice for the day you can tune out in the following manner.

1 Sit in Easy Pose, with the hands in Prayer Mudra. Offer your prayers up as you sing or chant the "Long-Time Sunshine" song:

May the long-time sun shine upon you
All love surround you
And the pure light within you
*Guide your way on.**

Then chant "Sat Naam" one or more times to tune out. ("Sat" is extended and drawn out, and "Naam" is short.)

2 Inhale deeply. Raise the hands over the head, or bring the hands to the Third Eye Point. Bend forward as you bow to the divine within you and all around you and in each of us.

*MUSIC: Many versions of this song titled "Long Time Sun" are available. Snatam Kaur has two that are great. Look for them on her albums titled *Grace*, and *Feeling Good Today!*

Glossary

Akashic record   Cosmic file of all thought, deed, and intention. The scriptures refer to it as the book of life.

Amrit vela   Ambrosial hours before dawn, when the devout celebrate the divine within and without. Typically 3-6 a.m. or 4-7 a.m.

Apana   The "downward breath" is the eliminative aspect of prana.

Aquarian age   Period of time beginning December 21, 2012. The age of experience. It is taught in yoga texts that this is the age that will welcome in the 1,000 years of peace.

Asana   The body positions of yoga.

Ashtanga   Eight beats, referring to mantras with eight syllables or eight words.

Bandh   Body Lock. There are four principal locks of Kundalini Yoga are Mul Bandh (Root Lock), Uddiyana Bandh (Diaphragm Lock), Jalandhar Bandh (Neck Lock), and Maha Bandh (the Great Lock, a combination of the other three locks).

Bhakti   One filled with devotion for his God or Guru. Bahkti Yoga is recognized as an exemplary path of yoga in itself.

Bij   Seed, referring to one or two syllable mantras that plant seeds in the psyche that grow to be great trees of consciousness when watered by consistent spiritual practice.

Chakra   "Lotus" or "wheel;" the seven energetic vortices created where the Ida and Pingala intersect across the Sushumna. Yogi Bhajan also taught that the Aura is the eighth chakra.

Covenant   A sacred two-way promise or agreement between God and a person or group of people.

Endowment   A special spiritual blessing of power given to worthy and faithful members of the Church in the temple.

Golden Chain   Divine lineage of spiritual masters that one connects with when chanting the Adi Mantra.

Gurmukhi	The language of many of the Kundalini mantras. It is the Sikh language of prayer. The word 'Gurmukhi' literally means "from the mouth of the Guru."
Guru	That which takes us from darkness to light, ignorance to knowledge. It can be a person, a teaching, or in its most subtle form, the Word.
Guru Ram Das	Patron saint of Kundalini Yoga. Translation means "humble servant of God."
Hatha Yoga	"Ha" = Sun and "tha" = Moon; hence "the union experienced when Sun and Moon channels (Ida and Pigala) harmonize."
Heart Center	Point of focus at the center of the chest, corresponding to the Heart Chakra.
Higher Self	Soul-consciousness relating to the upper chakras.
Ida	A major nadi. Coils around Sushmana and carries the female lunar current from the base of the spine to the left nostril.
Intuition	The ability to acquire knowledge without inference or the use of reason. The word intuition comes from the Latin verb *intueri* which is usually translated as to look inside. It is usually associated with the Third Eye.
Jap	Meditate!
Karma	Law of cause and effect.
Kirtan	Sacred music and chanting.
Kriya	It means: an action that leads to completeness. In Kundalini Yoga As Taught by Yogi Bhajan® a sequence of postures or yogic techniques in one posture to produce a codified effect or impact.
Kundalini	The latent divine potential of the human being, which when dormant lies coiled at the base of the spine.
Laya Yoga	Applied science of sound, rhythm, and locks. An integral part of Kundalini Yoga.
Logos	Divine Word as perceived by the ancient adepts.

Mahan Tantric	Mantel of the Master of White Tantric Yoga.
Mantra	Sounds or words that through repetition tune or direct the mind.
Meditation	In yoga there are different words for different specific kinds of meditation. In the west when we use the word meditation we usually refer to dhyan: deep concentration. Meditation releases reactions and unconscious habits and builds intuition and awareness of self.
Meridians	Channels of subtle energy, common to eastern practices such as acupuncture.
Mudra	Hand position that moves or seals energy. Many Kundalini kriyas specify a mudra.
Nadi	Non-physical channels of energy within the body similar to nerves.
Naam	Manifested identity of the essence. Literally "that which is not, now is born." Also referred to as the Word.
Navel Point	2 inches below the umbilicus, a major intersection of energetic channels in the body, starting point of the 72,000 nadis.
Niyams	"Five Yogic Observances" to which the yogic aspirant should adhere: purity, contentment, austerity, study, and recognition of the One.
Ojas	Subtlest refined essence of the cerebrospinal fluid.
Opposition	The opposite nature of this planet, also referred to as polarity. Opposition often seems like an obstacle to progress but can create potential.
Ordinance	Sacred acts with symbolic meanings, formally performed by the authority of the priesthood.
Pingala	Major nadi coiled around the Sushmana carrying the male solar current from the base of the spine through the right nostril.
Piscean Age	Period ending December 21, 2012. The age of information. A masculine, power-centered age.
Polarity	The presence or manifestation of two opposite or contrasting principles or tendencies.

Prana	The Life Force or Light of Christ that is in and through all things.
Pranayam	Literally to "lead the Life Force." Refers to the science of yogic breath control.
Pratyahar	"Withdrawal of the senses." It is synchronization with God.
Raj Yoga	The Royal Path or the yoga of mastery of the mind.
Sadhana	Daily spiritual practice especially during the Amrit Vela.
Sadhu	Yogi or yogini who has established a powerful spiritual practice, or "Sadhana."
Samadhi	State of self-realization; complete absorption within the Infinite.
Sanskrit	Earliest-known Indo-European language.
Sattva	One of the three conditions of matter, denoting purity and illumination
Shakti	Creative power. Associated with the feminine creative principle.
Silver cord	Energetic pathway from the base of the spine to the pituitary gland, or sixth chakra
Sushmana	Central spinal channel. The vertical nadi by which Kundalini ascends.
Tantra	"Length and breadth." The yogic science of expanding the parameters of the subtle energetic body and the psyche.
Tattvas	All phenomena in the universe are composed of the five elements. Each is associated with a behavior or quality, chakra, and sense: Earth (Greed, first chakra, smell), Water (Lust, second chakra, taste), Fire (Anger, third chakra, sight), Air (Attachment, fourth chakra, touch), and Ether (Pride, fifth chakra, sound).
Third Eye Point	A point of focus at the center of the brow, corresponding to the sixth chakra.
Vedas	Sacred text complied in India during the Vedic Period 3,000 years ago.

Yamas	The Five Yogic Abstinences: non-violence, truthfulness, not stealing, continence, and not being greedy.
Yogi	One who practices yoga and has achieved a high level of spiritual insight.
Yogini	A female master practitioner of yoga.

Muscle Testing/Intuition Chart

If you like numbers or are a scientist at heart, here is a little chart you can use to assess your vibration and progress with various virtues along your journey. As I mentioned in the chapter titled "Keep Up and You'll Be Kept Up," it is not helpful to assess your progress every day or even every month. Perhaps every nine months is a good time to assess yourself. Use this chart only if you think it will help you. Then relax and enjoy the journey.

0	100	200	300	400	500	600	700	800	900	1,000

VIRTUE	DATE	DATE
Overall Vibration		
Charity		
Meekness		
Humility		
Impersonal Obedience		
Personal Obedience		
Self Esteem		
Peace		

Use this scale to measure and track the suggested virtues or add your own intentions to the blank spaces provided. There are a few things that won't work with this scale, such as faith, which has no upper limit. I like to equate 1,000,000 units of faith with a grain of mustard seed, but there is no need to stop there. Make a graph and watch the numbers go up! Also, some virtues, like Faith, tend to fluctuate as much as fifteen percent, so ask for an average. You will notice that other virtues, such as Charity, remain very stable. Also, I have discovered that there is more than one kind of faith (childlike, experiential, and causal).

Other things to consider testing for is your percentage of Seeing Things As They Really Are. This is a 0–100 percent scale and it fluctuates, so ask for your average. Most people see less than one percent. You might also find it interesting to ask for your average while meditating or during other activities.

Usage Guide

Kundalini Yoga is based on excellence and exaltation and is a sacred science. Through it, the sacredness of the student is awakened. Kundalini Yoga is not illness based—as a system, it wasn't started to cure anything. Though it has enormous therapeutic benefits, it is not an inherently therapeutic model. None of the Kundalini Yoga kriyas are specifically designed for the diseases encountered in today's world. Even when Yogi Bhajan says that a certain kriya is for such and such, he is mostly speaking of prevention.

Kundalini Yoga and Meditation are not a substitute for medical care, chiropractic care, or a healthy lifestyle. However, numerous people have asked which meditations and kriyas are good for specific issues. In response, I am including this usage guide, which contains my ideas. However, remember to always trust your intuition. Also, it is important to ensure that part of your regular daily practice remains the same (see Keep Up, page 175). Finally, remember the importance of living a healthy and balanced life.

Issues	Suggestions
Abandonment	Healing Meditation; Nabhi Kriya
Abuse	Healing Meditation; Nabhi Kriya
Addiction	Meditation for Healing Addictions; Nabhi Kriya; Meditation for Strenthening the Arcline; massive amounts of Pranayam; a consistent practice of Kundalini Yoga
Anger	Fists of Anger Meditation; Kriya for Relieving Inner Anger; Meditation for Healing Addictions
Anxiety	Kriya for Relaxation and Releasing Fear; Meditation for Strengthening the Arcline; Technique for Managing Fears; Kriya to Throw Off Stress; Bring Mental Balance Meditation; a consistent practice of Kundalini Yoga and Meditation
Apathy	Basic Spinal Energy Series; chant Mul Mantra until you feel better
Autism/Asperger's	Sitali Pranayam; Ganputi Kriya; Healing Meditation; see *Sacred Therapies* in the Resources Section

Issues	Suggestions
Bad habits	Meditation for Healing Addictions
Breathing problems	All Pranayam
Celibacy	Sat Kriya; Kriya for Elevation; Frog Pose; Mahabandha; Meditation for Healing Addictions
Chain breaking	see Generational Healing
Charity	All Kundalini Yoga; a consistent daily practice; set the intention and keep up
Chastity	Meditation for Healing Addictions; Sat Kriya; Mahabandha; Frog Pose
Chronic pain	Long Deep Breathing; Sitali Pranayam; Alternate Nostril Breathing; Kirtan Kriya; Ganputi Kriya; depending where pain is, follow intuition with when chosing yoga kriyas
Circulatory system	Nervous System and Stamina; all Kundalini Yoga
Communication	Antar Naad Mudra (Meditation)
Confusion	Meditation for a Calm Heart; When You Don't Know What To Do (Meditation); Bring Mental Balance Meditation; cover your head
Constipation	Nabhi Kriya; Exercises to Create a Disease Free Body (yoga kriya)
Creativity	Adi Shakti Meditation
Depression	Mul Mantra; Bring Mental Balance Meditation; Kriya for Elevation; Kriya for Relieving Inner Anger
Desires	Kirtan Kriya
Digestive health	Nabhi Kriya; Uddiyanna Bhand; Exercises to Create a Disease Free Body

Issues	Suggestions
Disconnection	A consistent sadhana practice
Discouragement	Chant and play Mul Mantra
Divine connection	All Kundalini Yoga and Meditation; a consistent sadhana practice
Eating disorders	Meditation for Healing Addictions; Meditation for a Calm Heart; see Addictions
Faith	All Kundalini Yoga and Meditation; a consistent sadhana practice; set the intention and keep up
Family relationships	Meditation for a Calm Heart; Antar Naad Mudra (Meditations)
Fatigue	Basic Spinal Energy Series; Breath of Fire; Renew Your Nervous Systema and Build Stamina; a consistent daily practice in the ambrosial hours
Fear	Technique for Managing Fears; Kriya for Relaxation and Releasing Fear; chant and play mantras; Victory Breath
Fertility	Adi Shakti Meditation
Financial stress	Prosperity Meditation; Kriya for the Fourth Chakra
Forgiveness	Releasing Childhood Anger Meditation; Fists of Anger Meditation; Kriya for Relieving Inner Anger; Meditation for a Calm Heart; Kriya for the Fourth Chakra
Generational healing	Ganputi Kriya; Kirtan Kriya; all Kundalini Yoga works generationally backward and forward
Giving up	Chant Mul Mantra; Breath of Fire; Victory Breath; all Pranayam; keep up; see "Interference" in the Resources Section
Grief	Meditation for a Calm Heart; all Pranayam; chant Mul Mantra
Guilt	Meditation for a Calm Heart; chant Mul Mantra
Heartbreak	Breath of Fire; Kriya for the Fourth Chakra

Issues	Suggestions
Hope	Mul Mantra; a consistent sadhana practice
Hormone balance	Cat-Cow Pose; Exercises to Create a Disease-Free Body; Mahabhand; Kriya for Relieving Inner Anger; Adi Shakti Meditation
Identity	Nabhi Kriya; Sat Kriya; regularly chant or breathe Sat Nam until you vibrate it on every cell
Immune system strength	Exercises to Create a Disease Free Body, Breath of Fire
Insomnia	Kirtan Kriya; Long Deep Breathing; Left Nostril Breathing
Intuition	Adi Shakti Meditation
Irritable Bowel Syndrome	Sat Kriya,
Jealousy	Meditation for Healing Addictions; Kriya for the Fourth Chakra; Kriya for Relieving Inner Anger; Fists of Anger Meditation
Judging	Meditation for Healing Addictions; Kriya for the Fourth Chakra; Fists of Anger Meditation
Kidney Problems	Kriya for Relaxation and Releasing Fear; Technique for Managing Fears; Kriya to Throw Off Stress
Light of Christ	To get more light of Christ use any and all Pranayam
Liver problems	Fists of Anger Meditation; Kriya for Relieving Inner Anger; Meditation for Healing Addictions; Releasing Childhood Anger
Love	Kriya for the Forth Chakra, Kriya for Elevation, Awakening to Your Ten Bodies
Marital problems	Venus Kriyas, Kriya For Relieving Inner Anger
Meekness	Kriya for Elevation; Awakening to Your Ten Bodies; Consistent sadhana practice; Set the intention and keep up.

Issues	Suggestions
Miracles	A consistent daily practice; regularly play or chant the mantra Ardas Bahee
Mother-child issues	Adi Shakti Meditation; Releasing Childhood Anger
Negative beliefs	All Mantra; Bring Mental Balance Meditation
Negotiations	Antar Naad Mudra (Meditation)
Nervous system strength	Kriya for Nervous System and to Build Stamina
Neurotransmitter imbalance	Kirtan Kriya, Ganputi Kriya,
Overwhelm	Renew Your Nervous System and Build Stamina; a regular daily practice of Kundalini Yoga Meditation
Panic attacks	see Anxiety
Parenting	Meditation for Patience, consistent practice
Patience	Meditation for Patience
Peace	Meditation for a Calm Heart, Kriya for Elevation, Kriya for Relaxation and Releasing Fear
Phobias	Meditation for Healing Addictions
Pregnancy	Adi Shakti Meditation, see Pregnancy (page 282)
Premenstrual syndrome	Kirtan Kriya, Cat-Cow Pose, Basic Spinal Energy Series, Mul Mantra
Pride (Ego)	Fists of Anger Meditation; Kirya for Relieving Inner Anger; Releasing Childhood Anger Meditation; Meditation for Healing Addictions, Nhabi Kriya, Awakening to Your Ten Bodies
Procrastination	Meditation for Healing Addictions

Issues	Suggestions
Prosperity	Prosperity Meditation; Kriya for the Fourth Chakra; Releasing Childhood Anger
Protection from evil	Obedience; keep the commandments; play mantras at home and chant them; mantras like Wahe Guru, Aap Sahee Hoa, and Aad Guray Nameh are great for protection, but all kundalini mantras will raise the vibration; all Kundalini Yoga and Meditation; ssential Oils, especially Frankincense and Myrrh
Purification	All Kundalini Yoga and Meditation
Sabotage	Keep up a consistent practice; play and chant the mantra Aap Sahaee Hoa
Self-loathing, shame	Mul Mantra; Releasing Childhood Anger; Chant long Sat Nams; any anger meditation or kriya
Sexual problems	see Celibacy and Chastity
Sickness	Exercises to Create a Disease Free Body
Spiritual gifts	Adi Shakti Meditation; Kriya for Elevation; Awakening to Your Ten Bodies; any and all Kudnalini Yoga and Meditation practiced regularly
Spiritual guidance	A consistent sadhana practice
Stubbornness	Ganputi Kriya; Kriya for Elevation
Temper tantrums	Alternate Nostril Breathing; Sitali Pranayam; Long Deep Breathing
Victim energy	Nabhi Kriya; Kriya for Elevation
Weight loss	Renew Your Nervous System and Build Stamina; Ganputi Kriya; Awakening to Your Ten Bodies

Resources

ONLINE RESOURCES

http://www.3HO.org

http://www.kundaliniresearchinstitute.org

http://www.spiritvoyage.com
(Kundalini Yoga music, manuals, and other helpful products and information)

http://www.treeoflifekundaliniyoga.com

http://www.youtube.com/treeoflifekundalini

http://www.progressiveprophetess.com

http://www.zionconsciousness.com (podcast)

http://www.sikh.net

http://www.mormon.org

http://www.lds.org

BOOKS AND MANUALS ON KUNDALINI YOGA

Bountiful, Beautiful, Blissful: Experience the Natural Power of Pregnancy and Birth with Kundalini Yoga and Meditation by Gurmukh Kaur Khalsa (New York, NY: St. Martin's Press, 2003)

Exploring the Physical and Subtle Anatomy, by Nirmal Lumpkin NCTMB and Japa K. Khalsa DOM (Santa Cruz, NM: K.R.I., 2015)

Kundalini Yoga: The Flow of Eternal Power, by Shakti Parwha Kaur Khalsa (New York: Berkeley, 1996)

Meditation as Medicine: Activate the Power of Your Natural Healing Force, by Dharma Singh Khalsa and Cameron Stauth (New York: Fireside, 2001)

Praana, Praanee, Praanayam: Exploring the Breath Technology of Kundalini Yoga As Taught By Yogi Bhajan, by Yogi Bhajan and Harijot Kaur (Santa Cruz, NM: K.R.I,, 2006)

Sacred Therapies: The Kundalini Yoga Meditation Handbook for Mental Health, by David Shannahoff-Khalsa (New York: Norton, 2012)

Spirituality and Sexuality: With the Kundalini Yoga Sets by Yogi Bhajan, by Gururattan Kaur Khalsa (Sunbury, PA: Yoga Technology, 1989)

The Kundalini Yoga Experience: Bringing Body, Mind, and Spirit Together, by Dharam Singh Khalsa and Darryl O'Keeffe (New York: Fireside, 2002)

The Master's Touch: On Being A Sacred Teacher For The New Age, by Yogi Bhajan (Santa Cruz, NM: K.R.I., 2000)

BOOKS ON ESSENTIAL OILS

Modern Essentials: A Contemporary Guide to the Therapeutic Use of Essential Oils 5th ed., by AromaTools (Orem, UT: AromaTools, 2013)

Essential Oils for Pregnancy, Birth, and Babies, by Stephanie Fritz (Sierra Vista, AZ: Gently Born, 2012)

Emotions and Essential Oils, by Daniel McDonald (American Fork, UT: Enlighten, 2012)

RESOURCES FOR DEALING WITH INTERFERENCE

"Devils and Such," by Felice Austin (http://www.progressiveprophetess.blogspot.com/2013/05/devils-and-such.html)

"Understanding Spiritual and Evil in the Context of Psychotherapy," by Ronald Poulton (http://tamarasbook.blogspot.com/2008/12/fascinating-paper-on-evil-spirits.html)

Index

Photo Credit

Brook Andreoli 136, 193 (lotus pose), 195 (ego eradicator), 246-247, 292
Felice Austin cover, 126, 129, 151, 184, 191, 193-197, 199, 206-211, 225-228, 234-237, 248, 252-253, 257, 265-267, 271-273, 284 (butterfly)
Lani Axman 216-219
Jennifer Bacher 99
Hailey Bradshaw 204, 274-281
Shannon Durda 101
Mandi Felici 220-224, 244-245
Shannon Flores Photography 261, 286
Kami Larsen 290 (mom with baby)
Chelsea Proctor 163, 238-243, 254, 256, 268, 270, 288-289
Jamie Smith 164
Cali Stoddard 183
Alyse Thomson 282-285
Nancy Voyer 229-233, 255
Mandy Williams 26, 212-215, 251, 264, back cover (author photo)

Acknowledgements

I offer my thanks to the following:

My daughter, for bringing me to meditation when she was in my womb, and for being the shining light in my life. Lani, for being my editor, my friend, my confidant, my photographer, my model, and for dancing with me under the moon on the beach. Heather Farrell for meditating with me and encouraging me to write about meditation. Kylie Power for encouraging me to teach meditation to Mormons. Sierra Cory, for being my editor and being awesome. Suzy Bills for editing. Janice Madsen for keeping me organized and for paying attention to dreams. Lisa Underwood for having an open and loving heart, helping solve a few mysteries, and helping me get to Ojai. Hannah Worthington for being good, and for helping my daughter love "maths." Sheridan Ripley for being supportive from the beginning. Wendy Cleveland for being awesome. Mandi Felici for her open heart and her endless generosity. Jennifer Horne for following the spirit and for her generosity and friendship. Andrew Rasmussen for being great and getting me to do a podcast. Robyn Allgood for being the first of my friends to try it and stick with it. Emily Stevens, for being the other first one. Tana Clark for helping me see the full power of my intuition. Julie Petit, for posting a quote when I needed it. Breynn Arima, Carole Sneddon, Sarah Cooksley for being my overseas posse and for being awesome and trying something weird. Rachel Harris, for a million trillion things and years of friendship. The Cianciullis and Louine Hunter and the Thomases for helping us transition to the promised land. Especially Sophie Thomas, for being my daughter's best friend and playing with her for hours and hours. Kelsey Thomas, for babysitting. Hunter and Jaxson Thomas, for giving Phoebe big brothers. Buddy, for being Phoebe's stepdog. Jessica Jostes for recognizing her mission. Katy Willis, for writing the anatomy chapter and for her enthusiasm and awesomeness. Nancy Holbrook for being a powerful Jedi. Amanda Olsen for her spontaneous generosity and sponsorship. Kimberly Walker, for having an open heart and being willing to jump in with only a day's notice. Bonnie Hansen, for being lovely and taking every class I have offered. Brittney Walker for reading and commenting. Laura Stott Rogers, for reading me poetry when I couldn't write any more and for her sublime powers of poetic telepathy. The hawks who kept flying over me at just the right times. Joseph Smith for restoring the gospel of Jesus Christ to the earth. All the modern prophets of the LDS church. Abraham Lincoln for freeing the slaves. Yogi Bhajan for being a master and for having the guts and compassion to do what no one had ever done but what needed to be done. Harijiwan for being funny. Tej for being honest, though I didn't like it at the time. Navjot for being. Chelsea Proctor for photography. Mandy Williams for photography, inspiration, and artistic awesomeness. Lisa Frei and family (Chase and Hailey) for pictures and also for their openness and generosity. Paige Anderson for helping me when I needed it. Amy and Veiko for modeling at the last minute. Michelle and Dave Larsen for being so great to photograph and for their open hearts. Nicole Olsen for pointing me to the right scripture at the right time. Parmahansa Yogananda for writing thoughtfully about Jesus and his yoga. Snatam Kaur for making awesome music. Nirinjin Kaur and many others for doing the same. My mother for being my helper in the spirit world. My grandparents for leaving such a great legacy of strength and capacity and kindness. Everyone who submitted stories. Everyone who thought about submitting stories. Everyone who prayed for me during the process of writing this book. Everyone who donated money to rush this book to publication so that the world wouldn't have to wait another minute. For their generosity and support and friendship: Amy Byrd, Ashley B., Audrey Crozier, Beth Hughes, Bonnie Hansen, Brook Andreoli, Candace Evans, Carole Sneddon, Amy Thompson, Catherine Dagsland, Chablis Adams, Chelsea Shure, Cherise Sant, Daryl Austin, Debi Youngs, Hannah, Heather Ramanlal, Janet Kuester, Janine Busald, Jennifer Horne, Jennifer Lucas, Jenny Miller, Jessica Drollette, Jo Alterman, Karin Hardman, Katy Willis, Kelly Titmus, Lara Seaver, Laura Stott, Lisa Frei, Lisa Underwood, Lori Taylor, Mike and Rebecca Hansen, Maria Cranford, Michelle Larsen, Misha Strunk, Molly Tanuvasa, Nancy Cole, Natalie Permann, Ryan Call, Sarah Sussman, Shannon Flores, Steven Waters, Summer Turner, Tammy Olsen, Stacia Butler, Tawnie Larsen, and Z. Nielsen.

Made in the USA
Charleston, SC
05 July 2015